T H E   O P E N   E Y E

Books by Katharine Kuh

The Open Eye

. . . . IN PURSUIT OF ART

by Katharine Kuh

HARPER & ROW, PUBLISHERS

NEW YORK, EVANSTON, SAN FRANCISCO,
LONDON

1817

12 - 238

The article ''Clyfford Still'' first appeared in *Vogue*.

CONTENTS

ILLUSTRATIONS

I am sometimes called an art critic. Truthfully, I am not quite sure what the title means. I was trained as an art historian, a profession which is often anathema to artists and critics alike. Artists, of course, are understandably impatient with any peripheral activity that fails to provide appreciation for them individually; the only critic they admire is the one who admires their work. And, as a rule, they are suspicious of all art historians, lumping them together as hair-splitting Herr Doktors.

Some years ago, I spoke at a symposium organized by the American Federation of Arts and called ''The Critic and the Visual Arts.'' I recall that most of my talk dealt with unanswered questions, because, then as now, art criticism represented a hazy territory for me. Certain of these questions still seem relevant, and I now offer tentative answers.

''Is it dangerous to judge the art of today by standards of the past?'' I'm inclined to say no, it is not, though contemporary events can hardly be ignored.

''Can one be a valid critic of the past and yet not fully experience the present, or even suspect the future?'' This time I'm inclined to say yes, even if I don't quite know why, for now

I have a double standard, yet with modern art I proposed a single one. Perhaps because past art has been carefully sifted by time, it lives on its own terms.

"Can we turn the present into history before it is history?" When flying over the land we sometimes see the broad wing of our plane dominating the scene below. The big view becomes minuscule while the immediate one takes over. Here, then is the problem.

"Is it preferable to start with our own times and see the past in terms of present commitments? Should we move back from Pollock to Monet, from Cubism to African sculpture, from Léger to Poussin, from Giacometti to early Sardinian art? Should we reverse orthodox chronology in order better to understand both the past and the present?" This is a personal matter. I, myself, find a logical time sequence invaluable, but there are those who might accept the past more readily if introduced to it by the present.

"Is the art critic both commentator and reporter, a reporter who deals with facts and news?" To a certain extent yes, but if he limits himself to these latter priorities he remains solely a reporter, though even to report honestly about art is an occupation not to be scorned.

"Is the critic's role to encourage the artist or to encourage the public to understand the artist?" The two roles overlap.

"Must the critic be a gifted writer?" Surely the better he writes, the better he communicates. Who has written more persuasively about Rodin than Rilke, about Giacometti than Sartre, about Manet than Zola?

"Is the art critic a tastemaker, a molder of opinion, or is his function to recognize what is going on around him rather than to set himself up as an impresario?" Hopefully, he is not a disciple of any one system or any single way of seeing. He is unavoidably swayed by his own conditioning, but everything else being equal and, to be sure, it never is, the more encyclopedic his knowledge, the deeper his insight, and the richer his experience, the more reticent are his judgments. For us today these judgments are increasingly difficult. A Greek saw only what preceded Greek art, but now, since mass communication has opened up wider horizons and art history is accelerating in all directions, we are confronted by a maze of conflicting experiences.

The essays in this book, some of them briefly expanded, and, except for one, all selected from a monthly column in *Saturday Review,* have not made history in the art world, nor were they intended to. I discovered no new painters or sculptors; I named no new movements and hope I harmed no old ones. My column rarely attracted the attention of the "swingers." Frankly, I am considered rather square. My objective was simple: to write lucidly in nontechnical language for an intelligent but not necessarily highly informed audience about the intricacies of art as encountered throughout the world from earliest times until the present. I consider the art critic chiefly an interpreter, though this view finds little favor at present. Recently a college student wrote me questioning whether it was possible to discuss an artist's intentions. He felt the job of a critic was to describe and evaluate only the formal elements of a work of art. For him a drawing is nothing but line, a painting nothing but compositional elements, and for him a critic is nothing but an eye, yet rarely an eye open enough to see more than tangible dimensions. Today, many artists and critics would agree with him.

Divided into three sections, the book stresses people, places, and what I call "pros and cons," which are really personal opinions that sometimes encompass art history, sometimes criticism, but more often both, or can we separate the two? Under "people" I have included those artists and personalities connected with art who specially interest me. They form an unrelated group, yet each is a distinctive individual and for me an unforgettable one. Except for Andrew Wyeth, all have helped to steer me toward an "open eye."

In the section devoted to "places" I have wholeheartedly accepted the role of reporter, a reporter of integrity, I hope, but one not always free of bias. Take Alaska—for me a symbol of total involvement and failure. Ireland was sheer delight; the U.S.S.R. an engrossing experience but a fear-ridden one; Israel so full of contradictions, myths, and fervor as to challenge the most objective observer, and Yucatan—that triumph of grandeur. Al-

ways I approached these countries through their art and archaeology, neither of which can be divorced from geography, climate,
or history.

For more than forty years I have enjoyed a love affair with
art. It has been the focus of my life. When troubles came, I as-
suaged them temporarily in museums or on trips to parts of the
world where man's skills have left an indelible imprint. An itch-
ing foot and an incurable curiosity led me on wonderful junkets
over seas and lands including our own continent from its arctic
wastes to its tropical jungles. In the most unexpected places at
the most unexpected times this involvement with art came to my
rescue. It has provided friends, a livelihood, and a world of unfailing interest. I only wish the words in this book were eloquent
enough to do justice to the subject.

K.K.

PEOPLE

1. *Ivan Albright*

Nodding, joking, rushing, jerking, Ivan Albright piloted me through his new house in Woodstock, Vermont, or more correctly his two houses, one for children, grandchildren, and guests, the other chiefly for his wife and himself. In contrast to Chicago's Near North Side, where until recently the Albrights lived, this romantic and elegant colonial setting gives the lie to any further theory that the painter is a Midwestern-oriented artist. For years I thought so, but I was wrong. Nothing in his work has changed. The same pulverized, uncompromising images emerge from Vermont as came out of Chicago. A serene New England landscape threaded by the lovely Ottauquechee River affects him no more than did the bleak sprawl of an industrialized city.

Curiously, this man, who is obsessively immersed in his own painting and who apparently is uninfluenced by any contemporary movements, does not include even one of his works in either house, though both are filled with art from all periods. To see what he is doing, one must go to the studio, an authentic Albright landmark meticulously tailored to his specific needs. And his needs are not simple. For this painter who appears the very incarnation of nervous tension is perhaps the most patient, painstaking artist alive today. In his work nothing happens by chance. Each detail is planned, studied, and researched in depth. Even that tireless prober Edwin Dickinson has never devoted twenty-four years to one composition, as Albright did with "The Window."

And speaking of windows, in the new studio there are several which were specially designed so that, inch by inch, separate glass sections can be regulated to control the light. Albright dislikes bright light or, for that matter, any kind of cheerful, flat sunlight. He prefers cloudy, gray skies that allow brooding shadows to define form and yet suggest the unknown.

Despite his mercilessly detailed technique, one must not suppose that Albright is interested in the object per se. True, he stages elaborate setups for his compositions, going as far as to reproduce a drab wall, brick by brick, or to tear and resew a worn velveteen sleeve until each wrinkle has the desired consistency. But these visual facts are merely the raw material he manipulates and transforms. He is, paradoxically, an abstract artist who deals with reality only to destroy it by bending all images to his unique metaphysical bias. Projecting his own kind of ambiguous space, his own labyrinthine perspective, his own irrational light, he creates a jungle of insecurity.

Albright's methods, which at first glance appear literal, are in fact the reverse. He paints solely what he thinks, sometimes what he wants, but never what he sees. What he sees acts only as his point of departure. Attracted by the perversities of life, he infuses the commonplace with deceptive allusions. He once observed, "I like to see dust move and crawl over an object like a film." And, to be sure, his paintings have the touch of dusty death. But he is not concerned alone with dissolution. "Let's say I'm equally interested in growth and death. How can you divide them?"

Albright looks on the human body as man's tomb. "Without eyes the light would not hurt; without flesh the pain would not hurt; without legs our motion might accelerate. Without a body we might be men," he says. At best, he transcends human limitations by imperiously disregarding the laws of nature. He shows us human flesh, no matter how young, and inanimate objects, no matter how new, in a relentless journey toward extinction. He claims that when the artist moves, all things move with him. "If I stir, they stir. If I stand arrested, they become motionless." In short, he is the total impresario—to such an extreme that he prefers smooth board to canvas. Not wishing to fight the texture of woven cloth, he wants to weave his own painting. In an interview several years ago, Albright confessed, "I hope to control the observer, to make him move and think the way I want him to. . . . I want to jar the observer into thinking—I want to make him uncomfortable."

Working intensively for some three hours each day, he stops as soon as the painting "begins to look good." At that point he finds his critical faculties becoming blunted. More than any other artist I recall, he can appraise his own work with unflinching objectivity. He knows his strengths; he knows his weaknesses. For him, his two top paintings are "The Door" and "The Window." He spent long years on both, planning them in excruciating detail with endless preliminary drawings, notes, written directions, and three-dimensional setups. Conflict and turmoil distinguish every inch of the two compositions. Warring forces tip, tilt, slant, invert, twist, and foreshorten each object until the eye reels and the object, ceasing to be itself, takes on hallucinatory overtones. At the same time, the compositions, like tangled quagmires, dispense with ordinary boundaries. Sometimes it is virtually impossible to separate top from bottom or inside from outside in an Albright painting.

And that is precisely what he wants—to confuse and shock, to force re-evaluations. In a notebook of working directions for "The Window" he wrote, "Make the painting more accurate and more accurate and more accurate." But his idea of accuracy was less a realistic than a compulsive one. "The Window" for him was an experience to be seen simultaneously from outside and inside. He tells himself to "make a view of the window as if a man is walking by it." Then, in the next sentence, he demands that each object be seen from the inside in multiple combined positions. For only thus does Albright believe that simulated motion can be achieved—not as a finite action but as a creative transmuta-

Poor Room—There is no time, no end, no today, no yesterday, no tomorrow, only the forever, and forever, and forever, without end ("The Window") by Ivan Albright

Ivan Albright working on *Poor Room*—, late nineteen fifties

tion. With unorthodox freedom, he defines motion as the third dimension. Relying on physical findings for purely psychic effects, he has developed a kind of simultaneous vision that is a far remove from the structural emphasis of Cubism.

Albright claims that art concepts like motion, space, color, and form are all invented by man, and that without man they cease to exist. Though a door is not curved, if the mind envisions it that way, it is curved. Hence, he painted his famous "Door" as a slightly convex door-coffin combination. With the same speculative drive he questions the role of color, asking himself, "What is the nature of color anyway? Does it build up—does it add strength—does it add softness—what does it do? Why does a certain object have a definite color? Take all the color away from it —then put it back. What is the significance of its color?" The answer "is not in the eye, nor in reason." He implies that it comes only from one's own sensibility, one's cumulative experience. Just as the real transforms itself into the abstract for him, so dark and light merge. "Put everything in total darkness and you see nothing. Put everything in brilliant light and you see nothing." If Albright has a leitmotif it stems from his conviction that no single fact is as it seems.

In his youth, this artist, who was born in 1897, headed toward architecture but shifted to art after two years as a medical draftsman in World War I. The early surgical watercolors and drawings done rapidly on the spot in French base hospitals may seem antipathetic to Albright's subsequent mature style, partly because of the spontaneity with which they were executed, partly because they turned brutal wounds into the equivalents of growing plants. Instead of the dusty, almost dead plum color that characterizes so much of the later work ("maybe because I'm gloomy") we find here a veritable rainbow of iridescent hues. And yet there is continuity, for already the artist was rearranging nature to fit his needs. As later he was to invest the healthy with encroaching decay, so now in a world of death he made death live. These sketches remain an unforgettable indictment of war, both as documents and as exotic comments on the profligate destruction of the young.

One of my reasons for going to Vermont was to see a new painting Albright had started the previous fall. Already a year old, it would, he felt, require at least another five or six years to complete. (In early 1970, however, the picture had been on the way for four years, but Albright predicted another five to complete it.) Realizing that time can subvert the best-laid plans, he never names a work until it is finished. The new one is temporarily called *The Vermonter.* Except for two portraits (of his late father-in-law, Captain Joseph Medill Patterson, and of Mary Block) this is the artist's first figure painting in thirty-five years. The subject is a man in his middle seventies who comes regularly to the studio for long hours each week. Between visits, a dummy carefully constructed by Albright suffices, but for head, hands, and body articulation the sitter is indispensable. According to Albright he chose a model "who has lived and who feels as tired as I do." Could it be the artist paints himself as well as his sitter?

Tacked up on the studio wall is a crude chart with meaning for no one but the painter. Words and brief lines, both frequently crossed out or altered, act as directives. By the time the painting is finished, it is unlikely that any of the guideposts will remain as originally conceived. Nearby on an easel stands a "static drawing"—at least so Albright describes it. For me, it was neither a drawing nor static, but a superb charcoal, white chalk, and black pastel portrait on canvas. Albright considers it static only because it is closer to nature, to what one sees, than to the secret turbulence he feels invests all life. The background is naturalistic, the figure direct, three-dimensional, and harmonious.

And this is exactly what Albright does not want in the final composition. Relentlessly priming and questioning himself in his notebook, he suggests "moving model so light falls strongest on shoulder—then moving it back so light is stronger on face." Thus he makes his own arbitrary light. Next he directs himself to "put stubble of beard on pulsating flesh" and "have end of nose literally wriggle." Now he wants the cap to turn sharply in one direction, the head to turn in the opposite direction, as if the figure were caught in conflicting forces.

Even a modest silverpoint drawing of a bridge becomes the occasion for an entire book of sketches and notes. "Have bridge angle more than it does. Force more interesting rocks into view. Change their position and arrange them in stream so they make flow of water more rapid." The word is always "more," for Albright does not hold with the modern philosophy that less makes more. He deliberately exaggerates the multiplicity of life. Turner, it is said, was less interested in imitating nature than improving on it. Albright, I would guess, feels otherwise. He, too, changes nature, not to improve it, but to energize it with new meaning.

Except for Paul Klee, no modern artist has so frankly employed titles to underline the meaning of his work. What could be more evocative of guilt than the real name of "The Door": *That which I should have done I did not do?* Whether we see here a closed coffin lid, a closed door, or both, the same finality is implied. And, of course, ''The Window'' eventually became *Poor Room—There is no time, no end, no today, no yesterday, no tomorrow, only the forever, and forever, and forever, without end,* a title that might seem corny if it accompanied any other painting. A half-nude man in a bowler viewed against shabby furniture under a naked light bulb is called *And God Created Man in His Own Image* (*Room 203*). The title echoes the compassion implicit in the picture. In most of Albright's work, compassion plays a central role. The artist sympathizes with the human predicament he lays bare.

If the titles have poetic overtones, this is hardly surprising, for Albright has long written verse as ''a rest or reaction from painting,'' and, also, perhaps, as a way of exploring his attitudes toward art. In a poem about a painter, he observes, ''And the sky is not blue to him. . . . And the river is not held within its banks. . . . And the tree is not a tree to him. . . . And colors are not just colors to him. . . .''

2. *Why Wyeth?*

The emergence of Andrew Wyeth as a national culture idol is a phenomenon, but not an entirely surprising one. No time or place in history could be better adapted to the hero worship of this particular artist than present-day America. The very vitality that churns our cities into fevered conflict fills us with nostalgia for ''life on the farm.'' The more international our world, the more tormented it is by unrest, the more unstable our social fabric, the more, alas, we turn to oversimple solutions. It is easier to shout about ''law and order'' than to remedy the causes that turn these words into a national slogan.

Somehow I think of Wyeth's paintings as persistent, if gentle, evocations of that same mindless slogan. His ''law and order'' never envisions a universal structure. His paintings are washed in a colorless, finicky pigment that obliterates even their competent draftsmanship. And competent it is. Indeed, all Wyeth's work is competent, but nonetheless sentimental and episodic. He offers us first-rate illustrations of ''the good life,'' but these vignettes never rise above illustrations. Because his themes are systematically native, even regional, the public has come to think of him as the American symbol par excellence of healthy self-reliance. Not so many years ago it was Grant Wood who occupied this exalted position, but today his name is slipping.

Surely Edward Hopper was no less American than either of these men. He, too, dealt with the same pervasive solitude that underlies Wyeth's work; yet Hopper was not a romantic folk artist. He devoted himself to the dry, hard light and dry, hard life of our land, nor did he make a single concession to the incidental. His paintings have bones and sinews; they are built on a rigorous scaffold. Never pictorializations of specific events, they deliberately avoid overeasy emotional content. It is what Hopper omitted that created his illusion of loneliness; with Wyeth, it is what he includes.

This is not to say that all artists who concentrate on local incidents are captives of their material. Edwin Dickinson paints Cape Cod, but his sea, sand, and mist are philosophic statements about the evanescence of nature. Yet Wyeth's Chadds Ford, Pennsylvania, and Cushing, Maine, are Chadds Ford and Cushing. His poetry is diluted by idiosyncratic facts. The observer is rarely asked to soar; instead he is led along well-grooved ruts, which, no doubt, explains the idolatry of those who find Wyeth's work a reassuring escape from the demands of contemporary art and life. One cannot exaggerate the happy relief of certain observers who, when confronted by Wyeth's paintings, are challenged by no new isms, no new techniques, no puzzling multiple meanings. Like kindly little sermons at the village church, this artist's contrived compositions shine with moral rectitude. Their popular appeal seems to grow in direct proportion to the fad for novelty that proliferates in America today. And yet it is an anomaly in our country of astounding innovative technology that a painter so totally divorced from the present century could become a veritable patron saint.

In the United States there is no other native artist whose popularity can compare with Wyeth's, a curious situation when one considers how relatively unknown he is abroad. The American museums that patiently wait in line to pay astronomical thousands for his major compositions are not matched by foreign counterparts. Wyeth is a home product ill-suited for export, and perhaps that is precisely why he is so admired. In perilous times we are apt to creep back to the comforting protection of familiar surroundings. I once read about the comparative prices paid early this century by a Brussels museum for works of Breughel and Alfred Stevens. A topical genre scene by the latter brought well over $100,000, a Breughel, little more than one-tenth that sum. The Stevens, however, was unable to bridge the time gap and now is relegated to well-bred obscurity. This, I am afraid, is what will happen to Wyeth's homely chronicles as, to be sure, it is already happening to those of Grandma Moses. The rapture her paintings recently occasioned is fast evaporating.

Once when I visited the Virginia Museum in Richmond a newly acquired Wyeth, featured in a special room replete with sketches, photographs, and historical data, set me to wondering how this institution could justify such abject veneration. Surely before we elevate Wyeth to institutional homage we ought first to present in depth those nineteenth-century American proto-types who were his natural forebears and who, at times, seem more modern than he, and always more profound. Why rhap-sodize over Wyeth when Eakins and Homer did it far better, and did it at a period in our national development when their vision was meaningful?

Every age has its potboilers. Whether their emphasis is on nudes, rural scenes, or daily anecdotes, it is not the subject per se that makes them potboilers; it is the artist's handling of the subject. Bouguereau's slick nudes bore us no less than that painter's feeble efforts to resurrect the vigor of authentic classi-cism. True, every artist need not be an innovator, but merely to pretty up the past is scarcely enough. Yet, repeatedly, the very painters who do just this receive the warmest kudos.

Where Wyeth's work is concerned, we find thoughtful critics and artists whose stinging words contrast with the judgments of an overwhelmingly large lay audience. On one hand, we have adulation; on the other a slightly weary resignation. The en-thralled crowds that wormed their way through Wyeth's travel-ing retrospective exhibition were amazing not only for their numbers but for their seeming sophistication. His work, far from a magnet for simple country bumpkins, is "in" except for a few lonely voices. Because the layman understands it at a glance, he is apt to forgive clichés that are so disarmingly unpretentious and so skillfully executed that even the adamant hesitate to carp. Wyeth's amiable accomplishments sometimes camouflage his vacuous message.

And now comes a new cause for astonishment. Houghton Mifflin is publishing *The Work of Andrew Wyeth* in an edition of fifty thousand copies to sell for $75. The volume comprises 184 pages, 121 of which are faithful color reproductions. In addition, sketches and preparatory drawings are seen with the major works they influenced. And, as is often true, the spontaneous sketches frequently come off better than the final, frozen paintings; the sketches are more direct. In addition, Gambit, Inc., is issuing a limited edition of the book (250 copies) signed and numbered by the artist for the unprecedented price of $2,000 each. Even Rembrandt's signature could hardly compete. There is something almost obscene about this swollen sum for nothing more than reproductions which, because of their very nature, are intended for mass consumption. And reproductions, let me add, of works curiously unrelated to color. Were they, let's say, illustrations of paintings by Matisse or Bonnard, where subtle color nuances are crucial, one might more readily understand the need for such extravagance.

The book (I am referring to the trade edition) is handsomely and simply designed with reproductions which capture those tender textural fluctuations and expressive light that sometimes lift a Wyeth painting beyond its usual pedestrian format. Painstakingly supervised by the artist and his wife, this outsized (13-by-17-inch) volume is so heavy as to tax the muscles of an athlete in training. Here, at last, is a coffee-table book too large for the coffee table, and too cumbersome for the reader.

There is no doubt that Wyeth loves what he paints. He says, "If I have anything to offer, it is my emotional contact with the place where I live and the people I do." In the winter, he lives in Chadds Ford, Pennsylvania; in the summer, in Cushing, Maine. These small areas of America he examines with affectionate eyes, but he rarely has the ability to transform the specific into the general. One need only refer to the unfortunate text accompanying this book to realize how parochial is the artist's approach. Richard Meryman, staff writer for *Life,* took a year's leave to write about the places and people in Wyeth's pictures—about their characteristics, peculiarities, and relationships to the artist. Instead of allowing the works to speak for themselves, Mr. Meryman liberally quotes Wyeth as he describes in detail each incident that touched off a painting. His homily, filled with maudlin anecdotes, is an unqualified tribute to anti-intellectualism.

The more explicit the text, the more certain we become that Wyeth's painted reports of local events were conceived as glorified illustrations and not as the hallowed art most enthusiasts would have us believe. After all, Wyeth's father was a distinguished illustrator whose son was admittedly influenced by him, but N. C. Wyeth never claimed to be more than an illustrator. There is no cause to scorn accomplished illustrations; yet to confuse them with an art that is an extension rather than a repetition of life is a mistake. Though good reportage, whether graphic or literary, is important, it is not concerned with re-creation. It is concerned with facts.

Wyeth sees objective integrity as the key to art. For him, the only valid approach is through precise observation and precisely executed definition. Then alone, he reasons, does the full impact of a visual experience assert itself. He claims that honest presentation of the object leads to larger vision, but whether he achieves this larger vision is a moot question. In his portraits, which are often searching, he, unlike Ivan Albright, never includes an extra wrinkle, though every wrinkle he sees is conscientiously recorded. Albright turns his tortured exaggerations into obsessed abstractions; Wyeth deliberately limits himself to a reality his eyes can digest. His favorite sitters, it is true, are strongly individualistic, but even when he indulges their gnarled dignity, he never pushes them beyond their actual capacities. Wyeth shows us life as it is, or at least as he sees it, not as it might be.

At best, his work exudes a quiet loneliness and a sense of oblique light. If I were to choose the most successful painting in the book, it would be *Wind from the Sea,* done twenty-one years ago. Here, the elements of nature are not interrupted by visual small talk. The theme is the wind itself.

Once he reached his stride (and this was very early), Wyeth continued on an even keel. It is impossible to pinpoint any chronological stylistic development in his work. And yet, oddly enough, the publisher's blurb describes him as "an astounding painter whose art continues to move in new and surprising directions." When explaining why he feels no need to look beyond the two locales where he lives, Wyeth is quoted by Meryman as saying: "You know after travel you're never the same. You get more erudite, you get more knowledge. I might lose something very important to my work—maybe innocence." And maybe that would be the best thing that could happen to Andrew Wyeth.

Not unexpectedly this piece on Wyeth triggered a batch of angry letters. Some, of course, agreed with me, but others were so vehemently opposed as to become almost incoherent. It was as if a certain security had been peeled away. I can remember no other article I have written that occasioned such bitterness. Herewith a few typical excerpts from irate correspondents:

Is it possible that Andrew Wyeth once spurned a salacious proposition from Katharine Kuh? It is the only feasible explanation that comes to mind for the irresponsibly malicious, incredibly inept and embarrassingly revealing article . . .

Trying to account for Katharine Kuh's outburst I have concluded that:

1. She is recovering from a bout with the flu and is a bit woozy, or
2. She toured the back country and over-indulged in green apples, or
3. Mr. Wyeth refused to paint her portrait—(Hell hath no fury, etc.)

Now I ask a question—Why Kuh?

Perhaps to satisfy critics like K.K., Wyeth should loose a barrel of worms to wriggle over his undried canvases, give all his money to a prostitute, take himself off to some paradise island and drink himself to death on absinthe, but, of course, not before he cuts off one of his ears.

In February of 1970 Andrew Wyeth was honored by President and Mrs. Nixon with a dinner and a month-long exhibition at the White House. Said Mrs. Nixon, "I'm a great admirer of Andrew Wyeth and so is the President." Said Mr. Wyeth, "I've consistently admired President Nixon and everything he stands for." It all figures—not a surprise in a carload.

3. *Rembrandt*

For years I have gone along with the theory that Rembrandt was the first realistic painter of bourgeois life. And in a sense he was. He came from and understood the burghers of his period, even going so far as to endow his religious figures with sturdy Dutch characteristics. But the more one examines his work, the more one becomes convinced that realism or naturalism, call it what you will, held relatively little interest for him. At heart he was a visionary involved with the supramundane. His tool was light, an invented luminosity that made visible the invisible. Rembrandt was that dual-edged enigma—an unrealistic realist. He saw figures, faces, and landscapes much as they are; yet he revealed more than a tangible presence, playing his transcendental light not over man and nature alone but through them, for his was a light that pierced at once physically and psychically.

The Rembrandt exhibition at the Art Institute of Chicago once again confirms the dichotomy of this artist's vision. The juxtaposition of Rembrandt's paintings and drawings with those of his followers emphasizes his undeviating superiority, despite the fact that many of the master's more important canvases are missing. But nearly fifty drawings, most of them superlative, make up for the paucity of great paintings. The over-all tenor of the exhibition is scholarly. It poses certain problems and suggests certain solutions as it compares the master with his pupils. For this viewer, except in rare cases, Rembrandt towers above his contemporaries with decisive authority. Why a rapid sketch of his can make an ambitious composition by a follower seem puerile is a question the exhibition repeatedly posits. Also, it asks, what kind of studio, what kind of teaching, produced this impressive entourage of committed disciples, many not much younger than Rembrandt himself?

Like Caravaggio and Cézanne, Rembrandt totally changed the course of painting. After him nothing was the same. He was a catalyst, a landmark, a true forerunner, and, above all, a man who fully faced his own threatening identity. He was the artist who with the simplest means was able to convey the entire gamut of human experience.

Rembrandt's work presents certain imponderables, particu-larly today when authorities are reappraising long-established attributions. Portraits and compositions that for years were ac-cepted as his are now given to one or another of his followers, a fact that makes suspect my conclusion that he always stood taller than they. For who knows? Perhaps next month what we presently call Rembrandt will emerge as Barent Fabritius or Jan Lievens. And yet, despite these doubts, Rembrandt remains an overwhelming personality. Encroachment on the fringes of his work has only strengthened his stature. The real imponder-able, the haunting question, is more basic than that of attribu-tion. We ask what gives this artist such universal appeal. Why more than any other painter is he able to involve and hold his audience, an audience astonishingly wide, ranging from inno-cent neophytes to experienced scholars, from young to old, from abstractionists to stubborn realists? I recall several years ago interviewing seventeen contemporary painters and sculptors whose work represented a broad spectrum. I asked which artists of the past had meant the most to them. Rembrandt was con-spicuously the favorite.

What, then, sets him apart from his associates and, indeed,

from all other painters? We could say his humanity, his compassion, but these qualities are not his alone. Breughel, Daumier,
van Gogh, to mention a few artists at random, were equally concerned with the state of mankind. We could say it was his searching light and line that, interacting, created a new interior force,
but again there were others from El Greco to Giacometti who
devoted themselves to similar chimerical ends.

What makes Rembrandt incomparable is a combination of all
these attributes: his humanity, his light that is more than a
physical element as it shines through and isolates apocalyptic
encounters, plus—and the plus is big—his drive to expose the
living core of everything he touched, the core of man and individual men, of the earth itself. This he did with modest
means. In a tiny drawing, with a smudge or two, a sweeping
line, a few calligraphic pen strokes, he generated a spacious
landscape, moving, expanding before our eyes. Or take his in-
quiring self-portraits. He saw himself as young, middle-aged,
old, and finally sagging with wisdom. He recorded his image
with scrupulous probity, yet ventured beyond himself to mirror
in his own face all stages of human development. In reaching
for bare truths, he did not remove the supernatural from life,
nor did he permit any irrelevancy to obscure it. One feels that
with him the supernatural was daily fare, reflected in and raised
above the familiar.

Rembrandt is frequently identified with Shakespeare. Though
both men displayed matching profundity, Rembrandt was not
like Shakespeare. Less agile and less complicated, Rembrandt
was however no less obsessed with the human condition. Because
his canvases are opulently sonorous, they are sometimes compared to Beethoven's symphonies, but they are related no more
to music than to literature; they clearly belong to the visual
world. All three of these men represent the loftiest peaks of
Western civilization, and that is perhaps why we group them
together; also because their best work was dedicated to the veri-
ties of life.

In the Chicago show, it was Rembrandt's drawings that were
unforgettable. When viewed with those of skilled followers, his
have a dynamism that tames everything in sight. Since most of

his drawings were sketches and not intended as finished works, he allowed himself great latitude. His line is wildly free and imbued with a kind of impromptu brilliance which, when imitated, often turns into little more than technical fireworks. In seventeenth-century Holland, these spontaneous statements by Rembrandt must have seemed starkly revolutionary, and the truth is, they still do, despite his death three hundred years ago. He drew with awkward, virile pen strokes, capturing the essence, the very heart, of his subject. It is this probing intensity we miss in his pupils, who adopted his style but rarely attained his concentrated thrust.

Because of their condensed drama, Rembrandt's drawings are too engrossing to analyze. It is the miraculous event that holds us, not how it was done. And possibly this is the final criterion for all great art. Why parse Hamlet? Why worry about Rembrandt's line? The event I refer to is less connected with subject than with the transmutation of subject into visual equivalents. Thus, religious myths, human likenesses, and rural Dutch landscapes transcend their faithfully local renderings.

A case in point is *The Supper at Emmaus: The Vanishing of Christ,* a pen, ink, and wash drawing that depicts the Bible legend described by Luke. Here what galvanizes us is not the story but the conception. To make an absent figure the pivot of an entire composition is a heroic tour de force. Instead of Christ, a blazing light replaces Him, dominating the scene with occult radiance. For the light is Christ, or should we say it is His afterglow; yet it is likewise Rembrandt's light, a power that elevates his work to metaphysical heights. The artist's candid approach to immediate surroundings and his lack of affectation confused his followers, who misjudged him for a realist. They took him literally, rarely recognizing the earthy mysticism that eluded their grasp.

To compare Rembrandt's *Female Nude Seated on a Stool* with Govert Flinck's *Seated Female Nude* is an interesting exercise. The Flinck drawing is earlier and probably not influenced by Rembrandt, though later Flinck was to adopt the master's style. The two drawings speak for themselves. One adheres strictly to seventeenth-century stereotypes, to discreet, sculpturesque drapery and theatrical gestures. Flinck's figure is well drawn but easily forgotten; it is one of many. Rembrandt's heavy, unbeautiful woman seen against flickering shadows is unique. She does not posture; she sits firmly on a modest stool; yet for some reason her thick, bare body has a dignity and humanity lacking in

Female Nude Seated on a Stool, by Rembrandt

Flinck's idealized version. Rembrandt's nude, carefully observed and undoubtedly drawn from life, seems singularly vulnerable, her drooping head and ungainly torso touched by melancholy. Two centuries later, figures like this were to influence van Gogh, another Dutch disciple of the greatest Dutchman of them all.

In his maturity, Rembrandt was progressively less concerned with established art conventions. By this time he was completely

Seated Female Nude, by Govert Flinck

The Supper at Emmaus: The Vanishing of Christ, by Rembrandt

his own man, though his popular image had faded somewhat. His late self-portraits give eloquent evidence of pitiless integrity and patient intelligence. With no vestige of self-indulgence or sentimentality he envisioned his own face as the map of mankind, endowing it with unexpected pragmatism. One recognizes in Goya a contempt for the human race, but Rembrandt's searing honesty was mellowed by what must have been faith in his fellow men.

The media he depended on were merely the servants of his

vision. It is true that paint, ink, wash were important to him, but they were not prime factors. Unlike numerous artists today, the medium was never his message. The new methods he invented grew out of his need to communicate through his work. At present, the reverse is often true. Methods and meaning are now implicit in and limited to the material itself, be it plastic, wood, movement, or color.

It was light that Rembrandt zealously liberated, manipulating it to his own ends. He conceived of this fluctuating element as a potent central motif and as the star performer in many of his paintings. With arbitrary light, surging pigment, and a wide orchestration of line, his work became a touchstone for modern Expressionism. Who, before Rembrandt, eliminated all conventional traditions and allowed a painted picture to look like a painting, even though it was not restricted to purely physical properties? Who, before him, so completely rethought religious symbolism as to identify it with the daily life of his period, and for that matter with the life of all periods? This man virtually changed the iconography of Western art without diminishing its fervor. He made religious legends accessible to us all, because, though never rationalizing the unattainable, he related it to our common knowledge.

And so we continue to cherish him. He has revealed the age-old secrets that eluded us when presented earlier in hieratic stylizations. He was able to transmit past wisdom in terms of our own aspirations. Though everything there is to say about Rembrandt has already been said, it bears repeating. For he remains an untarnished force in our lives.

4. *Clyfford Still*

Clyfford Still is an enigma and a challenge. Sometimes denounced, he is more often recognized as a pivotal figure in the American Abstract Expressionist movement, though his own work does not always conform to the school he sparked. Because he has stubbornly protected his privacy, his name is hardly a household word, but among artists and the knowing he remains a potent force and an elusive one. For years, he has personally avoided the "in" art scene, nor has he shown his canvases except in rare instances. He is very much a man who walks alone. The only other illustrious American painter to absent himself so pointedly is Mark Tobey. Yet both artists seem to be thriving, their late work often their best.

Those who resent Still most are frequently the very men he has influenced. Dates are bandied back and forth to prove "who did what first." Whether Clyfford Still or John Doe turned out the earliest "black painting" is of no great moment. What does matter is that certain dense, dark canvases by Still, some dating from almost thirty years ago, opened the way to important discoveries. Beneath opaque blacks and other nocturnal colors he compressed energies that finally fermented into a molten existence of their own. With him pigment and color were already one, but it was the surging undercurrents that turned his paintings into living organisms. He seemed to squeeze light out of black. His canvases no longer represented nature but, charged with the immutable laws of nature, asserted their own physical identity.

It was especially these early works that changed the course of contemporary American painting, a fact that struck me forcibly when I recently visited Still in New Windsor, a small Maryland retirement town midway between Baltimore and Gettysburg. There the artist lives in an unlikely turn-of-the-century mansion decorated with white columns and next to a funeral parlor. The whole setting has an aura of serenity; it looks like a place to come home to. When I saw Still a few years earlier, he was established on a nearby farm where the barn served as studio and the modest house as home. In the latter, ceilings were too low and rooms too limited to see his paintings properly, but the adjacent barn with its ample white walls was a perfect setting. I remember walking in on a damp winter day, the barn empty except for three vast late canvases that illuminated the bare interior with a kind of exaltation.

Still has kept the farm and, when weather permits, continues to paint in the barn, for there size presents no problem. He can be as expansive as he wants, and, as a rule, his sumptuous canvases demand the sweep of unrestricted space. Because of inadequate heat at the farm, winter finds him working in the New Windsor house, a large house, let me add, that is dedicated to his paintings. Living space for himself and his family is comfortable, but top billing goes to the studio and to other rooms piled high with stretched canvases plus hundreds of rolled ones, some of them thirteen feet long.

In this curiously anachronistic building with its stained-glass windows and panels of oak and maple, the artist's work takes on an uninterrupted flow. Many of the paintings might be safer in a warehouse, but Still seems to need them around him both as recapitulations of the past and as clues to the future. I think if he could have his way, he would sell nothing and keep intact the entire record of his life. For the paintings are his life. He says,

"They are my way of growing and thinking; they're my auto-biography." He sees them as an "extension of his mind and heart and hand." They are the center of his being; he would sacrifice anything to protect their integrity. And he is fortunate that both his wife and daughter feel the same. So the pictures remain at home to be studied, compared, and cherished.

It is, however, a bit unnerving to realize that most of this man's life work is preserved in an anonymous Maryland town where fire could inflict serious damage and where neighbors probably have no idea that a legendary figure is living next door. Still has deliberately ordered his life this way. After eleven years in New York, he moved to the Maryland farm in 1961, not because his painting was suffering from city life but because he himself was suffering from lack of fresh air and from a sense of feeling "crowded and pressed." Born sixty-five years ago in North Dakota, and raised alternately in Spokane, Washington, and on a homestead in southern Alberta, Canada, he has never gotten the West out of his system. It represents a "free mobility" that permeates his thinking, yet environment does not directly affect his work. The hills of Maryland, the prairies of Canada, the East, the West are never source material for him. It was the spirit of the West, Still claims, that got into his bones. Except perhaps for the size of successive studios, no other surroundings ever circumscribed his canvases.

Freedom is Clyfford Still's password. His late paintings are totally liberated; they defy gravity as they lift off and soar, the viewer soaring with them. Measured, open, and often trembling with light, these canvases have an exuberance rarely found in his early work. It is almost as if they mirror the emancipation that an isolated life and increasing technical proficiency can generate. In order to remain free, Still has resigned three life-time university sinecures and avoided all commercialized pit-falls. He wants no intrusions, no art gossip, no press views, no cockail parties, no openings or closings, no novelties, no petty competition. He is dead set on his own course, and this, to be sure, is his ultimate freedom. He is his own man; he belongs to himself and believes in himself.

A show in 1969 at the Marlborough Gallery was Still's first

New York exhibition in eighteen years, a vacuum not due to lack of offers. As a matter of fact, he was importuned by a procession of dealers who recognized him as the seminal influence he is. There are, indeed, very few Abstract Expressionist painters from either the first or second generations of the movement who have not been swayed by him at one time or another. Only Willem de Kooning with his strong European orientation remained immune, and Jackson Pollock, whose attack was too obsessive to permit or need outside implementation.

The show at Marlborough did not pretend to be a complete survey, nor was it organized by the artist, but nonetheless the forty-five works, stemming from 1943 to 1966, provided clear evidence of Still's impact on his period. One found a wide variety of expression, from sonorously orchestrated curtains of color to shredded firmaments either suspended on or dashing across open areas of unpainted canvas. One found depths of red, blue, or earth brown gashed by cleavages more luminous than linear. Some works were closed as if locked away; others were open, permitting one to look in, through, and beyond. Almost always Still's paintings are conceived vertically. Stretching up, they seem to escape finite boundaries. In many cases they are too disciplined to qualify as orthodox Abstract Expressionism, and yet they are. For, once Still puts brush to canvas, his paint begins to churn under its own steam and take on an activist role.

To understand this artist fully, one should start at the beginning, as early as 1925, and follow his progression. It is not single works that stand out; it is a sequence of hard-won battles. In his youth he turned to established European movements, notably Cubism and Surrealism, but eventually he escaped to find his own roots. At New Windsor, two oils (one a farm scene, the other an accomplished still-life of rocks) painted when Still was twenty-one and living on his father's homestead farm in Canada suggest that the young artist had already mastered the more frustrating technicalities. He knew how to draw, and later this basic skill was to give sinews to every brushstroke he raced across a canvas, a fact that came home to me as we were having coffee in the living room. Hanging there was a recent black calligraphic composition bristling with electricity. Only a superb draftsman could have invested a painted surface with such vitality. The work is an authentic kinetic explosion that puts to shame those tame neon experiments that twinkle in museums and galleries these days.

The two 1925 canvases reminded Still of his past, of his growing-up years on isolated plains in Canada where winter averaged twenty below zero and summer often reached one hundred degrees, where in a severe home environment there was no hint of art. From the beginning he had to dig everything out for himself, stealing time to draw and paint between farm chores. He still remembers his first trip to New York when he was twenty. On a bleak autumn morning he arrived at the Metropolitan Museum of Art, waiting in the rain for the museum to open. Unprepared for the then dreary installations and murky light, he was disappointed, but disappointed even more because these long awaited European masterpieces seemed alien to him. They represented a world apart from his. He also recalls enrolling at the Art Students League and pulling out after forty-five minutes, persuaded that the rudiments he was offered there he had already absorbed at home.

Though Still taught for many years—in Washington, California (where he influenced an entire generation), and Virginia—he is convinced that traditional art education is useless. Each man must find his own way. When I asked him what his main thrust had been, he answered "self-discovery," but he made clear that for him self-discovery was less concerned with finding out about himself than with creating himself. One gathers that only through his work does he exist and grow. He cannot divide his life, nor does he want to. All of which no doubt explains why Still is so vulnerable and so often alienated from colleagues he once respected. He demands the same purity from them that he exacts from himself. With naïve trust he expects the present-day art jungle to face up to the highest ideals of history. He sees art as a moral force and hence is bitter when he finds this trust betrayed. For him, "art is the only aristocracy left where a man takes full responsibility."

Numerous fellow painters of his generation seem bent on self-destruction. For some reason they have flirted with and, alas, often succumbed to, early death. Many of them have lived with the same untidy spontaneity that invests their tumultuous "action" paintings. Not so Clyfford Still. He has consciously structured an ordered life, and though he personally is sometimes angry with the state of the world and the state of art, his work usually rises above specific emotions. The artist himself remains vigorous, his step light, his face lean and alert. For him, life is still a miracle. And, not surprisingly, his recent work reflects this optimism. Often it is as fresh and stabbing as if he were painting it before our eyes.

Still deals with painted imponderables. Space becomes a yawning void in which volumes sweep upward with such tense velocity as to exaggerate the boundless areas they move through. This invented geography of the mind is an interrelated experience. No one element lives alone. No color, no brushstroke, no void, no surface detail is separate from the whole. The artist put it better when he said, "I never wanted color to be color. I never wanted texture to be texture, or images to become shapes. I wanted them all to fuse together into a living spirit." Basic to this fusion is Still's sheer power of paint. Pigment can be cool and thin, but more often it boils. Not interested in concealing the stamp of his own hand, he freely admits that for him "the paint is the instrument." The pigment becomes life, like a majestic river of controlled lava. It is little wonder this artist claims Rembrandt as "one of his early gods."

There are times when Clyfford Still reminds me of Mies van der Rohe, not that their work is in any way similar—only their attitude toward their work. Mies once dismissed a prospective client who, bored with his austere purity, wanted him to come up with a new architectural formula. "What do you think I've been doing all my life?" he asked. Like him, Still thinks of each work as an inevitable link to the next. The paintings are never accidental, but the connections between them inexorably direct the course they must follow. Also like Mies, as he grows older, Still refines, intensifies, at times reassesses, but never feels the need to perform new tricks. Somehow both men, I think, have understood their place in history.

Except for the paintings in New Windsor, there are only

two other important concentrations of the artist's work—a fine group in Buffalo, New York, at the Albright-Knox Art Gallery and the ones at Marlborough. In 1964 Still gave the Buffalo gallery thirty-one canvases ranging from 1937 to 1963. In addition, the museum had earlier acquired two. These thirty-three works join together as a splended résumé, but nothing quite equals the experience of visiting the Maryland house. There, Mrs. Still and Clyfford's daughter, Sandra, are cataloguing and photographing, both in color and black-and-white, each individual work, a number that will probably total between fifteen hundred and two thousand.

Before the photographic operation got started, Mrs. Still customarily made small, faithful sketches of each rolled canvas for identification purposes. Many can still be seen attached to bulky canvas bundles. For the paintings remain nameless, as they should. They are not about life; they lead their own lives.

5. *Mies van der Rohe*

Ludwig Mies van der Rohe was born in Aachen, Germany, in 1886 and died in Chicago in 1969. As director of the Bauhaus in Dessau and Berlin from 1930 to 1933, and as director of the Illinois Institute of Technology's School of Architecture in Chicago from 1938 until he retired in 1958, Mies made history as an educator. But more important is the history he made as a builder.

The following interview took place in 1964 at Mies's Chicago office. On a nearby wall hung an enlarged photograph of a 1919 Berlin drawing, a project for a glass skyscraper that was never built. Opposite stood the scale model of a modern art museum then being constructed in West Berlin. Though separated by forty-five years, these two buildings were each characterized by the same flawless purity, the same uncompromising clarity that we recognize as Mies van der Rohe's signature.

QUESTION : Which do you consider your most important building ?

MIES : My whole life has been a search for good architecture. Everything I've read (and I've read a lot in my life) was

directed toward finding an answer to the question of truth.
What is this thing called truth? Everyone uses the word but
who can really explain it? To learn that truth is relative requires a long search. It took me years to find out, to find out
how to make a clear, honest construction. My entire life has
been one trip in that direction—so no single building stands
out.

In the beginning I worked with small units. At the time I
started I still had to grow up. When I was young, mostly
small houses came my way. Of my European work, the
Tugendhat House (Brno, Czechoslovakia, 1930) is considered
outstanding, but I think only because it was the first modern
house to use rich materials, to have great elegance. At that
time modern buildings were still austerely functional. I personally don't consider the Tugendhat House more important
than other works that I designed considerably earlier.

Another example is the German Pavilion at the Barcelona
Exposition, built a half year earlier. You know, there were
already seventeen enormous general buildings—really palaces
—planned for the exhibition when representatives of the German government heard that France and England were each
putting up separate national pavilions. So they decided to have
one, too. I asked, "For what purpose?" They said, "We
don't know—just build a pavilion, but not too much glass!"
If I'd used brick, the pavilion would have been equally good
architecture (I like brick), but I doubt if it would have become as celebrated, for this was really the first modern building to use rich materials, even before the Tugendhat House.

QUESTION: Which projects have you designed that you most regret were never built?

MIES: I never regret. I knew, for instance, that the glass skyscraper I designed in Germany around 1920 would never be
built. I designed it for a competition. As a matter of fact,
nothing was built; the whole project was dropped. I realized
that at the time Germany was not ready for my design, but
I was interested in the idea. I did it for that reason, not to win
a competition.

Much later—in Chicago in 1954—I designed a square building with no interior columns, 720 feet by 720 feet, planned as a convention hall. I'll tell you why I particularly wanted to design that building. When I was young I started with simple brick structures, then went on to larger buildings like the Barcelona pavilion and then to office buildings. I had already tried to solve these various types of construction, but during my life one type was still missing—an enormous open building. Of course, by this time I'd put up Crown Hall at Illinois Institute of Technology; yet I had never designed a structure of really monumental quality until the convention hall.

QUESTION: Would it be possible for this design to be used elsewhere?

MIES: Of course. I don't feel site is that important. I am first interested in a good building; then I place it in the best possible spot.

QUESTION: What is a good building?

MIES: That's the question I'm pursuing—the question of truth. Long ago I knew that architecture had to be related to our time, but now I feel it can only be the expression of our civilization.

QUESTION: Are you saying that your architecture is a reaction against the chaos around us?

MIES: Yes, in a sense, but it is more than that. It is very difficult to define our civilization. And it is far different to put this thought into words than to build it.

QUESTION: Do you design for yourself or for your client?

MIES: I build not for myself, not for my client. I build for the sake of architecture.

QUESTION: Do you consider over-all design more important than the needs of people using your buildings?

MIES: I think personal needs are taken care of in all my build-

ings, but not personal whims. There is an aphorism by Goethe:
"It is neither core nor shell—it is all one." The interior and
exterior of my buildings are one—you can't divorce them.
The outside takes care of the inside.

Modern buildings of our time are so huge that one must
group them. Often the space between these buildings is as
important as the buildings themselves. I'm working now
on a project for San Francisco, a group of three structures—
two apartment buildings and one for recreation. Important
to me is how these buildings are related to each other. You
can see an example of this here in Chicago. In the group of
apartments between 860 and 900 Lake Shore Drive we purposely opened up the surrounding and intervening space; now
this space is being filled up with additional buildings. How
ridiculous!

QUESTION: From your experience as director of the Bauhaus
and later of the School of Architecture at Illinois Institute
of Technology, do you feel that architecture can be taught?
MIES: You can teach students how to work; you can teach them
technique—how to use reason; you can even give them a sense
of proportions, of order. You can teach them general principles. If a man knows these principles, he is at least able to
reach his potential, and this differs, of course, for each student. But the different potentials are not the teacher's problem. As far as I was concerned, every student working under
me was given the same problem—only in order to make the
general principles clearer.

Some students you simply cannot teach. What's important
is not to act as if everyone's a genius. As I have often said,
architecture starts when you carefully put two bricks together.
There it begins.

When I came to the Illinois Institute of Technology I figured we'd have about twenty students a year and if there
were two good ones each year, that meant ten in five years. I
thought we really only needed two good ones to change Chicago.

QUESTION: From the beginning did you start in the direction you have consistently followed?

MIES: Yes—I've simply tried to make my direction clearer and clearer. I feel my work has become clearer. I don't think every building I put up needs to be different, since I always apply the same principles. For me novelty has no interest, none whatsoever.

QUESTION: What were the most important influences on your work?

MIES: I thought a lot and I controlled my thoughts in my work —and I controlled my work through my thoughts. I read voraciously when I was young—philosophy, natural science, sociology. I wasted a lot of time on sociology; I don't believe it has much to do with building—it's another problem. My father was a stone mason, so it was natural that I would either continue his work or turn to building. I had no conventional architectural education. I worked under a few good architects; I read a few good books—and that's about it.

QUESTION: What architecture from the past has impressed you the most?

MIES: I was impressed by Romanesque and Gothic cathedrals, by Roman aqueducts, by the Pitti Palace in Florence, and by modern suspension bridges. They're still the best buildings in New York.

QUESTION: Has living in Chicago these many years affected your work? Has the proximity of the so-called Chicago school changed your thinking in any way?

MIES: I really don't know the Chicago school. You see, I never walk; I always take taxis back and forth to work. I rarely see the city. In 1912 when I was working in The Hague I first saw a drawing by Louis Sullivan of one of his buildings. It interested me. Before I came to Chicago I also knew about Frank Lloyd Wright and particularly about the Robie house. If you remember, I wrote about Wright in the Museum of Modern Art catalogue for my 1947 exhibition. [Excerpt:

"At this moment (1910) so critical for us, the exhibition of Frank Lloyd Wright came to Berlin. . . . The encounter was destined to prove of great significance to the European development. The work of this great master presented an architectural world of unexpected force, clarity of language, and disconcerting richness of form. . . . Here again, at long last, genuine organic architecture flowered."]

[In discussing Sullivan and Wright a few years ago, Mies was quoted in the British magazine *Architectural Design* as saying that their work was "very interesting and very important. . . . Yet we would not do what Sullivan did. We see things with different eyes, because it is a different time. Sullivan still believed in the façade. It was still the old architecture. He did not consider that just the structure could be enough. Now we would go on for our own time—and we would make architecture with the structure only. Likewise with Wright. He was different from Sullivan, and we for equal reasons are different from Wright."]

As to your question, no; living in Chicago has had no effect on me. When I first arrived, I immediately went to the campus of the then Armour Institute (now the Illinois Institute of Technology). I felt I ought to turn around and go home.

QUESTION: Speaking of campuses, how important is continuity of design?

MIES: I firmly believe a campus must have unity. Allowing every building or group of buildings to be designed by a different architect is sometimes considered democratic, but from my point of view this is just an excuse to avoid the responsibility of accepting one clear idea. The only American campus worth the name was built by Thomas Jefferson at the University of Virginia.

QUESTION: What should be the relationship of architecture to sculpture and architecture to painting?

MIES: What I like most is to come on a fine work of art and

then find a place for it. But first the architecture must be good. I do not believe that sculpture or painting can be included in the original design of a building. To start with, the architect must work alone, because I believe above all in the clear structure itself. Here I differ from Corbusier. Since he is also a painter he tends to incorporate color in his buildings; I prefer natural materials.

In the initial design of my buildings I do not believe there can be cooperation between the artist and the architect. The reason is simple: my structural objectives always have an objective character, never subjective. I get along well with artists, but their work has nothing to do with my work.

6. *Alfred Barr: Modern Art's Durable Crusader*

More years ago than I like to remember, when I was a student at Vassar College, a remarkable, somewhat emaciated young man appeared on campus to instruct us in rudimentary art history. He was a fervent teacher who turned what I had selected as a snap course into a three-dimensional—and, for me, unforgettable—experience. It was not just orthodox art history—it was art's vital relation to the life of its time that he stressed. Later when I was a curator at the Art Institute of Chicago and he was top man at New York's Museum of Modern Art, I worked again with him on joint exhibition projects, and as at Vassar, I never failed to learn from Alfred Barr.

Once, in anticipation of a trip to the Soviet Union, I gathered together available reading matter on Russian painting by the same Mr. Barr, a name we have come to associate with the immediate present and not with the fine points of earlier Slavic art. Even the sternest Soviet experts grudgingly respect his knowledge of their own nineteenth century, a period extravagantly admired by them and too little known by most of us in the Western world. I have even heard that once, when visiting the U.S.S.R., Mr. Barr was invited to lecture on this very subject to a Soviet audience.

Unlike many modern specialists, he presumably finds it helpful to explore the past before appraising the present. And, indeed, how can one hope to evaluate even so obvious a movement as Socialist Realism without studying its sources, ambiguous as they may be? After all, the history of art is sometimes less dull than those contemporary critics claim who think that all art worth discussing started with Cézanne and that all historians are incurably blinded by dates and data.

Over the years I have never failed to marvel when eminent print curators extol Mr. Barr's proficiency in their difficult field, notably where old masters are concerned; when bridge enthusiasts tell me he is a whiz at their game; when accomplished musicians admire his understanding of their profession; and when ornithologists salute his informed bird-watching skills. What makes all this the more impressive, of course, is Alfred Barr's encyclopedic grounding in his own field of modern art plus his unique contribution to its acceptance, enjoyment, and understanding—not only throughout America but all over Europe, Latin America, and Asia. Surely no one in the present century has so acutely changed our attitudes toward the art of our times, toward museums and their practices, toward art publications (an area much enriched by Mr. Barr's own perceptive writings), and, above all, toward the meaning of the word "art." He was, I believe, the first to envision it as a far more inclusive term than merely a label for painting, sculpture, and graphics. It was largely he who incorporated architecture, industrial design, photography, and the film into the daily life of our museums.

Mr. Barr does not indulge in the usual art clichés, nor does he make oracular statements that lend themselves to instant publicity. Instead he examines each work probingly in terms of itself. Though sometimes accused of tastemaking, he is too interested in meanings to accept so shallow a role. With missionary zeal he has conscientiously tried to explain the art of our times by weaving it into the context of all art. If occasionally he hoped to cubbyhole present trends a bit too neatly before they had jelled, more often he predicted the future with clairvoyant sensibility. What better proof than the permanent collection of the Museum of Modern Art, unquestionably the best survey of its kind in the world? Mr. Barr is also responsible for several of that museum's most useful innovations and services, many of which are now standard practice throughout America and Europe. Every modern gallery models itself to some extent on this pioneer New York prototype. Even the Metropolitan is beginning to borrow certain of Mr. Barr's techniques, an interesting full-circle phenomenon, since it was the Metropolitan's stubborn conservatism that originally spawned the Museum of Modern Art.

And now, alas, Mr. Barr is retiring after thirty-nine productive years, first as director and subsequently as director of collections. One wonders where sniping critics, disgruntled artists, and occasional envious colleagues will direct their potshots now that Alfred Barr is no longer there to act as a favorite target. One also wonders when the American art world will be graced again with so erudite, thoughtful, and creative a champion.

Because Mr. Barr has been written about voluminously, both pro and con, I decided it would be interesting to hear what he has to say about himself and about the museum he, more than anyone else, helped to establish. So I posed to him a number of questions, to which he responded with characteristic candor, modesty, and courtesy. Here are my questions and his answers.

Q. What do you feel are the most important contributions the Museum of Modern Art has made since it was founded nearly forty years ago?

A. (1) Establishment in 1929 of a new museum in New York, a very great city which had an active art community but lacked a museum devoted enough and strong enough to take responsibility for an area avoided by the Metropolitan Museum, namely the recent past (which, of course, includes the present).

(2) The Museum's serious concern for certain highly important arts of our time generally ignored by art museums—namely the film, photography, architecture and city planning, design in industrial design, consumer goods, typography, and graphic arts.

(3) Encouragement of universities to accept the modern arts as a proper field for scholarly study and publication.

(4) The Museum's collections.

(5) The exhibition program both within the walls of the Museum and, perhaps more important, the distribution of exhibitions throughout the country and abroad on a scale not previously attempted.

(6) Seven exhibitions (and publications) from 1933 to 1954 of primitive and pre-Columbian art, which in that period rarely appeared in art museums or in the history of art curricula of universities but which were—and are—almost as deeply involved in the taste and aesthetics of our century as are abstract art and Surrealism.

(7) The most beautiful garden on Manhattan.

Q. Are there projects you envisioned for the Museum that still wait to be done?

A. The projects I "envisioned" in 1929, and many others I did not foresee, such as circulating exhibitions here and abroad, a great library, a publishing house—all these and others thrive or are about to.

The Museum chronically needs more space for exhibiting its collections in all departments, especially in prints and drawings, photography, architecture and design, and painting of the past decade. In a few years there will be more gallery space.

The Museum is developing its educational and scholarly facilities, particularly the library and archives; making accessible all the works of art in the collection which cannot be shown in the galleries; planning complete catalogues of the collections with the intention to keep them up to date; establishing greater rapport with schools and universities; studying the problematical methods of how best to help the public understand art.

Q. Where should the Museum of Modern Art head from here? Where does its future lie?

A. I think the near future of the Museum of Modern Art lies in solving the problems which it faces and in developing the programs which it already has under way; but I assume—indeed, I hope—that there will be new problems and programs which none of us has foreseen.

Q. Does the present existence of numerous modern museums in New York change the role of the Museum of Modern Art?

A. I do not think the lively presence of other New York museums concerned with modern art need change the role of the Museum of Modern Art. The four or five other institutions in Manhattan are scarcely enough to meet the public's demand and the encouragement of artists. Weekend crowds are often too big for the comfort of people and the safety of the works of art.

The Museum of Modern Art does compete with other museums in temporary loan shows; it competes much less in showing continuously visible collections of prints, drawings, photography, architecture and design, and the recurrent programs from the film collection. (Other enterprises, such as the very active international program, are, of course, not visible to the New York public.)

Q. Because modern art has become fashionable, is there less need to promote it as vigorously as heretofore?

A. Yes, there is less need to promote modern art than there was three decades ago. But even then, I did not think of the Museum as promoting twentieth-century painting any more than the Metropolitan Museum promoted quattrocento painting.

Q. What part of your work at the Museum have you most enjoyed?

A. Seeing dreams come true.

Q. What part have you least enjoyed?

A. Fund-raising, interruptions, allocating too sparse gallery space, rejecting unwanted gifts, and, worst of all, in recent years seeing so few exhibitions outside the Museum.

Q. What has been your guiding acquisition policy?
A. (1) Securing the best works by the best artists.
   (2) Collecting their work in breadth and depth and in all relevant media.
   (3) Collecting good work by secondary artists.
   (4) Taking chances with the work of young artists.
   (5) Searching for good work throughout the world.
   (6) Other things being equal, selecting paintings with vertical formats rather than horizontal—the vertical takes less wall space.

Q. Where exhibitions and acquisitions are concerned, should a museum stress what its staff considers best or merely what is going on?
A. The staff should try hard to discern the best of what is going on and act without partisanship.

Q. Do you know of any modern collection that from an over-all point of view can compare qualitatively and quantitatively with the Museum of Modern Art's?
A. No.

Q. After your many years at the Museum what do you consider the authentic role of the modern art critic?
A. I'm not sure how to answer "authentic role." Obviously, critics have different functions, such as reporting and criticizing, and in different degrees. I believe that fundamentally the critic of contemporary art ought to like "what is going on" more than he dislikes it. If he does not like it, he should retire. Art thrives on enthusiasm.

Q. What are your personal plans for the future? Will you be writing extensively and, if so, in what specific areas?
A. Finish scandalously delayed prefaces and appendices for a new edition of the catalogue *Painting and Sculpture in the*

Museum Collections; with James Thrall Soby, initiate a series
of short monographs on works in the collection of special
interest and importance, the series to be published in honor
of Mrs. Simon Guggenheim; write confidential notes on works
in the collection of painting and sculpture for the use of
future curators in case they should be interested; revise for
republication monographs on Picasso and Matisse.

7. *Moholy-Nagy*

When László Moholy-Nagy went to Chicago in 1937 as director of the New Bauhaus, he was forty-two years old. Nine years later he died of leukemia, but in the interval he made an indelible imprint on Chicago and, indeed, on the entire country. I remember meeting him a day or two after he arrived from Europe, where he was already known as a professor at the Bauhaus and as an artist who had experimented with new forms of painting, photography, sound and documentary films, as well as theater and commercial design. He was like a charged dynamo; ideas poured out of him a mile a minute. And we listened, hypnotized. Moholy made us feel that anything was possible; for him, everything was.

Already he was prophesying the end of easel painting, arguing that modern technology and the new architecture were bound to make the orthodox framed picture obsolete, a prediction that has very nearly come to pass. He foretold, too, that art works eventually would be designed by painters and sculptors, but manufactured by machinery, a common practice today. As early as 1922 Moholy tested this idea with his now famous *Telephone Pictures*, so called because he phoned all descriptive specifica-

tions about them to a sign company, which in turn carried out
his orders in three different sizes. The resulting abstractions,
distinguished by a spare spatial purity, conjure up both the past
and the future. We think of the Russian Suprematists, Malevich
and El Lissitzky, both of whom strongly influenced Moholy's
early work; we also think of present-day Minimalists and their
starkly reduced means. For Moholy was no less an inheritor than
an activator. His *Telephone Pictures,* repeated in three descending sizes, removed the capital ''A'' from art as they investigated
possibilities related to scale, duplication, and industrial fabrica-
tion. Other European artists, notably Marcel Duchamp even
earlier, were likewise proposing an art divorced from the human
hand; they had become suspicious of rich Gallic pigment and
aggressively personal expression.

All of which makes it difficult to understand why Moholy
remained a painter to the end. True, his most interesting work
was often not on canvas. Obsessed as he was with the idea of
space, and later with space and light, he attempted at times to
paint with light, exploring all manner of new materials, such as
neolith, Galalith, trolit, colon, rhodoit, and Plexiglas. Probing
indefatigably for that most volatile of all elements—speeding luminosity—he hoped to capture it in layers of transparent, translucent, light-sensitized substances.

Why our century more than any other has produced an art so
concerned with space and light has never been fully explained.
Vastly accelerated forms of communication and transportation,
new artificial intensifications of light, and the whole syndrome of
space exploration are obvious stimuli. Yet, surely an emphasis
on two such abstract elements is not based solely on modern science and technology but perhaps also on the unconscious need
to escape the stifling materialism this very science and technology have created.

Moholy was a Hungarian, yet he was every inch an international figure by the time he left England for Chicago. Intermittently he had lived in his own country, Germany, Austria,
Holland, and Britain. Curiously, he was less affected by the
great painters of the Bauhaus than by the philosophy of that
school. He felt that art must be an integrated experience, in-

tegrated with daily living, with producing and consuming. For him it was never an isolated or precious encounter; it was available to and mandatory for everyone. In the Institute of Design, the process of making art was irrevocably tied up with the process of seeing and using it. At that school, let me add, no cleavage existed between the fine and commercial arts. All was one. All evolved from the interrelationships of nature, man, and modern technology.

Moholy was convinced that visual order would eventually result in social good. Like the Russian Suprematists and Constructivists who flourished during the early years of the U.S.S.R., he equated art with ethics. That the Soviet Union has completely repudiated this way of thinking is evidenced by the all-powerful Socialist Realist movement, which intersperses propaganda with kindergarten banalities. All visual order is gone. But oddly enough, it is the West that continues to build on these earlier revolutionary conceptions. If Moholy's optimistic idealism is somewhat moribund today, his insistence on the union of art and science is very much alive.

The purer Moholy's work, the better, for at heart he was not an easel painter. His oils on canvas rarely approximated the fugitive vision he pursued. They were too heavy-handed, too romantic for the clarity of his thinking. In other media, however, he succeeded with a brilliance that foretold much of today's scene.

His drawings, even those on canvas, have a terse economy, a velocity that transforms them into restless space notations. His remarkable *Light-Space Modulator Machine,* developed between 1921 and 1930, is a mobile construction of steel, plastic, and wood that predated the current enthusiasm for kinetic art by almost a half century. Here Moholy substituted electrically propelled light for brush and paint. This assemblance of metal rods, screens, spheres, and diagonals was motorized and eventually became the central motif in a pioneer film called *Light-Play Black-White-Gray.* The artist's widow, Sibyl Moholy-Nagy, comments that the film "now seems almost like the cardiogram of Moholy's creative heart." For with this work he hit his stride; it was here he conquered light.

I recall the first time the film was shown in Chicago. For me it was an exhilarating experience, and reassuring proof that light and space in art differ from light and space in tangible surroundings. Though still ephemeral, real light and real space have more than an illusory existence; in art they result from purely metaphysical investigations that recognize no boundaries. Here, at last, we find unrestricted freedom. We come to understand real space and light more intensely after confronting their aesthetic equivalents. For only then do we accept the ambiguities that make these visual experiences more than visual. After all, we exist in space; we feel the warmth of light; we do not merely see these phenomena.

Later, Moholy simplified his *Space Modulators,* though he still used a variety of materials in multiple layers, thus hoping to incorporate real shadows, real transparencies, and real, if limited, space. Certain of the younger artists today accept Moholy's tradition, at least in part. Take Donald Judd, who says, "Three dimensions are real space. That gets rid of illusionism. . . ." But Moholy never tried to eliminate all illusionism. He realized that art must remain a transmutation, though at the same time an experience in its own right. His best works were often dependent on physically tangible substances. He saluted the neon tube and doubtless would have used it had it been readily available, for I am sure he would have considered the light-giving tube superior to its painted image. Still, the tube as such could not have been the end aim for him; he was after a more complex structure where tubes merely acted as accessories.

He was after those positive and negative reactions of substance and shadow, of form and reflection, of speed and rest, of black, white, and gray, of sound, silence, and echo. In his *Space and Light Modulators* he sent light streaking along edges of Plexiglas and chrome-plated steel. His most memorable works became vehicles for choreographed luminosity, especially the Chicago series. I can still see the Moholys' first apartment on Astor Street, where the long entrance hall was lined with his earlier paintings from Europe, often dark, precise canvases in the tradition of the Suprematists and the Constructivists. He remained a Constructivist in Chicago, but here his plastic sculpture, his transparent looping constructions, his painted designs incised on Plexiglas and reflected on surfaces underneath became entirely his own.

Moholy's American output differs not so much in emphasis as in means, though it is usually gayer, brighter, faster, less inhibited. No single work stands out, for he was more interested in ideas than in any specific production. As an educator, too, he was more concerned with over-all conceptions than with individual students. His Chicago work incorporated a new world that he never ceased to probe. I can think of no other European artist except Léger who so fully understood this country and who was able to reflect its spirit so intuitively. In Moholy's late convoluted plastic sculpture, form ceased to exist. He no longer painted with light; he drew with it. Sharp transparent edges acted as luminous conveyers for nervous racing highlights. At this point, he was vaporizing, reducing, reorganizing, and remaking his surroundings. If single works are sometimes disappointing, their multiple impact is triumphant.

Moholy's life was snuffed out too early. Some artists die young but have said their say. He hadn't. At the apex of his career and still far in advance of his own generation, he worked avidly until the last day. He and we are deprived of knowing what he would have done next. Moholy wrote widely and well. One need only read two of his books—*The New Vision* and *Vision in Motion*—to recognize how much this versatile, vital man bequeathed to us.

8. *Delacroix*

The Delacroix exhibition at the Louvre is, as the French say, formidable. Building up step by step, it leaves one breathless, partly because of sheer size (almost seven hundred works, including paintings, watercolors, and drawings) but chiefly because of the artist's inexhaustible powers of invention. Not many painters in history could survive such complete exposure.

If today Delacroix's subjects seem overromantic, even alien, there is no denying that his methods set the pace for much of modern art. Present-day eyes tend to look more sympathetically on the honest realism of his contemporary, Gustave Courbet, but it would be folly to underestimate Delacroix merely because he infused a hard-earned freedom with extravagant and occasional high-flown gestures. No artist in the nineteenth century, a century of glory for French painting, broke ground more courageously than he. Technically a consummate innovator, he remained something of an anomaly, imposing electrifying new methods on familiar trappings. As Maurice Serullaz, commissioner general of the exhibition, observed in the catalogue, Delacroix was at once the last great Renaissance master and the first great modern one.

Recalling Turner, who also outpaced the Impressionists, Delacroix as early as 1826 was breaking color into stabs of startling luminosity. The following year he produced several extraordinary studies so full of light and sensuous color that they could have been painted by Renoir a good half century later. Indeed, it is no exaggeration to say that in Delacroix one finds the antecedents of every important nineteenth-century French artist who came after him, not to mention the Dutchman van Gogh, and later Picasso, with his *Women of Algiers.*

For me, heretofore only a dutiful admirer of Delacroix, the show was a revelation, particularly the profusion of oil, watercolor, and pencil sketches, often produced at white heat by a hand so mercurial as to defy analysis. At best, Delacroix's work bristles with speed, air, light, and emotion. At its least interesting, an occasional composition merited little more than official salon recognition. And yet even when the artist was patently overdramatic, the magnitude of his feeling, the opulence of his palette justified what in anyone else might have become pretentious posturing. Key works in the exhibition were documented with multiple studies so juxtaposed as to permit simultaneous comparison. To see innumerable preliminary sketches next to great final compositions, starting with the 1822 *Dante and Virgil* and continuing through the late fluid *Lion Hunt,* is to realize how tirelessly Delacroix experimented.

The more informal the study, the more exciting its execution. In his drawings—nervous, taut, agitated—each furious line communicates unbounded energy. There are pencil sketches that dance with flexibility; there are tempera paintings where a racing brush turns conventional subjects into streaks of emotion; there are small watercolor landscapes of surpassing tenderness; there are tiny interiors filled with vast space; there are forms that defy definition as they merge into a surging, moving mass; there are penetrating portraits and, above all, densely interwoven compositions. This master visionary found no tour de force beyond his means.

Not surprisingly, he was less interested in still-life than in more active subjects. Like Rubens, to whom he was prodigiously indebted, Delacroix was drawn to daring baroque compositions filled with figures plunging in and out of shadowy depths. Again and again, his brooding skies are offset by those glowing reds that have become his virtual trademark. In the North African paintings, mysterious shadows are often relieved by contrasting areas of piercing sunlight. The late works produced before his death are characterized by a lighter palette, looser brushstrokes, and an increasing emphasis on luminosity as a source of emotion. The exhibition is tangible proof of how vitally the Impressionists were influenced by this artist, as were the Post-Impressionists and even the Expressionists of our own century.

The Louvre's collection of Delacroix is staggering. Many of the top oils, most of the myriad drawings, watercolors, and sketchbooks in the show belong to this museum. In comparison, representation from other countries is feeble, though the United States is by far the largest lender outside of France. But it is only in the artist's native land that one can begin to take his full measure. I recall once seeing a Delacroix show at Venice which, in light of the present survey, provided little more than a shadowy introduction. Reminiscent of the great Caravaggio exhibition that made history in Milan some years ago, this inclusive panorama of Delacroix at the Louvre has been organized on a comprehensive scale with understanding, with imagination, and, best of all, *con amore*.

In addition, the Bibliothèque Nationale honored the centennial of Delacroix's death with a survey of his prints, while at his home and studio in the Rue Furstenberg an exhibition called "Delacroix, Citizen of Paris" gave an intimate picture of the man himself. Among the letters, memorabilia, portraits of and by his friends, souvenirs of Morocco, personal belongings, and documents, appeared such illustrious names as Géricault, Bonington, Victor Hugo, Balzac, Daumier, Alexandre Dumas, George Sand, and of course Chopin, whom Delacroix particularly cherished. As a climax to this absorbing auxiliary exhibit, Fantin-Latour's now famous canvas *Hommage à Delacroix* proved once again how dynamically this artist had captured the imagination of his contemporaries. Painted the year Delacroix died, the composition includes ten distinguished men grouped around a large portrait of their idol, among them Whistler, Manet, Legros, Bracquemond, and Fantin-Latour himself.

Here one senses the world of Eugène Delacroix, urbane, cultivated, steeped in history, supremely civilized. Printmaker, mural painter, draftsman par excellence, gifted writer, as evidenced by his remarkable *Journal,* indefatigable traveler, and, not least, Gallic to his fingertips, Delacroix emerges from these joint exhibitions as a complete personality in the round and as an artist of unbelievable fecundity.

9. *Walter Arensberg and Marcel Duchamp*

"How one would like to know what Duchamp thought of the Arensbergs," wrote John Walker, director emeritus of the National Gallery of Art, in a recent issue of *SR*. What Duchamp thought was never recorded, nor was it likely to be, for he was not one to show his hand, but about twenty-two years ago I spent several weeks with Walter and Louise Arensberg when Duchamp was visiting in their Hollywood home. If fragmentary memories of those days do not provide definitive information on Duchamp's private opinions, they do, at least, reveal something about the quixotic Walter Arensberg. He and his wife had known Duchamp for many years, but since leaving New York and settling in Hollywood they saw him infrequently, a serious deprivation for Walter, who found Marcel equally stimulating as a person and an artist. Indeed, I can remember no one he consistently referred to with as much affection or respect. And this was unusual, because Arensberg's private likes and dislikes were highly volatile. The friend he revered one week could be peremptorily cast out the next; his enthusiasms were prodigious, but so too were his doubts.

At the California house, Duchamp was always present in principle if not in person, for his most important paintings spearheaded the Arensbergs' pioneer collection of twentieth-century art, a collection that had superb concentrations of the Cubists, Dadaists, Klee, Miró, and, above all, Brancusi and Duchamp. These works, many of which Marcel had tracked down for the Arensbergs long before the names of the men who made them became household words, were eventually left to the Philadelphia Museum of Art, where they can now be seen in less cluttered but also, alas, less charismatic surroundings. From the Arensbergs' entrance hall, glowing with Brancusi's voluptuous brass *Princess,* to the butler's pantry with its Futurist painting by Joseph Stella, to the smallest closet dense with pictures, that house was Nirvana for me. It was full of unexplained mysteries and delights from which I have never fully recovered, though in the end I was banished from it, as were so many others. Duchamp alone seems to have survived the ups and downs of that mercurial ménage.

His visit, which lasted about a week, was, I believe, the first he had made to the Hollywood house and thus the first chance for him to see his own work after many years. I was in the living room when he arrived. There and in an adjoining garden room he dispassionately examined everything in sight, including paintings by his colleagues and key ones he himself had produced in another life some thirty-five years earlier. Here were his three versions of *Nude Descending a Staircase, Chess Players, The King and Queen Surrounded by Swift Nudes, The Bride,* two versions of *Chocolate Grinder,* plus a few less radical works, preparatory sketches, "Ready-Mades," and his only unbroken glass. He looked quietly, intently—the Arensbergs nervously following his slightest move. Finally, turning to *The King and Queen,* he said, "This one still holds up." And that was all. What he thought about his other paintings he kept to himself.

A postscript: Early in 1970 one of the *Chocolate Grinders* and a 1910 Cézannesque portrait of the artist's father were inexplicably lost en route to a show in New York. I shudder to think of Walter Arensberg's reactions had he been alive. For him each painting in the collection had special importance, and in this case both *were* pivotal works—notably *Chocolate Grinder,* a subtle forerunner of Pop art. Despite its deceptive simplicity, this picture's metaphysical content became fully evident only after the composition was finally incorporated in *The Large Glass (the Bride Stripped Bare by Her Bachelors, Even)*. And in addition *Chocolate Grinder* was one of the first experiments to handle a commonplace object with the same deference that Poussin might have brought to a goddess or Piero to a saint. The other lost picture, the portrait of Duchamp's father, is less of a ground-breaker, yet it is interesting as an auto-biographical document and as a beautifully painted canvas. Both stolen pictures were eventually recovered.

I recall a day at the Arensbergs' shortly before Duchamp arrived when I was upstairs working on a projected catalogue of the collection. I heard shouts below—Walter calling his wife. "Lou, Lou, see what I've got!" He was beside himself, prancing around the living room in an absolute ecstasy. And there on a fine Oriental rug (the house was full of them and also of strange tattered curtains) stood two newly acquired Brancusis —*Torso of a Young Man* in wood and a small version of *The Fish*. Both came from next door, where the dealer Earl Stendahl lived in lordly fashion and operated a quite fantastic gallery devoted to splendid examples of modern art and to mountains of pre-Columbian stone carvings and terra-cotta sculpture, some in relatively good condition, some literally in pieces. Just how Stendahl maneuvered this vast and, I should judge, forbidden cargo across the border was never fully explained. Once Duchamp and I went with Walter to see Stendahl's workshop, where a European craftsman was patching, restoring, reconstituting, and repairing masks, idols, sun gods, and Terrascan dogs. Duchamp, inscrutable as always, observed everything and said nothing, though at one point I thought I heard him muttering, "Dangereux, dangereux." No dealer could have asked for a more convenient neighbor than Walter Arensberg, who made daily excursions to the house next door and rarely came back empty-handed. As Duchamp might have said, it was a perfect "Ready-Made."

Arensberg always reminded me of the finest vintage champagne—heady, slightly biting, demanding, temperamental, and effervescent. He changed his mind not from day to day, but from hour to hour, so one never knew whether there would be a warm handclasp or a frigid dismissal. Earlier he had been a poet and journalist, but during the years I knew him, he was absorbed in proving that Bacon had written Shakespeare. He also expended untold energy debating where he should leave his collection. There was scarcely a day he did not receive important museum directors, trustees, or university presidents who were competing for his favor, all of which I think he immensely enjoyed. Leading his victims on unmercifully, he charmed them with his courtly manners, but he left them dangling. This problem of the collection's final disposition (the Arensbergs had no children) naturally concerned Duchamp, since many of his outstanding works were involved. He found Walter's cat-and-mouse technique a bit unnerving.

One entire upstairs section of the house was reserved for the Bacon-Shakespeare enterprise. Here, like human computers, several ladies were forever dealing with some kind of mathematical codes. I never could figure out what they were doing, but in a confidential moment Arensberg told me that seven years of work once had to be thrown out because of a single incorrect number which had escaped detection all that time. I believe he had even hoped to investigate one or the other of those famous gentlemen's graves in order to unearth corroborating data. In conversation, instead of referring to Bacon by name, Arensberg substituted "the writer of Shakespeare's plays."

Louise Arensberg was delicate, taut, and strong-minded but for some reason always seemed to be wringing her hands. It was as if she nursed some nameless grief. Friends hinted that she had sparked the move to California in order to rescue Walter from the excitement, late hours, and convivial life of New York, where Duchamp's electrifying presence may have interfered with the seclusion she wanted. Not just Duchamp came night after night to the Arensbergs but many other members of the avant-garde as well—Picabia, Man Ray, Joseph Stella, Charles Demuth, and Morton Schamberg, each of whom was later well represented on the walls of the Hollywood house. Edgard Varèse, Isadora Duncan, and William Carlos Williams were also frequent visitors. Pre-Dadaist little reviews and startling new exhibitions were launched here while every conceivable facet of contemporary thought was argued from dinner to dawn. During a few brief years the Arensbergs' apartment acted as the most provocative salon New York has known, unless later the Cedar Bar could compete. In 1913 when the Armory Show astonished New York, the Arensbergs were living in or near Boston. Walter visited the exhibition, was transfixed by it, and actually forgot to go home for several days. The following year the Arensbergs moved to New York, where Duchamp stayed with them from time to time. I often wondered whether Walter's obsession with Bacon was a compensation for the life he had renounced and the poetry he ceased to write.

Duchamp threaded his way through these vague tensions with the cool grace that distinguished everything he did. I was charmed to find chocolate bars on his bedside table when I catalogued works in his room. There were also paintings under the bed, for large as the house was, its walls could not accommodate the omniverous collection. Suspecting the diet of dates and nuts the Arensbergs favored was inadequate (I must confess I was often hungry myself), I asked Duchamp if that explained the Hershey bars. He assured me they were a habit of his, an endearing habit, I thought, for the twentieth century's most cerebral artist. The Arensberg house was far from any store. I never quite figured out how a new supply of chocolates appeared each day. At that time Hollywood was the movie capital of the world, a vulgar commercialized hubbub in a beautiful setting. No two men could have been more alien to this garish scene than Duchamp and Arensberg. The latter claimed he and his wife settled there precisely because the atmosphere was so antipathetic to any form of time-consuming sociability. He used to say, "I love to live in a vacuum."

Before dinner each evening Arensberg disappeared, returning with outsized highball glasses filled with a little bourbon, a lot of ginger ale, and a touch of ice. Yet even this could not quench the investigative conversations that took place at meals. I remember one luncheon of cheese, dates, and nuts (the only person I ever encountered more addicted to health food was also a collector—the Baroness Gourgaud, who ate quantities of what looked like uncooked grass). Discussion that day turned to the accidental in art, a phenomenon Duchamp considered basic. For him the planned and the unplanned interacted dynamically as they contradicted each other. Arensberg, less convinced, felt the accidental only seemed accidental—that it was actually always predetermined, even if unconsciously. Duchamp mentioned his own experiment, *3 stoppages étalon,* where he had allowed threads to fall spontaneously and then become the source of an antiartistic arrangement. Wasn't this a salute to the accidental? he asked, but Arensberg felt it was a conceptual idea that Duchamp, and only Duchamp, could have instigated. The way the threads fell was accidental, he admitted, yet the impulse to create an accident was not by chance. On and on they went, probing, questioning, and examining every ideographic nuance. Walter Arensberg searched for hidden meanings (usually erotic ones) in paintings and sculpture; Duchamp found them intuitively, for, after all, he was the artist par excellence who had created the climate for hidden meanings.

Arensberg took Duchamp and me on a sightseeing trip around Los Angeles with specific emphasis on Frank Lloyd Wright's buildings. His contempt for this architect, whom he considered an impostor, was acute. Duchamp remained impervious but attentive no matter how emotional Walter's outbursts became. More remarkable was the artist's sang-froid in the face of Arensberg's driving habits. As our host boiled over at the thought of Wright, his handling of the car became more and more eccentric. He usually removed both hands from the wheel in order to regale us with proper dramatizations. Duchamp listened, responded, and apparently never noticed our mortal danger, or, if he did, was not averse to it.

The artist, with impeccable good manners, moved in and out of the house so silently I doubt if the Arensbergs knew that almost daily he was seeing his old friend Man Ray, who at that time was living nearby but was not welcome because of a recent falling-out with Walter. Duchamp pursued his own way without fanfare or aggression, but one felt that no one, not even the tumultuous Walter Arensberg, could divert him. The week of

Duchamp's visit was a shot in the arm for Arensberg. Both men were iconoclasts. They seemed to understand and complement each other. It was impossible to know what Duchamp thought of his host, but what Walter thought of his guest was more than clear. Duchamp was the spark plug that ignited him.

And the same was true of Katherine Dreier, another Duchamp devotee and collector who likewise was mesmerized by him. Years later he took me to visit her in Milford, Connecticut, where for the first time I saw *The Large Glass*. Miss Dreier called him Dee and was a bit peremptory with him but hung on his every word. Driving back to New York, Duchamp discussed collectors and their frustrations, wondering aloud whether their possessions were not actually a form of "Ready-Made" art. Surely Walter Arensberg's were. His own vast store of creativity had somehow been diverted, yet I can recall no one, except perhaps an occasional painter or sculptor, who could immerse himself so deeply in art, understand it so clairvoyantly, and discuss it so hypnotically. Suspicious, ambivalent, acquisitive, inquisitive, urbane, scholarly, alternately drunk with delight or opaque with doubt, Walter Arensberg is a memory difficult to expunge.

All of which brought him to mind when I recently visited the Philadelphia Museum of Art to see Duchamp's last incredible work of art. How Walter Arensberg would have appreciated it! Everything he prized is there—a disquieting ambiguity, an overlay of meanings, eroticism in its fullest sense, secrecy, paradoxes, irony, and always the unexpected. But possibly secrecy is the cornerstone of this new work, a three-dimensional mixed-media assemblage called *Etant Donnés: 1° la chute d'eau, 2° le gaz d'éclairage,* which, when translated, roughly means *Given: 1. the waterfall, 2. the illuminating gas.* Dealing with many aspects of the life forces that drive us, *Etant Donnés* was secretly conceived and carried out by Duchamp over a period of twenty years from 1946 to 1966. For a long time he had been advising artists to go underground; he scrupulously followed his own advice. Viewers can only see this work separately. One looks through two deliberately uncomfortable holes to find a complex and exquisitely crafted world, a world of illusion and

Marcel Duchamp and Katharine Kuh, 1951

reality, a world of theory and tangibility, a world of philosophy and Eros, a world of secret meanings and erogenous frankness, a world Walter Arensberg would have loved, and a world any intelligent member of the twentieth century should see and ponder.

PLACES

10. *The Circuitous Odyssey of Irish Art*

"This country of ours is no sand bank thrown up by some recent caprice of earth. It is an ancient land, honoured in the archives of civilization. If we live influenced by wind and sun and tree, and not by the passions and deeds of the past, we are a thriftless and a hopeless people."

These are the words of Thomas Davis, a respected nineteenth-century Irish patriot who early realized that his native land was rooted in more than the idiosyncrasies of man and nature. And he was right, for Ireland has too long been identified with whimsey, leprechauns, and romantic landscapes. To be sure, the countryside is as green as advertised and often touchingly unspoiled by modern commercialization, but, with the exception of a few gaunt and barren stretches, this lovely land is not visually spectacular. For scenic wonders you must go elsewhere, though an absence of billboards and a slightly haunted, weather-beaten terrain are undeniably endearing.

What you do find here is a wealth of art and archaeology, both sidetracked at times for more banal tourist attractions. You are less apt to see the high crosses at Monasterboice than to kiss the Blarney Stone, and less apt to explore a remarkable

Bronze Age tomb at Fourknocks than to eat a mock ''medieval banquet'' in Limerick. Even in Dublin, that most elegant and eloquent European city, fluorescent eighteenth-century interiors opulent with plasterwork are frequently overlooked.

For it is true that ''the passions and deeds of the past,'' as revealed through nearly five thousand years of art, give Ireland its special psyche. Not much farther from New York than San Francisco, Dublin offers layer upon layer of superimposed civilizations, all within a fifty-mile radius. Nearby are extensive prehistoric cemeteries crowded with megalithic monuments; within a stone's throw are well-preserved medieval round towers, carved high crosses, rambling remains of Norman castles, and inimitable examples of eighteenth-century Georgian architecture. Neighboring County Meath swarms with ruins from all periods. Condensed into an area of only a few miles, a microcosm of Ireland's art unfolds in baffling profusion.

Everywhere one is struck by contradictions that repeat themselves so insistently as to become a form of continuity. Irish art is abstracted to an astonishing degree, yet it often deals with familiar aspects of nature—with plants, animals, birds, and fish. Irish art is assertively Christian, but pagan symbols are rarely absent. Irish architecture combines exterior restraint with interior extravagance. Irish decoration is exuberantly quixotic, though meticulously organized. Its immense fecundity is tempered by strict controls. Over-all design is apt to be austere, but this very severity can encompass a delirious elaboration of decorative invention.

If it is the earliest monuments one wants, then the road leads north from Dublin for about thirty miles to the banks of the Boyne River, where an amazing burial complex of Bronze Age tombs involves a wide area. Many mounds have not yet been excavated, but of those that have, the most memorable is Newgrange, a large communal grave covering nearly an acre. Built of colossal unhewn stones, some carved with interlacing designs, this multiple burial chamber is mute evidence that well over four thousand years ago Ireland was inhabited by a people dedicated to some mysterious cult of the dead, yet a people sufficiently advanced to cope with monumental boulders of prodigious weight. How these early men managed to maneuver such formidable stone slabs in the vaults, niches, and passageways of their tombs is no more puzzling than why they invariably chose prominent hilltops for their burial sites.

Newgrange, like most ancient excavations, arouses acute frustrations. Who were these people, these master builders? Why did they decorate certain stones and not others? What did their double and triple interlacing spirals, their rhythmic zigzag incisions and repetitive geometric designs mean? How did they use the great rock basins that appear repeatedly in their tombs? And why were their burial mounds surrounded by circles of large isolated monoliths? One questions whether these free-standing rocks, reminiscent of Stonehenge, were intended as records of important events, as possible grave markers, or merely as objects of ritual worship. One questions, too, whether the monoliths celebrated the importance of death, or the majesty of nature, or both.

The entire Slane Valley near the Boyne River is one far-flung stone necropolis where collective tombs presumably sheltered the bodies of tribal leaders. The most interesting mounds, notably Newgrange, Dowth, and Knowth, lead to cruciform interior chambers via long passageways roofed with stone. In the central sanctuaries, boulder against boulder build up to awesome false domes that breed claustrophobic anxieties. For a show of sheer atavistic power, I know of few rivals. Perhaps it is the massive crudity of the stones as opposed to the ingenuity of their deployment that confounds us.

Knowth, as yet only partially excavated, is something of an archaeological wonder, for it is possible that this passage grave may help unravel the origins of Ireland's Bronze Age settlers. According to Dr. George Eogan, archaeologist at Dublin's University College and at present in charge of excavations at Knowth, "The discovery in July 1967 of the chamber here was a major and spectacular find. We encountered for the first time an important burial passageway that seems to have been substantially untouched since it was originally sealed more than four thousand years ago. The shape of Knowth differs from other known passage graves in Ireland. The only site where similar

tombs are found is in Brittany, making one believe that the ancestors of this tomb were Breton.''

Heretofore, the Iberian peninsula seemed the most likely
source of migrations to Ireland, though some scholars suspected
these migrations had filtered through Brittany. Now, patient
detective work on a single site begins to clarify a perplexing
secret. As the ruins in Ireland add revealing chapters to the
story of Western civilization, they also pose new problems. Why
did art in this country consistently feature interlacing designs?
Surely there is no reason to believe that craftsmen in early
Christian days were familiar with the Boyne Valley tombs,
which were not opened until centuries later. Granted that occasional stones from ancient dolmens (a simple post-and-lintel
type of prehistoric tomb) might have found their way into
Christian buildings, still such accidents hardly account for a
stylistic phenomenon that embraced thousands of years.

Only a few miles from Newgrange and Knowth in the town
of Kells, one is catapulted forward some 3,500 years to the
final flowering of Early Christian Celtic art. Here at Kells, in the
market place, I encountered my first high cross and am still
wondering why this humble monument moved me so poignantly.
Perhaps its modest scale and defenseless weathered carvings
were partially responsible; also, its simple cruciform shape
deftly interwoven with Ireland's ubiquitous circle. Alive with
agitated Bible stories in high relief, the cross becomes a self-
contained stone sermon in serial form. Every empty gap not
filled by scriptural figures is decorated with sinuous linear
ornaments borrowed from the more flexible arts of manuscript
illumination and metalwork. Nothing daunted these stone-carv-
ers; they handled their obdurate material with a consummate
disregard for its resistance. That the Market Cross of Kells
served as a gallows in 1798 struck me as a shocking duplication
of past history and as an ironic comment on the meaning of
religion.

Other high crosses can be found nearby in the cemetery at
Kells, and even finer ones in Monasterboice, less than thirty
miles away. These latter—also covered with vigorous scriptural
scenes—are located in an isolated graveyard where they are

Cross of Muiredach at Monasterboice, County Louth

dominated by the towering Cross of Muiredach, one of the largest in Ireland. Thought to have been named after an abbot of Monasterboice, the cross is 18 feet high and, though crisply carved in almost full relief, is suffering from erosion by wind and rain. The same tragedy is re-enacted all over Ireland. Everywhere, exterior stone sculpture shows signs of serious deterioration. To remove these handsome outdoor carvings from their original sites is to subvert their meaning, but to allow them to waste away is to forfeit an important slice of Ireland's art and history.

Irish high crosses answered several needs. They acted as boundary markers, as sanctuary and dedicatory monuments, and as instruments for instructing the faithful. Because early Celtic church architecture was heavy, dark, and rarely of commanding presence, the crosses substituted as decorative rallying points in monastic communities. Today they loom over their smaller, more modern prototypes, for most of them are located in cemeteries still or only recently in use.

The graveyards at Kells and Monasterboice also shelter two of Ireland's unique round towers, structures peculiar to this country. Dozens are sprinkled throughout the land, and a more frankly phallic symbol I cannot imagine. Intended as belfries, watchtowers, and places of refuge, these ninth- and tenth-century tapered cone-capped ''campaniles'' act as aggressive vertical demarcations in a gently rolling landscape. One cannot forget them. As a rule they stand alone, but often they have been adopted by later church buildings and skillfully incorporated into the new structures.

The Christian Church did not borrow alone from its own past; as each civilization depends on preceding ones, it made use of pagan monuments, too. In Ireland this interrelationship is more conspicuous than usual because, within a restricted radius, one encounters a virtual galaxy of overlapping cultures. Who is to say, after all, just how much the ninth-century Viking invaders brought to Ireland and just how much they took home, for there is no doubt that their minutely fluent coloristic carvings recall Celtic design. For that matter, so do certain Melanesian patterns, though here there is presumably no direct connection; intertwining spirals may well be a universal symbol. A short tour of Dublin and its environs is enough to prove how strong was this sense of continual give and take—between pagans and Christians, Danes and Irish, English and Irish, Protestants and Catholics. The constant political upheavals that scar Ireland's history were mirrored and magnified in its art.

On a beach not far from the ruins at Newgrange, an intricate eighth-century pin, known as the Tara Brooch, was discovered about 120 years ago. This find is said to have spearheaded a native arts-and-crafts revival, but the fact remains that no nine-teenth- or twentieth-century Irish artist has faintly approxi-mated the brilliance of Early Christian Celtic design.

The Tara Brooch and a breathtaking group of other ancient Celtic works are on view in Dublin's National Museum. Gold necklaces from as early as 1500 B.C. have the twisting, writhing rhythms of obsessed snakes. Bracelets, horse bits, bells, reli-quaries, belts, and dress fasteners, all bursting with irrepressible vitality, are small, yet of such life-giving intensity as to seem monumental. Spanning thousands of years from prehistory to the Middle Ages, the museum collection offers a panorama of Ireland's heritage, a heritage of extraordinary ebullience. Early Christian Irish treasures are at once more subtle and more sophisticated than their continental European counterparts.

Merely to examine the Tara Brooch is to realize the technical agility this gossamer object demanded. Combining chiseled gilt bronze, enameled silver, red and blue glass, gold filigree, and bands of amber, the small pin suggests a modern surrealist as-semblage, less because of its myriad materials than because of its optical deceptions. Here one finds characteristic scrolls, spirals, and animal heads growing out of one another in way-ward succession.

It is likely that Irish manuscript illuminations—among the most celebrated in history—borrowed heavily from early Celtic metal designs. The manuscripts permitted an even more ecstatic use of interlacing spirals. Witness the Book of Durrow from the Library of Trinity College. As if kinetically energized, illumi-nations in this volume unwind themselves from continuous, knotted, interwoven strips of color where neither beginning nor end can be found. From a century later—about A.D. 800—come the imperious animal drawings of the Book of Armagh. Leaping out of vellum pages, these imaginary creatures have the electrically alive quality typical of Irish art at its best.

Most extraordinary is the Book of Kells, that inspired, intoxicated dedication to fantasy. Here everything becomes illusory. Nothing is what it seems. Animals break loose from the letters they form; columns turn into chimerical monsters; entanglement is denser than human eye can penetrate. A kind of organized insanity prevails. Certain pages, especially the stylized nonfigurative ones, seem drunk with movement, yet there is always the restraint of a calculated design. For it is only within the confines of predetermined boundaries that proliferation reigns. In the Book of Kells, the Irish horror of a vacuum reaches its climax. Surfaces boiling with convoluted details metamorphose into curiously disciplined form. Though numerous monks from a large scriptorium worked on this unfinished masterpiece, still the book maintains its own personal style throughout—a style that many years later may well have affected Art Nouveau, though the latter seems clumsy in comparison.

Liam de Paor, a Dublin authority on Early Christian Irish art, suggests, "If we examine Irish laws contemporary with art of the seventh, eighth, and ninth centuries, we will find the same pattern revealed in the mentality of the lawyers, the same love of complexity and intricacy. These men explored all possible eventualities and many impossible eventualities. At this time the Irish upper class was polygamous and yet Catholic. Laws concerning the rights of their multiple wives were as involved as designs in the Book of Kells."

The Irish, who in the past—almost until the nineteenth century—were frequent innovators in the visual arts, seem to have retreated during the last 150 years, an inexplicable anomaly in light of their literary leadership during the same period. I recall visiting a commercial gallery on St. Stephen's Green where the eighteenth-century plaster ceilings were more exciting than the contemporary Irish paintings, though the latter, it is true, were often poetic and competent. Today one searches in vain for the dynamic momentum that fired earlier Celtic artists.

Then, too, both important art museums in Dublin, the Municipal Gallery of Modern Art and the National Gallery, offer the public little contact with present-day art, either foreign or homegrown. In the Municipal Gallery there are some fine nineteenth-century European paintings from the Lane Collection, but half of these, due to unfortunate legal technicalities, must be exchanged every five years with London's National Gallery. As for Irish nineteenth-century artists, I was impressed by Nathaniel Hone, though admittedly his gutty, light-struck landscapes owe more to Constable and the Barbizon school than to Ireland. If the generous representation of Jack Yeats in both museums is a clue to his reputation, then he seems to be the country's most honored twentieth-century artist. A bit too passionately expressionist for my taste, his compulsive brushwork and inflammatory color have the total commitment we associate with Irish fervor. In any case, Celtic genius, with the exception of manuscript illumination, seems more at home in stone, metal, and plaster than on canvas and paper, and this despite its predominantly linear character.

The best paintings in the country are usually not Irish. Most of them can be found in the National Gallery, an interesting, if shabby, museum in need of a coat of paint and of some careful weeding. Distinguished by a number of noteworthy pictures and by an occasional jolting attribution (such as an easel painting labeled Michelangelo), the gallery is rich in Turner watercolors, in Poussin canvases (no less than four), and in a recently acquired School of Avignon *Annunciation,* a sublime work.

Irish architecture has understandably been dominated by British influences since the Norman invasion of 1170. The country is dotted with Norman abbeys and castles, many of them in ruins. Frequently these ivy-encrusted remains are more romantic than architecturally illustrious, though the castle at Trim, the largest Anglo-Norman fortress in Ireland, is a majestic pile worth seeing. Regally located on the Boyne River, the castle rears itself up above an ancient town to remind us of past English glories. Not surprisingly, the invaders tended to stifle native volatility. It was to take more than five hundred years for Irish exuberance to reassert itself.

If there is little modern painting, there is also little or no indigenous modern architecture in Ireland, unless those numerous small stone and whitewashed stucco farmhouses can be so considered. Except for domestic Arab dwellings, I know of few structures as organically pure as these traditional cottages with their useful thatched roofs. Form never followed function with more reassuring results. The only distinguished present day architecture worth mentioning is an addition (designed by an Englishman) to Trinity College's famous library. The new structure is a frankly contemporary concrete building, yet it adapts itself to the mellow harmony of a historic background. Trinity's campus, with its stately, measured architecture, is no less impressive than the roster of its illustrious graduates. The old buildings are stern, their proportions noble. They look like what they are—halls of learning.

It is not for modern architecture we go to Dublin; it is for the city's unparalleled succession of eighteenth-century Georgian squares and streets. There are few capitals in the world that have retained their own identity to the degree Dublin has. If modern Dublin is impersonal and not even interesting enough to be ugly, eighteenth-century Dublin continues to live with extraordinary validity. Here, size bows to proportion, and space has human, yet princely dimensions. The best streets—and there are many—present a handsome geometric unity. House after house, blending in uninterrupted sequence, fronts, as a rule, on well-planted squares. Upper Mount Street leading into Merrion Square is sometimes considered the world's longest and finest extant Georgian vista. Here, where uniformity has structural meaning, variety shows itself only in doorways, fanlights, and wrought-iron details.

But today even Dublin is threatened by the bulldozer. Four years ago, a peerless mile of eighteenth-century domestic architecture was marred by the destruction of an entire block to accommodate modern premises for an electric company. Now further disruption is under consideration. The two main canals which originally defined Dublin's boundaries and provided access to horse-drawn barges may shortly be converted into covered sewers. These beautiful open waterways, together with the River Liffey, are part of the city's authentic anatomy—an anatomy which makes sense, since water, parks, and squares all act as foils for Dublin's densely organized masonry. Worried townsmen have coined the phrase, "Ireland's Heritage, Dublin's Sewer."

The capital abounds in Palladian buildings, mostly still in use. Among the best is the Custom House, which appropriately imposes itself upon the Liffey. You cannot go far in Dublin without coming face to face with this impressive landmark. Everywhere you are confronted by an eighteenth-century past that seems singularly well tuned to present-day Irish life, or is it possible that present-day Dublin is well tuned to the past precisely because so much of the past remains?

The Irish countryside is presently blossoming with reconditioned eighteenth-century Palladian mansions. The earliest and largest of these is Castletown, at Cellbridge near Dublin. As a prototype for the many that followed, this vast residence is set in a luxurious park with vistas terminating occasionally in obelisks and teahouses. The scale of such buildings and their surroundings is surprisingly lavish—and so also, I would judge, were the lives of their owners. Desmond Guinness, president of the Irish Georgian Society, is largely responsible for the preservation of Castletown and of numerous other eighteenth-century monuments. He feels "there was always greater love of show in Irish Palladian than in English," due partly, I would guess, to the more theatrical temperament of the Irish, and partly to a proud people's need to outdo its conqueror. Mr. Guinness also finds that "English Georgian design seems dead and lifeless when compared to Irish." He questions why Irish silver "is more sought after" than English. "Is it," he asks, "because it is rarer or because it is better?" Guinness himself lives in a house that suggests a provocative contraction of Irish architectural history, for he has transformed the interior of a Norman castle into a Georgian home while leaving the outside strictly medieval. The result is both amusing and comfortable.

As for the eighteenth-century silver he mentions, there is a wealth of it in the National Museum, where even deplorably crowded, poorly lighted cases cannot obscure the touch of madness that turns swirling surface designs into a kind of personal choreography. Everything intertwines—scrolls, swans, pheasants, grapes, and flowers all lead from and to one another, creating a web of interrelations. The silver, like the best of Irish art, has line, style, and potency.

Even more densely overgrown is Ireland's rococo plasterwork, which, at least in spirit if not in form, parallels Early Christian Celtic design. One finds the same excesses, the same free imagination and horror of a vacuum, though nearly a thousand years separate the two styles. The stuccodores, who flourished in the second half of the eighteenth century, were influenced by Italian plasterers, but soon converted traditional European design into their own mercurial images. Dublin is full of walls and ceilings that flow, sprout, blossom, and twist with painted plaster sculpture, sometimes in almost full relief. Putti, scrolls, leaves, animals, and, above all, birds assiduously follow us up stairways and dance over crowded ceilings.

It is difficult to describe the gulf that divides exterior simplicity from interior abundance. Take, for example, the building known as 86 St. Stephen's Green, now part of University College. Outside, it is well proportioned, forbidding, and dignified. Inside, the visitor is caught up in a tangle of plaster flowers, musical instruments, and multitudes of soaring, singing, swooping birds. Probably from the hand of Robert West, who earlier, it is thought, collaborated on Dublin's marvelous cherub-infested Rotunda Chapel, this plaster maze transcends decoration to become authentic sculpture. No wonder James Joyce, once a student at this college, developed layers of language as evasively circuitous as the stucco images on his classroom walls. In Ireland, less is not more; more is more.

11. *Art in the Soviet Union, 1963*

One day in the spring of 1963 I found myself in Moscow, sitting across a table from two important Soviet painters who seemed the complete antithesis of each other but who in conversation differed not one iota. Neither uttered a word that failed to echo verbatim the statements of Chairman Khrushchev in his now famous March 8 speech cracking down on cultural freedom. The two men were Vladimir Serov, a pudgy, neatly dressed painter of fifty-three who looked more like a prosperous storekeeper than the recently appointed president of Russia's most powerful art organization, and A. A. Deineka, eleven years Serov's senior, a man of rough-hewn features, unclouded blue eyes, and magnetic presence. I had come to the National Academy of Art in Moscow to interview its new president, along with one of its veteran academicians, but this meeting, supervised by two interpreters, two critics, and the administrative director of the organization, was scarcely an informal chat. Even the long conference table posed a gulf between Serov, Deineka, and myself.

When I asked, "Do you feel that art must be a tool of government?" Deineka promptly replied, "I believe there's no art on earth that is not connected with government. Some artists think they're independent, but they're not, so long as they must rely on stock exchanges and selling and buying—all, of course, reflections of their government." Serov went further. For him, "This question does not exist because here art is an expression of the people and the government serves only the people. I believe our artists in the U.S.S.R. are freer than yours in the U.S.A. because ours are doing what they want." (A moot question, I must say, since today any expression counter to Soviet regulations is indefatigably suppressed.) "I know a number of Western painters who must produce abstract works because these are the only ones they can sell. I consider these men slaves of the dollar. I believe that no real artist would paint with his feet or spit on a canvas purely for the sake of sensation."

"But," I asked, "isn't it possible to hold other views than yours and still remain an authentic artist?" Serov replied, "I am positive that only realism is what I can believe in; it is the only human approach to art." In Kiev a Ukrainian critic was more categorical. He told me, "Either it's realism or it's not art." Still trying to find some point of rapprochement, I questioned Serov on the meaning of realism. I recalled that a bare seven years ago, images of Stalin were virtually the trademark of Soviet art but that today, except for three monuments in Tbilisi, any graphic evidence that he had lived or left his signature on Russia had been eradicated. What kind of realism was this, I asked, that permitted a complete visual denial of history? (Privately, I found myself speculating about those innumerable obsequious images of Stalin now banished to the same storages that house the avant-garde works he himself had excommunicated. Never before has politics produced stranger bedfellows. And now in 1970, Khrushchev's likeness is seen even less than Stalin's. In the Soviet Union everything is "out" that isn't "in.") Serov's answer was a model of ambiguity: "Though it is true that today we are no longer permitted to see Stalin in our paintings and sculpture, this does not mean our principles have changed. The fact that we recently added certain historical facts to our knowledge about Stalin only enriches Socialist Realism."

I heard similar statements at every turn. In a scant few months the cultural thaw of recent years had frozen into impenetrable ice. The Iron Curtain had become an iron wall, with all forms of modern art outlawed and with fear the password—fear of diversity, of personal expression, of experimentation, of anything, in fact, that might lead to official displeasure. Under the circumstances, artists had reason to be alarmed, but the government's jittery behavior seemed curiously disproportionate to the dangers involved. After all, why all these recent denouncements about a few mildly unorthodox works, why this accelerated hammering away at Western "formalism"? (Formalism, in the U.S.S.R., might be described as any kind of modern art that strays from the Soviet concept of realism.) Surely, only extreme insecurity can account for such exaggerated emotions. The revival of drastic curbs on artists and writers is especially surprising in a country where standards of living are on the upgrade and where the suppression of a growing intelligentsia might lead to serious explosions.

My hope was to discover why the cultural blackout had occurred at precisely this time. But to investigate art in the Soviet Union is to court suspicion even when contacts are limited to painters and critics of spotless party allegiance. Had it not been for the Soviet-American Institute, I would have met no one, seen nothing, bruised my head against endless brick walls, and come away more battered, if perhaps less shattered. It was only through the cooperation of this group that I was able to visit art studios, schools, and artists' unions, to meet painters, critics, curators, students, and teachers—though each was scrupulously hand-picked. And yet there was always some nagging anxiety that I might speak or write in terms hostile to Soviet policy. I found that fear is a communicable disease. After meeting it in others for several weeks I began to develop symptoms myself, and even now I worry that the truth, as I saw it, may prove hazardous to the people who helped me. Today an open exchange of ideas on art is impossible in the U.S.S.R. From the lowliest neophyte to the most celebrated winner of the Lenin Prize, answers to my questions were exasperatingly uniform. The chant was always the same: "Art has a single aim—to serve the people and promote Communism.'' That other opinions exist is manifest, but to air them, let alone be seen discussing them with a Western journalist, would be more than foolhardy, even dangerous. Yet, who can deny that dissident artists in the Republic of Georgia were safer last spring than integrationists in the state of Georgia?

As far as I could gather, the blistering new discipline resulted from various provocations, not least from the steady rise of younger progressive forces, increasingly aware of the outside world and frankly bored with an overdose of propaganda. To appreciate how radical this attitude was is to remember that art behind the Iron Curtain has always been regarded as a potent political weapon. For those in the West who look on paintings and sculpture as a release from the materialistic humdrum world of reality, who consider personal expression synonymous with creativity, it is almost impossible to accept the Russian definition. Yet the nub of our dilemma is exactly here. Because the word ''art'' has divergent meanings for our two countries, comparative judgments are frustrating (and this is true, no less, of such terms as ''peace'' and ''democracy'').

Russian painting, once it broke with the icon tradition, was rarely free from political or nationalistic implications. In the eighteenth century, art was limited almost exclusively to artificial court portraits, while in the following century it concerned itself less with honoring than with attacking court life. Later, a self-conscious Slavic revival focused on early icons and native folklore. Russian art has always been torn between the East and the West, between outside influences and a fanatical nationalism. Save for the apocalyptic years between 1909 and the early twenties, painting and sculpture, unlike Russian literature, never made international history. The government, influenced by past traditions and deeply suspicious of the West, understandably rejected the very artists most respected by the rest of the world—Kandinsky, Malevich, Chagall, Tatlin, Lissitzky, Gabo, and Pevsner. As usual, fear was the reason. According to the communist critic Chegodaev, ''Such art as Kandinsky's is based on the desire not to be understood. It is important to show the public only art they can understand. Formalism is not as innocent as it seems, for it expresses certain hostilities toward life. Take Cubism, which I find cold, analytic, egoistic. It denies life, harmony, and beauty.'' Mr. Chegodaev did not make clear what he meant by life, harmony, or beauty, nor did he agree when I suggested that these terms might hold different meanings for different people. As for that, in my eyes, the very humanism he advocates is suppressed by the current Soviet obsession with undeviating uniformity.

Kandinsky and his illustrious contemporaries, though widely admired in Europe and America as pioneer Russian artists, were no doubt too theoretical and (ironically) too revolutionary for the average Soviet citizen of the twenties, who was still struggling with the basic problems of literacy. Indeed, most of these artists were too advanced for the average citizen of any country at that time, but today it seems shocking that educated young Russians have never been allowed to learn about their own world-renowned painters, or about such international figures as Brancusi, Modigliani, Marcel Duchamp, or even Freud. Not one student I spoke to had ever heard these names. A bare forty-five years ago, approximately 80 per cent of the population in the U.S.S.R. was illiterate. Now, virtually everyone can read and write, and presumably should be able to make up his own mind about art.

It was not alone to protect sources of political indoctrination that Khrushchev resurrected Stalin-like controls, but also to eliminate the infiltration of ''demoralizing'' Western ideas. His own instinctive distaste for any modern form of expression may have weighted the scales. But probably the most potent pressure came from the artists themselves, from intensely reactionary painters and sculptors who hoped to stave off displacement as long as possible. A new building recently opened in Moscow must have chilled their blood. The Kremlin Palace of Congresses is the first Soviet structure to depend on the spacious, light-swept discoveries of contemporary architecture. This totally modern hall, which could not conceivably accommodate the stale, heavy-handed art of the Stalin era, is a tangible symbol of danger. The old guard had reason to tremble.

When I asked Serov what happens to artists whose work does

not conform to official demands, he assured me that "all our painters are educated to believe in the principles of Socialist Realism. Those few who do not acknowledge these principles are neither liked nor understood by the people, and accordingly their exhibitions are not well attended. The psychology of a Soviet artist," Serov continued, "differs from that of a Western one, for should the work of one of our artists not be liked by the people, this knowledge depresses him more than being deprived of his livelihood—and causes him to change his views."

A cynical statement, particularly in light of recent official attacks on individual artists who have been forced into various types of retirement, even into mental homes. I think of the thirty-nine-year-old sculptor Ernst Neizvestny, whose work I am unable to judge since no single evidence of it was anywhere to be found, nor was he. Substituting "immature" for the Nazis' "decadent," Soviet critics apply the adjective to almost any art that fails to meet their rigid requirements. In discussing the moody, expressionist canvases of Robert Falk, who died five years ago and who was conspicuous for having never knuckled down to the powers that be, Laktionov, a winner of the Stalin Prize and a favorite of Khrushchev's, granted that "Falk may have had some ability, but for me he was an ignorant and immature artist." Though only a few months earlier, Falk's paintings were shown in most of the country's major museums and were widely admired, today a single comment by Khrushchev has implacably removed them from sight. I even heard murmurs that Dostoevsky was "immature" because his image of Russian life was warped by human frailties. In this period of mass taboos, it was not too surprising to find modern works of international reputation locked away from public view, but when the Deputy Director of the Russian Museum in Leningrad denied me access to the museum's sizable collection of paintings by Pavlo Filonov, an important native artist, I was dismayed and appealed to reason. How could I, at my age and after considerable exposure to modern art, be poisoned by the fanciful semisurrealist pictures of a man now dead over twenty years? Yet the director was adamant—and I was the loser, for it is only in Russia that one can see Filonov's work.

Surreptitiously one night I was taken by an American friend

to view the paintings and drawings of several gifted young modern artists, but not to meet the men themselves. That might have proved "embarrassing" for them. I came away sick at heart that works of genuine merit must be surrounded by such absurd cloak-and-dagger secrecy. This, of course, is not to say that all so-called modern painting in Russia is interesting, but when it is, one regrets that the artist for his own security must remain bleakly anonymous. Nor shall I soon forget a painter from the remote Central Asian city of Alma-Ata, who, along with some eight hundred other delegates from the U.S.S.R. and satellite countries, was in Moscow for the Second Artists' Congress. He assured me that "the artist must not feel personally; he must feel only as his society feels." He also mentioned that certain painters in his local union had been bitten by "formalistic germs and were rightly criticized but not punished by the Congress." Whether these virtuous words were merely diplomatic sops or reflections of bona fide feeling is anyone's guess.

For example, how explain Deineka? Here is a man who in 1928 painted a composition called *Defense of Petrograd.* Depending on rhythmic juxtaposition of silhouettes, a daring two-level design, and deliberate elimination of unnecessary detail, he made the canvas a moving testament to early Soviet history. It is painful to find the same artist after thirty-three years so debased as to produce a pompous scene titled *Cosmos Explorers,* which, again using figures on multiple levels, adds up to little more than a shoddy advertisement even Madison Avenue would spurn. Its threadbare realism recalls American Pop art, and why not? The painting was, to be sure, produced for mass consumption, a phenomenon that also attracts the Pop artists. The net results of Soviet Socialist Realism and American New Realism are often the same, though one school works tongue-in-cheek, the other for the glory of "the Party." Indeed, what stumps me is how incredibly bourgeois Soviet art has become. The country itself—huge, vigorous, powerful, enormously alive, full of contrasts and surprises—is far more exciting than the decorous, cheery illustrations that supposedly are faithful reflections of it. Too often realism is confused with wishful thinking.

As for Serov's vapid painting of 1954, *The Winter Palace Is*

Defense of Petrograd, by A. A. Deineka, 1928

"I think it's pretty much a secret how an artist paints his picture—an equation of some unknown components. Every picture has its social background. I myself was a participant in the Civil War and and some of the figures in this painting were portraits of real people I knew who also were fighting. I was especially interested in the siege of Petrograd because I was deeply impressed by the heroism of the people there. I myself fought in the south—but war is always war; there is more grief than joy. This particular painting was one of many depicting the Civil War. I made another series connected with the Second World War. War was our life—and it was only natural that an artist would depict it."—A. A. DEINEKA

Taken, I was amazed to see that this potboiler had become a favorite model for copyists. One "handmade" replica particularly caught my eye, a brightly colored copy by a Chinese Communist student. That young painters behind the Iron Curtain turn to such banal sources for inspiration is doubly astonishing when one thinks of the magnificent Rembrandts, Poussins, Cézannes, and Titians readily available in the Hermitage.

For me, the most interesting, albeit baffling, encounter of my trip took place in Moscow when I visited Pavel Korin, a seventy-one-year-old painter who two days later was to be awarded the Lenin Prize. A man of frail personal beauty and courtly manners, he lived in what was extreme luxury for a Russian. Let

Cosmos Explorers, by A. A. Deineka, 1961

The Winter Palace Is Taken, by Vladimir Serov

"This is one of a large series of paintings I've been working on all my life. At the time I painted it I was living in the country, but my family was a family of revolutionaries and that is why this theme became my consuming interest. The background for the picture was taken directly from the Winter Palace, though the episode was invented but might have and possibly did take place. The painting shows a soldier and a worker resting after the palace was taken. My prime aim was to use a small episode to express a larger idea—an historic event."—VLADIMIR SEROV me add that the only studios I was permitted to visit were, I am sure, equally atypical. Korin's home, however, was unique. Filled with fine antique furniture, baroque chandeliers, and a superb collection of rare icons, it seemed strangely out of tune with the middle-class Soviet materialism that now prevails.

Next door, in an immense studio, the artist showed me a series of larger-than-life-size portraits painted as preparatory sketches for a picture to have been called *Vanishing Russia*. These figures of forlorn ecclesiastics dramatized the tragedy of castoff men and women caught between two alien worlds. Relying chiefly on black, white, and gray, Korin invested his portraits with sober compassion. The entire group was done between the late twenties and the middle thirties. It is noteworthy that Korin chose to show me only paintings produced more than a quarter century ago, suggesting that he, like Deineka, felt freer before the Stalin era. It is also interesting that the final painting was never executed. There in the studio, as a perplexing reminder, stands the largest bare canvas I have ever seen. On this subject Korin was vague, but he did mention that his champion, Maxim Gorky, died in 1936. I surmised that without the writer's protection (at one time Gorky exercised considerable influence over Stalin) it would have been extremely hazardous for Korin to risk an important religious composition.

When I asked the painter which artists of the past he most admired, he listed Tintoretto, Velásquez, Goya, Michelangelo, and Raphael. Then he stunned me by adding the Russian Alexander Ivanov as the top painter of the nineteenth century. Finding this man's work little better than a simpering imitation of Raphael, I countered with the name of Cézanne. He agreed that Cézanne was influential but regretted that he saw "in him the beginnings of the same disease that poisoned the artists who came after him." To identify these narrow words with Korin's erudition and with the cultivated environment he had created for himself was discouraging. I felt that nowhere in that vast country was it possible to find a point of mutual understanding. This sensitive man, far more than his aggressively dogmatic colleagues, made me realize how deep was the chasm between us.

The painter Laktionov received me in his temporary studio

located at a surgical hospital where he was working on a portrait group of four distinguished doctors. With Serov, he represents the most rigidly conservative element in Soviet art. For him painting is above all an agile craft to be used for the good of the Party. Like Korin, he too considered a Russian artist, this time Repin, the greatest of all nineteenth-century painters. Moreover, only Rembrandt, he felt, had ever surpassed him. That a man as urbane as Laktionov could be so brazenly provincial (though Repin undeniably was an able artist) is almost unthinkable, but everywhere in the U.S.S.R. I encountered this same regionalism. If the West gravely underestimated nineteenth-century Russian painting, opinion at home smugly elevates it to such heights as to obscure all trace of accepted history. Where American artists are concerned, most Russians know only Rockwell Kent. The Pushkin Museum of Western Art in Moscow included no other painter from the United States.

Present-day sculpture in the Soviet Union struck me as even more depressing than painting. You simply cannot escape from it; in the Metro, on public buildings, in every city square the visitor is confronted by magnified Soviet heroes or Nazi-like athletic specimens. And everywhere one finds deified images of Lenin exhorting and activating the people. Soviet art preaches without end and, alas, without benefit of humor.

Mention of the omnipresent Lenin recalls an episode in Tbilisi, where a People's Artist, whose studio I was visiting, evaded a question of mine by quoting Lenin on art. When I suggested that great political leaders are not necessarily valid aesthetic arbiters, his face froze. He insisted every family must have a father whose word is final. That Russians expect to be told rather than to find out for themselves is hardly a new idea, but to what extent personal investigation has been sacrificed to prescribed directives is highlighted in their art. Soviet painters and sculptors become woefully tedious not because they are propagandists. So also were Goya, Daumier, and Posada, but these men worked from inner convictions to satisfy their own beliefs —never under orders from above. An unforgettable Russian film I saw in Kiev, called *The Third Time,* was frankly based on propaganda but went beyond indoctrination to become art.

I felt that everyone connected with the production was emotionally involved. I only wish I could say as much for Soviet painting and sculpture.

If art in the U.S.S.R. is a grim business these days, it has not been relegated to a back seat. Museums are jammed and well run, art schools have prodigious waiting lists, painters and sculptors are honored as top citizens provided they docilely follow the rules, and productivity (a word better suited to Soviet art than creativity) is prolific. Were it not for splendid museums and churches (most of the latter have been turned into museums), the average Russian would find himself aesthetically starved. The enthusiastic attendance at museums, historical monuments, theaters, ballets, and concerts indicates an avid public hunger. In the museums one encounters hundreds of tours conducted by tireless docents; one sees adults and children pouring in and poring over works of art. I was repeatedly touched by the dedication of the curatorial staffs, often composed of highly experienced scholars.

Most art museums are equipped with research libraries, photographic studios, restoration departments, and, above all, extensive educational programs. Last year, the Tretyakov, a museum devoted to Russian art, organized more than six hundred lectures in Moscow and throughout the country. The Russian Museum in Leningrad plans about fifteen temporary exhibitions annually, includes a staff of twenty-five working exclusively on educational programming, and has seventeen specialists in its restoration department (a considerably larger number than one would find in an equivalent American museum). The Pushkin Museum in Moscow offers serious adult students a two-year night course based on its permanent collection, the class consisting of lectures, seminars, and group discussions. This museum has also organized a Young Art Lovers Club for members between thirteen and seventeen. These four hundred youngsters are taken on art tours of Leningrad and Vladimir as well as to important local exhibitions in Moscow. In addition, the Pushkin provides studios for them and shows their work from time to time.

For me, the most indelible experience in the Soviet Union

was the Hermitage. Situated on the banks of the Neva in Leningrad, a city of ineffable beauty, this fabulous storehouse of masterpieces has only one rival—the Louvre. In the Hermitage entire rooms are devoted to single masters—to Poussin, Rubens, Van Dyck, and Titian. As for Rembrandt, the array of his canvases is nothing less than staggering. One is dumfounded by the inordinate buying habits of the czars and especially of Catherine the Great. On the third floor, inherited from the famous Morosov and Shschukin collections, are gallery after gallery of magnificent Renoirs, Monets, Gauguins, van Goghs, Matisses, and early Picassos. But here the sequence ends abruptly. As one staff member sadly observed, ''What we're lacking is modern art. The last date of an important painting in the Hermitage is 1914.'' During its brief forty-five years, the Soviet government has chalked up an enviable record in art restoration, but its acquisition policy has been far less progressive. Whether this fifty-year gap in the collection can ever be filled is extremely doubtful.

The Hermitage, reputedly the world's largest art museum, stretches for blocks and employs about 1,000 people, among them 350 in the curatorial, restoration, and education departments. Last year's attendance figures topped two million. The evacuation of the museum during the war was a saga of poignant courage and admirable organization. Of the 1,750,000 art objects handled, practically nothing was damaged or lost. The first train, packed to the rafters with masterpieces, left Leningrad at the beginning of July 1941, the second at the end of the month. The third train never left; by that time the city was surrounded.

Art restoration in the Soviet Union is on an unprecedented scale. Specialists in the conservation of icons, frescoes, oil paintings, watercolors, and other media are provided with up-to-date equipment and are trained in advanced techniques. The Russians do not advocate wholesale cleaning and repainting, but adhere as closely as possible to the artist's original intention. I visited several restoration laboratories, where I was shown written, photographic, and X-ray records evidencing careful research. The modern scientific achievements of these conservation studios contrast sharply with the outmoded techniques of the artists' studios. It would seem that wherever ideological content is not at stake, progress is possible.

Architectural restoration is also impressive. In cities like Kiev and Leningrad, where outstanding historical monuments were decimated during the war, reconstruction is patient, painstaking, and thorough. The wondrous Byzantine frescoes of Kiev's Saint Sophia, an eleventh-century church of austere beauty, are slowly coming back to life, as are the icons and frescoes in the churches of the Kremlin. One of the finest architectural restorations is taking place at Pavlovsk, some eighteen miles from Leningrad and only a mile or two from Rastrelli's renowned Ekaterinsky Palace at Pushkin. The latter, also under reconstruction, was conceived on such a colossal scale and with such heedless opulence as to make one question why the Revolution delayed so long. The Summer Palace at Pavlovsk, though smaller, is hardly a modest establishment. Built under Palladian influence for Catherine the Great's demented son Paul, it is being restored with meticulous care. Constantly, one senses modern Russia's preoccupation with her bloody and profligate past. These faithful reconstructions, along with the incomparable crown jewels in the Kremlin, act as living historical indictments.

If senseless excesses are an indictment of the czars, then we must hold the Communists responsible for sheer ugliness. No words can describe the miles of dreary barracks-like buildings that house the country's exploding urban population. Architectural design, as we know it, is nonexistent. The best of these tenements are inferior to our worst lower-income housing projects, but it is only fair to add that slums and ghettos, as we know them, do not exist. Russia's urgent need for living space immediately after the war explains the lack of certain architectural refinements, but not the unnecessary vulgarity that assails the eye at every turn. Except for the Palace of Congresses, new buildings fluctuate between Stalin's phony neo-Gothic monstrosities that recall early "Balaban and Katz," and the unornamented, unrelieved, drab utilitarianism of more recent days. That the human soul can exist in such neat squalor is a tribute to its powers of endurance.

What makes the situation more distressing is the contrast between past and present. The dramatic sense of spacious grandeur that marks the Kremlin, the Trinity-Sergius Monastery at Zagorsk, and the whole of eighteenth-century Leningrad has been lost along with the idea of architecture as an expression of life. Even the handsome new Palace of Congresses, which by rights should have climaxed a long perspective, is squashed within the Kremlin walls.

At the Repin Institute in Leningrad, the country's largest art school, students of architecture enjoy greater freedom than their colleagues in the fine arts. On exhibition were one or two plans for contemporary public buildings that could have held their own in any international competition. Though theater designs seemed less progressive, they still permitted some experimentation. A student from North Vietnam was developing an ingenious revolving stage which, if not new in concept, was still a reflection of the current century. The same can scarcely be said of the fine-arts curriculum. Here life classes provide a thorough grounding in anatomy, devoted teachers give unstintingly of themselves, but not the slightest hint of present-day thinking exists. The diploma students, so called because before graduating they must spend their entire sixth year on one final work of art, usually embark on ostentatious compositions that all seem stamped from identical molds. One young man was doing his diploma painting on the siege of Sevastopol; another was at work on a group of bouncing young athletes. This is about the spread—from Soviet history to idealized versions of Soviet life.

At the Leningrad Union of Soviet Artists, a group of paintings executed during the Nazi siege of the city was being shown again after twenty years. These anemic reports had captured none of the furious glory that marked those heroic days. Russian artists tend to describe war chauvinistically with romantic blow-by-blow accounts of national trials and victories. The West does it better. For us the horror of modern destruction is symbolized by a new visual language, a language of dematerialization that is anathema in the U.S.S.R., where peace is incongruously on every tongue but war is depicted as the ultimate achievement.

The director of the Stroganov Institute, an industrial-art

school in Moscow, told me that the year before six thousand students had applied for two hundred vacancies. To my amazement, he also said interior decorating was the most popular course, though I personally saw no evidence that this training was being put to use in a country where furniture design and room interiors were invariably graceless. In every school I visited, the relationship of art students and faculty reflected an easy camaraderie, a mature respect for each other. The warm interest most instructors show for their classes suggests that teaching is a proud profession in the U.S.S.R. and not merely an economic stopgap for artists.

Like architecture, graphics and book illustrations are given a bit more leeway than painting and sculpture. In Tbilisi one Sunday afternoon I attended an art opening where speeches, television cameras, and a sizable crowd paid respect to a graphic exhibition from Lithuania. The children's books, inexpensive and charmingly illustrated, were the high point of the show, though for me it was the work of a young printmaker from Vilna who dared to express an idea rather than a fact. His print, called *Morning,* was one of the few contemporary compositions I saw in Russia that substituted a spark of symbolism for straight illustration. In a country where man is commonly shown dominating nature, it was a pleasure to find two small figures so transported by the majesty of their surroundings that they turned into symbols of joy rather than "workers in the field." It seems strange that on canvas symbolism becomes a sin but in a puppet show it is not questioned. At the Obraztsoz Puppet Theatre, a parody combined pungent symbols, rubber puppets, and live actors in a sophisticated take-off on the creation of the world. Unfortunately, none of this humor seems to have rubbed off on other kinds of modern folk art or craft. A brief tangle with thousands of May Day posters persuaded me that these illustrations were at best a century behind the times. So, too, were the tasteless ceramics and textiles I saw everywhere.

Why the Russian people have never developed a visual tradition comparable to their literary one is a provocative question. Perhaps because the artists of this country have leaned heavily on literature, their work often seems better adapted to words than to paint. Ambivalence, too, about the outside world debilitated them. Turning to Byzantium, to Europe, to the East, native artists also periodically turned away from all foreign influences in the hope of finding themselves. Even the dazzling Scythian gold in the Hermitage shows evidence of Greece. No people ever imported their art more extensively than the Russians, or denied their neighbors more jealously.

Soviet artists have limited their sights chiefly to two native influences—to the fifteenth-century humanism of Russia's most celebrated icon painter, Rublev, and to nineteenth-century nationalism. In the latter they find an emphasis on realism, on dramatic gesture, and literal transcription of history that is close to their hearts. Indeed, the avowed ambition of present-day artists is to model themselves on their nineteenth-century predecessors. The tragedy is that as yet not one of them has caught up with the earlier men—with the variety, vitality, and sweeping imagination of Repin (who, by the way, was clearly influenced by French Impressionism), with the lyrical landscapes of Levitan, with the daring extravagance of Surikov, and, most noticeably, with the searching inventions of Vrubel. In a country where science and technology are geared to the future, art is stubbornly chained to the past.

On rereading this piece after seven years, I recall how bitterly I resented the restrictions that limited my activities in the Soviet Union. Everything I did, everywhere I went was accompanied by almost insurmountable difficulties. As an American, an art enthusiast, and a journalist I had three strikes against me, especially at the time I was there when all forms of cultural freedom had been stifled following Khrushchev's abrupt closing of the Manège exhibition. He considered this mildly modern show a threat and labeled it "degenerate," a word often substituted in the U.S.S.R. for "Western."

During the weeks I spent there I never stirred without discreet or obvious, as the case might be, "escorts"; my suitcases were rifled daily; my hotel room taped. Almost every night, particularly in Moscow and Kiev, I was awakened two or three times by harassing telephone calls. All surveillance was open and inflicted, I presume, to intimidate me, as indeed it did, but even more it infuriated me. I felt constantly fenced in.

Two episodes provide capsule pictures of what went on. One day three young boys followed me through several galleries in the Hermitage and finally asked whether I had any new jazz records. Everywhere I traveled behind the Iron Curtain there was this same consuming desire for popular Western music which at that time was off-bounds in the U.S.S.R. I told the boys no, but instead gave them each a ballpoint pen. Pronto a plainclothesman materialized and forced them to return the pens. Later they waited for me outside the museum and suggested I come to one of their homes to hear their records. In another country I might have gone, but by this time I trusted no one in the U.S.S.R., not even children. The constant taboos had pretty well brainwashed me. And it *was* just possible that the plainclothesman had planted a trap.

The other episode took place in the bar of Leningrad's Artists' Union, where I was having drinks with two officials of the organization. In came a slightly tipsy, pretty woman and a bearded man. She asked me if I was an American and when I said yes she gave me a chocolate beautifully wrapped in gold paper. In turn I gave her a lipstick. She and her companion were delighted. They spoke a little English and it looked like we might become friends—but, again pronto, out of nowhere appeared a stern authoritarian who forced both of them to leave the bar immediately. As they waved goodbye the bearded man called out wistfully in broken English, ''Bravo Jack London.''

At times, I must confess, it was somewhat flattering to be considered so dangerous. For where, except behind the Iron Curtain, is art feared as a potent secret weapon and art critics as polluters of the public mind? And why the Russian people accept those acres of dreadful Socialist Realist paintings is a mystery to me. That the population hasn't long ago revolted against such banality is proof of its patient forbearance.

Some months after my article on the U.S.S.R. appeared in *Saturday Review*, a delegation of Soviet officials visited the United States, among them Vladimir Kemenov, general director of a Russian graphic-arts exhibit then on display in New York.

Having read my piece, he objected strenuously to my estimate of art in his country. *Saturday Review* suggested that Kemenov and I enter into an exchange of letters—each of us sending the other five questions which in turn would be published in the magazine along with our candid answers, thus permitting the Russian to put his point of view before an American audience. He agreed. I sent my questions; I waited for his. They never came. Apparently mine enraged him (particularly my reference to Nazism). Here are the five questions I sent along with my covering letter.

Nov. 11, 1963

Mr. Vladimir Semenovich Kemenov
Soviet Graphic Arts Exhibition
Time and Life Building
New York, N.Y.

Dear Mr. Kemenov:

These are questions that puzzled me deeply while I was in the Soviet Union and also since I have returned. I send them to you in all friendship and with the warm hope that by discussing our differences we will come to understand each other better. I look forward to seeing you again and I hope at greater length than was possible at the opening of your exhibition. Meanwhile I will try to answer your questions to the best of my ability.

Sincerely,
Katharine Kuh
Art Editor

Enc.
KK : ms

1. Why do you call Soviet art realistic when much of what I saw in the U.S.S.R. did not reflect life as it is there, but as you want it to be? Doesn't realism demand an uncompromising honesty related solely to the truth? Why then does one only see the optimistic side of life in Soviet art and never any indication of the failings and bureaucratic

abuses that we both know exist in your country as well as
in mine?

2. Ought not large masses of the people be trusted to see all
kinds of art and then make up their own minds? Why do
you keep hidden from the Soviet people the work of some
of their own early twentieth-century painters and sculptors
who are considered great pioneers not only in the U.S.A.
but throughout much of the world? (I refer, of course, to
Kandinsky, Chagall, Gabo, Pevsner, Malevich, etc.) Is it
wise to treat millions of adults like children, giving them
no chance to see, compare, reject, or understand various
approaches to art?

3. Much as I tried, why was I never allowed during my entire
trip to the U.S.S.R. to interview any of the liberal younger
artists who had recently been denounced by Khrushchev
and the Party? Or, at least, why was I not permitted to see
their work?

4. Why do you in the Soviet Union consider valuable only art
that is approved of and understood by the majority of your
people? Haven't the greatest artists often been underestimated in their own time? How about Rembrandt and van
Gogh? And do you feel that throughout history the most
significant paintings and sculpture were produced solely
for the masses? Didn't Velásquez work for a king and
Michelangelo for a pope? Weren't Goya and Daumier the
true social propagandists because they painted from inner
conviction uninfluenced by government regulations?

5. Since I realize how violently the Soviet Union abhors what
the Nazis stood for, I question why the U.S.S.R. follows
many of the same dogmatic principles that strangled
German art under the Nazis—the same emphasis on un-
swerving nationalism, on literal propaganda, on physical
prowess, on magnified idealized portraits of Party leaders?
Though the ultimate aims of the two countries are drastically different, why does a revolutionary nation like the
Soviet Union stress in its art the same kind of materialism
that the reactionary Nazis did?

12. *The Mystifying Maya*

No ruins in the world are more extensive, more apocryphal, more abstruse, more demanding than the Mayan remains on our own continent. The fact that many of these heroic monuments are relatively near at hand and still in the process of being explored makes them doubly inviting. Each unexcavated mound, and there are virtually thousands, gives promise of added revelations. History on the Peninsula of Yucatan, so fluid as to unravel before our very eyes, is enriched, confused, and revised by almost daily discoveries. This is a living archaeology, an archaeology that still provides clues to the past with astonishing immediacy. During the past two decades alone, graphic evidence of influential but relatively unknown cultures has emerged from total jungle oblivion.

There are few other such accessible outposts where in a comparatively restricted area one can pursue the entire gamut of a complicated ancient civilization. But the Peninsula of Yucatan, including as it does the Mexican states of Quintana Roo, Campeche, Yucatan, and (stretching a point) parts of Chiapas, offers a seemingly inexhaustible supply of Mayan relics—some restored, others shrouded in dense jungle growth. Starting with

Palenque in the rain forests of Chiapas and ending with the walled city of Tulum on the Caribbean, the legendary Mayan world unfolds from its earliest beginnings through its classical florescence to inevitable decay. This is not to suggest that the entire Mayan civilization was restricted to the Yucatan Peninsula, for there are also important sites in Guatemala and Honduras. And each site excels for a different reason—Copán and Quiriguá for their magnificent carved stelae, Palenque for the refinement of its stucco work, Tikal for its monumental scale, Bonampak for its wealth of recently discovered frescoes. Even so, the whole chronological story of the Maya can be witnessed step by step within the limestone confines of a peninsula only a stone's throw away from New Orleans and Florida.

If Mayan artists were strictly bound by mythic rites, they still allowed themselves greater freedom within these limitations than did most early Meso-Americans. Why we can only conjecture, but perhaps, because their land was isolated by water and a difficult terrain, they were better able to pursue a comparatively peaceful life, to expand, to experiment in art and science, to maintain their own idiosyncratic identity. Though certain over-all Mayan characteristics prevailed, they were tempered by surprising variety. And it is this variety that poses a multitude of questions. No one even knows where these people came from. Until a few years ago, archaeologists were at a loss to find uninterruptedly occupied cities that might provide hints to the continuity of Mayan life. Now, at last, two such sites have turned up, one at Dzibilchaltun near Mérida, capital of the state of Yucatan, the other at Izamal, forty-odd miles east of the capital. In each case, one drives under a relentless sun through flat fields of henequen, Yucatan's number-one crop, to reach ruins only partially excavated but illuminating for the new light they throw on the ambiguous world of the Maya.

Unlike such famous ceremonial centers as Uxmal, Chichén Itzá, Copán, Tikal, and Palenque, all of which were occupied for only a few centuries and then abruptly deserted, Dzibilchaltun was settled continuously from about 2000 B.C. until the Spanish conquest and even later. Why the other cities were abandoned is anybody's guess. Each Middle American authority has a dif-

ferent theory but none is foolproof. Some claim the sites were
evacuated because of epidemics, because of water or soil exhaus-
tion, because of wars or unaccountable ceremonial practices.
Dzibilchaltun, located less than ten miles from Mérida and for
centuries buried beneath a scrubby jungle, was totally unknown
until 1956. Covering an immense area and numbering hundreds
of unexcavated mounds, the city, like most of its neighbors,
sprawls geometrically around spacious plazas and connecting
causeways.

Why this settlement was continuously inhabited during almost
forty centuries and others nearby were summarily deserted is
baffling. Could the Mayan cities have been established and main-
tained for different ceremonial roles? Could their longevity have
depended on varying functions? There is, of course, little doubt
that the ruins seen today are the remains of religious centers.
These towering buildings never housed ordinary citizens. They
were consecrated to a pantheon of perplexing gods who demanded constant propitiation from a special priest-noble group,
a group that dominated the life of Yucatan's theocratic city-
states. Presumably, the common man, a maize farmer as a rule,
lived on the outskirts of the temple area in a perishable small
hut similar to the primitive thatched ones found everywhere on
the peninsula today. At Uxmal, a so-called nunnery is ornamented with carvings of just such windowless little dwellings.
Indeed, wherever one looks, the past is mirrored in the present.
Unlike contemporary Greeks, Mayan Indians of today strongly
resemble their ancient ancestors in both appearance and habits.
Though the wheel and beast of burden are now known, jungle
roads still teem with small, patient men, their backs bent under
loads suspended from their foreheads by leather thongs. One
cannot help but associate these figures with the hordes of human
pack animals who must have laboriously hauled the prodigious
monoliths that form the backbone of Mayan architecture.

For me, even more interesting than Dzibilchaltun was Izamal,
a dusty town baking in the blazing sun, glorified on one side by
a large colonial convent and on the other by a partly restored
pyramid of impressive dimensions. Here pyramid, convent, and
native town combine to tell an abbreviated story of Yucatan. The

present, alas, cannot compete with its illustrious past. Izamal's heritage has a continuing poignancy, for the nobly proportioned, now shabby Spanish convent was erected over yet another pre-Cortesian structure, obliterating the latter completely, though telltale stones in the courtyard are reminders (as at Cholula) of buried treasure.

The Yucatec archaeologist Victor Segovia, who was restoring Izamal's pyramid, a landmark known as El Cerro ("The Hill"), told me that a year earlier the Club Intimos, a local men's organization, decided something must be done about Izamal's mound if the town was to attract its quota of visitors. So, between the club and the Mexican government, funds were allocated, and the job was started. El Cerro, occupied continuously for some three thousand years, has turned out to be the fourth largest (in volume, not height) pre-Columbian pyramid in existence. Only the one at Cholula and those of the Sun and Moon exceed it. The ruin is approached from vast artificial terraces topped by an enormous squat pyramidal structure that doubtless originally served as the base for a ceremonial temple. Access to terraces and pyramid is by the Cyclopean Stairway, so called because of its gigantic monolithic stones. The scale is princely and so also is the conception of this massive man-made hill.

Segovia is in love with the ruin. He affectionately compares it to a rotund Mayan lady, but for me it is utterly masculine—heavy, aggressive, and indomitably permanent despite its recent re-emergence. Now Segovia wants to investigate, if only circumspectly, the temple under the convent, but he doubts whether the citizens of Izamal will permit even a cursory look, fearing, as they might, desecration to the church—an ironic twist since it was the church that originally engulfed their civilization.

Rightfully, one should start a visit to Yucatan by going elsewhere first—to Villahermosa, the capital of Tabasco, for here in a still unexploited river town one finds spectacular Olmec carvings that predated and influenced the Maya. Flourishing around 800 to 500 B.C., the Olmecs ("People of the Rubber Country") produced an art that is nothing short of staggering. Along with the Chavin of Peru, they represent the most ancient known culture of the New World. From southern Veracruz and the eastern tip of Tabasco, including the neighborhood of La Venta, which sometimes lends its name to Olmec sculpture, come monuments of unrivaled majesty. Memories of Villahermosa still haunt me, especially those colossal stone heads in the city's two museums—the Museum of Tabasco, which, by the way, is second only in quantity and quality to Mexico City's National Museum of Anthropology, and the Park of La Venta, an outdoor installation where altars, godlike animals, and outsized portraits are deployed in a natural jungle setting. For sheer grandeur and unflinching emotional expression, Olmec art has few parallels.

These carvings go beyond symbols of emotion to grapple with a kind of brutal reality. Nowhere else in Middle America does sculpture expose so directly the human condition. In the bodiless portrait heads we discover not the usual archaisms but a naturalism that presupposes at once an understanding of man and of the supernatural, for these monstrous creatures were more than ordinary mortals. In Olmec art there is no clutter, no unnecessary hieratic detail which is later to invest and at times to overwhelm Meso-American carvings. Here there is a freedom, a frank handling of rounded form, an approach more closely related to personal observation than to prescribed stylizations.

The heads, somewhat Negroid with their blunt noses and swollen lips, are topped by curious helmet-like caps that may have been worn in ritualistic ball games similar to those subsequently popular with the Maya. What, we continually ask, were these inscrutable bodiless faces doing there in the jungle? Though one head was discovered as early as 1871, most of them, along with other Olmec carvings, were finally exhumed less than twenty years ago, and, like Izamal and Dzibilchaltun, are drastically changing our understanding of Middle American history. Could it be that these mystery men were the true progenitors of the Maya?

The Olmecs also carved strange votive altars that recall certain Buddha figures from Ceylon, but the connection is probably purely coincidental. And everywhere one encounters the werejaguar, half human baby, half monster—a snarling Olmec obsession. Some anthropologists feel this image was the father of all Meso-American rain gods, deities of crucial importance in a land where water was an urgent necessity. In addition, we know the Maya associated jaguars with water, because these animals were agile swimmers and generally hunted near rivers. Earlier, the Olmecs had embroidered this idea by including the watery tears of weeping infantile behemoths.

Of all pre-Columbian riddles, the unheralded flowering of the Olmecs is the most bewildering. Stones for their monolithic carvings, in some instances weighing more than twenty-five tons, were transported at least sixty miles from the nearest possible quarry. Considering that metal tools, transport animals, and wheeled vehicles were unknown, this operation was no less a triumph than a trial for the manpower involved—sometimes slaves, sometimes ordinary citizens working off their taxes. Certain scholars believe the Olmecs even used an early form of the Mayan language, but as yet there is no solid proof of any ethnic relationship. The entire Olmec culture seems to have vanished (who knows why?) around the seventh century A.D.

Less than a hundred miles from Villahermosa is the Mayan city of Palenque. Maturing later than the Olmec civilization but earlier than those of Uxmal and Chichén Itzá, this site is for me second only to the Acropolis in terms of unadulterated beauty. Located in a dense rain forest on the side of a luxuriant jungle hill, the ruin suggests poetic Chinese paintings where nature and architecture are fused in philosophic reverie. Never have structures and landscape been more happily married. One comes upon Palenque slowly. Then suddenly there it is, shining beneath a humid sun. All great Mayan ruins are touched by magic, but Palenque more than most. On natural protuberances, artificial hills form even higher bases for temples oriented around plazas and often surmounted by elegant openwork roof combs that give added loftiness to an already soaring city. It is possible, too, that these lacy decorations may have acted as reinforcing supports for interior corbeled arches.

Steep flights of ceremonial stairs reach up in the hypnotic vertical rhythm that makes each Mayan city a mesmerizing experience. Unnaturally shallow, the steps multiply repetitiously, astounding the modern visitor who cannot help but wonder whether Indian feet were small enough for such abbreviated treads. Was the traffic up and down on tiptoe? One wonders, too, were the priests and nobles carried up on litters? And did the ever-present stairs act overtime as glorified bleachers?

What was this superhuman drive for height, this need to rise above the jungle, to dominate nature? If the Maya wanted a miniature mountain, they made one. If there was no water, they supplied cisterns (as at Uxmal and Kabah). In Chichén Itzá they may even have altered the famous *cenote* (underground well), for its walls form a suspiciously perfect circle, readily adapted to the dramatic rites that took place there and often involved human sacrifice. Though most Mayan cities were located in low jungle country, their frequent pyramidal structures appear vaguely related to erupting volcanoes. Did the Maya travel widely? Without wheels? Always walking? Did their network of roads extend as far as the mountainous highlands?

It was more probably a need to reach the unattainable, to approximate the land of the gods that made the Maya (and the Egyptians) elevate their shrines so insistently. We know these people were able astronomers and mathematicians. In Palenque and Chichén Itzá sophisticated observatories bear witness to this. Like many religions, theirs, too, associated supernatural events with the awesome workings of the firmament.

Some years ago, the distinguished archaeologist Alberto Ruz Lhuillier made an epic discovery at Palenque, one that again reversed previous assumptions. In the Temple of the Inscriptions he found a hidden circuitous passage leading down to the richly carved tomb of a high priest or noble. For the first time, scholars realized the pyramids of Latin America were not always elevated bases for temples. Paralleling the pyramids of Egypt, they served as semideified burial crypts, at least on occasion. But there is no reason to believe that the Maya were in contact with Egypt, though Thor Heyerdahl has recently investigated this possibility.

Palenque is renowned for the refinement of its art. Within the ruin compound an excellent small museum preserves the more fugitive sculpture found on the site. Here, because necessary natural resources were available, stucco work reached its apex.

Fragmentary reliefs with hints of color are still intact on certain buildings, reminding us that Mayan architecture was once brilliantly painted and must have created dazzling, if garish effects. Today, the stucco reliefs at Palenque are badly eroded, but from what remains we recognize the cultivated urbanity that characterized this site. Modeling in stucco made possible far more sensitive surface nuances than carving in stone. A group of stucco portrait heads in the Palenque museum are among the most touchingly humanistic works to be found in all of Latin America. Tender, even compassionate, they celebrate the value of the individual, a conception rarely associated with the pomp surrounding supramundane rites. Why, one wonders, were the Maya more than most Middle Americans able to make contact with an interior world while yet living in a rigorously ceremonial one?

Palenque is also famous as the site where Mayan archaeology got its start, for here in the late eighteenth century a Spanish priest first officially investigated the ruins. Since then, a number of intrepid travelers and scholars have studied the city. Notable was the Frenchman Count Jean Frederic Waldeck, who came to Palenque in the early nineteenth century and established himself in a structure named for him, the Templo del Conde. Incidentally, all Mayan buildings today have similarly irrelevant names, usually supplied by local Indians and, more often than not, inaccurate. Nunneries, churches, castles, palaces—these are all invented modern labels. A few years after Count Waldeck's visit, that tenacious New York lawyer John Lloyd Stephens arrived with his English companion, Frederick Catherwood, and together they assembled the most valuable and painstaking early record of Middle American ruins.

Stephens' text is full of adventure, romance, fortitude, and facts; Catherwood's drawings are models of selfless accuracy. Archaeologists still use this double record as a reliable guide, and any intelligent visitor will not fail to read the various volumes of Stephens' *Incidents of Travel in Central America, Chiapas, and Yucatan.* To imagine the difficulties these men endured is to realize how even today ticks, mosquitoes, heat, and jungle rot can irritate the hardiest enthusiast, once he strikes out on his own.

The first detailed story of the Maya was Diego de Landa's *Relación de las Cosas de Yucatán,* a sixteenth-century document by a Franciscan bishop who arrived in time to see some of the Mayan cities still functioning. That he likewise was responsible for stamping out the entire legacy of Mayan literature is a fact not readily forgotten or forgiven. With sublime Christian arrogance, Landa signed the order in 1562 that incinerated hundreds of Mayan codices. In that conflagration, much of Mayan history expired.

Only three codices still remain, one in Madrid, one in Paris, and the most beautiful in Dresden. At the Tabasco Museum in Villahermosa, facsimiles of these vigorous, folded books are sad reminders that no original codices remain on the soil where they were produced, a fact which implies what might have happened to all pre-Spanish art had most of it not been carved from stone. Elegant, sure, and explosively alive, the draftsmanship in the three codices (especially in the one at Dresden) is amazingly free, despite unfailing stylizations. Students have long tried to decode the Mayan glyphs. Though certain dates, astronomical data, and religious dicta have emerged, many experts seriously doubt that Mayan writing can ever be fully transcribed. Like the "written" languages of Egypt and China, these hieroglyphics are not based on an alphabet. And, of course, no equivalent of the Rosetta stone exists. We hear frequent rumors that Soviet scientists are at work interpreting the Dresden codex with electrical computers, but one questions whether it is possible to decipher poetic metaphors with modern machines. It is even doubtful whether the Maya themselves, with the exception of specially educated priests and nobles, could decode their own writings.

Thus, the secrets are compounded in a never-ending conundrum. Question after question presents itself. Why do nineteenth-century Haida carvings from British Columbia resemble those of the Maya? Was there any connection? Why do both seem vaguely Oriental—also true of Olmec art? How was it possible that a highly advanced civilization never discovered the wheel, metal, transport animals, or the arch? The Maya did, it is true, repeatedly depend on false or corbeled arches, chiefly to attain greater height, but such arches carried no load. Walls remained massive, and fenestration, except for occasional small windows, was practically unknown. Interiors were everywhere dank, meager, awkward, and rarely pierced by light.

In contrast, exterior space was sumptuous. Since Mayan cities were ceremonial centers, and since the climate was warm, important public events took place outdoors. To fly over Chichén Itzá is to recognize with what measured order the designers of this kaleidoscopic city alternated weighted solids with open areas. Though certain sections of Chichén are Mayan, much of it is Maya-Toltec, for during the eleventh century the Toltecs arrived as conquerors from Central Mexico and made Chichén Itzá their super-showplace. Mayan influence, however, was never totally erased. The cross-pollination of these two cultures is a testament to the boundless creativity of indigenous American art. If the Maya were more subtle artists, the Toltecs were more adventuresome engineers. Mayan buildings were basically rectangular and compact. Related to the minor arts—in form to pottery design, in surface ornamentation to woven textiles—they show a strong monolithic emphasis. Columns and openings other than doors were rare. The Toltecs, in contrast, concentrated on oppositions of colonnade and wall, of space and form. With them, porches and pillars became more frequent. Everywhere open vistas challenged impenetrable masses.

Having visited Chichén Itzá more than thirty years ago, I returned recently to find it extensively restored and even mightier than I remembered. What stand out indelibly are its irrevocable order, its careful city planning, and above all, two magnificent monuments—the Ball Court and the Castillo. The former, a compound found often in Middle American sites, was reputedly the setting for symbolic religious games. There exists no other ball court as large, as flawlessly resolved, as the one at Chichén Itzá. In truth, I know of few outdoor areas that can offer such a breath-taking sweep of organized space. Nearby stands the Castillo, a familiar pyramid topped by a temple. But this structure is unique; it seems to soar, yet remains earth-bound, a reminder that early American vision was at once cabalistic and pragmatic. I got my first view of the Castillo this trip from a hotel balcony some two miles away. In the sunset light the pyramid became a floating mirage. Largely unornamented, it is comparable to the Parthenon, though no two buildings could differ more diametrically. What they share is the impact of perfect proportions and meticulous restraint.

Aesthetically superior, at least for me, to any pyramid in the New World or Egypt, the Castillo is built solidly over an earlier structure. This stacking of architecture is a familiar oddity on the Yucatan Peninsula. Wherever modern excavation permits, it is possible to investigate the inner temple as well as the outer one. And for that matter, there are often more than two structural levels. Uxmal's Pyramid of the Magician (so named because of a local myth) looks like a tribute to never-never land as it builds up and out in an eccentric complex of five superimposed layers. Lacking bulldozers and rarely daunted by technicalities, the Mayan architect resolutely filled in already existing temples, using the last one as a convenient support for the next. What remains today are visual genealogical cross sections of Mayan history. The constant compulsion to obliterate the old with large superimpositions was possibly related to the same obsession that forced the Maya to abandon their great cities at the peak of development. It was almost as if they deserted a supreme achievement before it could desert them.

Because Mayan architecture was built in stages from period to period, it tended to be asymmetrical, its very inconsistencies providing a kind of unexpected fallibility. The temple on top of Chichén's Castillo is placed slightly to one side and is all the more interesting for it. The buildings that constitute the Nunnery quadrangle at Uxmal differ in dimensions and decorative motifs but remain successfully integrated. It is this independence, this ability to exploit the accidents of life, that gives Mayan art a vitality sometimes lacking in other more formalized (and, let me add, more brutal) Mexican cultures.

The gods that preyed on the Maya were legion, but the most powerful were predictably representatives of rain, maize, sun, and death, though with Maya-Toltecs the plumed serpent always remained an ubiquitous totem. The rain god Chac, an understandably authoritative deity in arid Yucatan, very nearly became the leitmotif of Mayan architectural sculpture. Grotesque masks of Chac with long snake-like (or could it be lightning-like?) noses everywhere act as fanatical decorative images. Not even the twentieth century can surpass these deliberately abstracted symbols. On the Governor's Palace at Uxmal, masks of Chac are so interwoven that one design embraces another to create sinuous snake-like patterns winding through a complex frieze and finally intermeshing on the corners of the building in simulated columns. At Kabah, too, the exotic Temple of the Masks, which is literally covered from top to bottom with Chacs carved in high relief, puts modern surrealism to shame. For excessive extravagance, Kabah is unprecedented.

As John Stephens noted, Mayan relief sculpture resembles stone mosaics, each separately carved piece contributing to the whole but no single piece an entity in itself. Singularly enhanced by Yucatan's brilliant light, these decorative friezes at times approximate Near Eastern techniques in their coloristic precision. Ornaments and structure intermingle with fertile exuberance. Doors metamorphose into the gaping jaws of gods, as sculpture and architecture join in supernatural orgies. And always, external design skillfully adapts itself to rectangular demands.

At Uxmal, the archaeologist Cesar Saenz was directing restoration on the Pyramid of the Magician when he unearthed two sensational finds. Closely resembling the Reina de (Queen of) Uxmal—a much admired sculpture found earlier in the same pyramid and now on view in Mexico City's National Museum of Anthropology—the two carvings represent conventionalized serpents with human heads clutched in their open mouths, a Mayan concept of man's origin, perhaps. But there is nothing queen-like about these sculptures, and, indeed, female figures rarely appear in official Mayan art. Yet, from cemeteries on the island of Jaina off the coast of Campeche, from Mayapan and other sites come small ceramic figurines, often of women, that reveal a verve and informality, a realism and sensuality quite at odds with the hieratic symbolism we commonly associate with pre-

Cortesian sculpture. Tiny images of nursing mothers, dancers, acrobats, and musicians all combine to prove that life among the Maya was not limited to occult priestly habits.

In stark contrast to these small clay figures, the huge plumed serpents of Chichén Itzá coil up and down stairway balustrades, their rattles and feathers triumphantly covering columns, walls, and doorways. The Maya-Toltecs, with almost Freudian insistence, reproduced the serpent everywhere, relating it both to semideified leaders and, more practically, to agriculture. They inflated its transcendental powers by adding the feathers of that rare and precious bird, the quetzal—a creature of jewel-like beauty. Despite images of lascivious eagles and tigers devouring human hearts, of open-jawed snakes recoiling to attack, these ancient people exalted to godship what they needed more than what they feared. Above all, they needed rain and other favorable conditions for the cultivation of corn, a crop on which their very lives depended.

If Middle American Indians were involved with water and maize as symbols of life, they were also irrevocably preoccupied with death. Grinning skulls interlaced with bones parade in frantic processions across their buildings. The tradition continues today. In Mérida's native market I paid eight cents for one of the few handmade products not rendered obsolete by modern plastics—a leering papier-mâché skull closely identified with more accomplished versions of the past. The painter Carlos Mérida, who is part Mayan, once observed that death was incidental in his country but accidental in mine. At the moment, we had just witnessed the death of a young Indian, shot for stealing a chicken in a small Mexican town. Yet, death was never incidental for Carlos Mérida's ancestors; it was a major event even more consequential than birth. In fact, it was a logical continuation of birth, a concomitant of life that required ceaseless attention and prevention.

If the Maya was obsessed with death, he was equally obsessed with time, and possibly for the same reason. Calendar stones and stelae painstakingly record the dates of outstanding events. The here, the now, the past were all documented mathematically for the future; the Maya transformed the abstract idea of time into a positive fact. For him there were hours to plant and hours to reap; there were days to worship and days to die. But hours, days, and finite time were always ordered from above. Life, too, and death were controlled by whims of the gods. Only through the intervention of all-powerful deities could the Maya hope to survive in a land tormented by numberless hazards.

One day I flew across an endless sea of jungle to reach the Caribbean and the walled city of Tulum, a marvelous stronghold of gray stone ruins from the Maya-Toltec period. Gone is the original painted stucco finish; gone, too, most of the frescoes that ornamented this architecture. But on the inner temple of one small building, a group of chastely drawn gods, serpents, flowers, fruit, and ears of corn recalls the highly controlled hands that created the Mayan codices. Though these frescoes have been somewhat restored, they are fast disintegrating in Tulum's damp heat. And with the codices gone, Yucatan can ill afford to lose further Mayan paintings.

At Tulum, new questions arise. Why was this particular city walled? Why are its temple doors so low that only a dwarf could pass through them comfortably? And why was the site so involved with the Descending God, a winged deity forever plunging earthward? Almost every building honors this image, which has been associated with the setting sun, but more often with the bee, an insect of importance both for its honey and its wax. In the museum at Mérida, I recall a terra-cotta sculpture of the Descending God holding what looked like a honeycomb. In Tulum, there on the sea, a humble diving creature seems to have taken precedence over water and corn, over jaguar, serpent, and eagle.

It is these interminable puzzles that make Mayan art a web of chimerical conjecture. All is speculative, especially those thousands of unexplored mounds. In Yucatan, what we do not know is as engrossing as what we do.

13. *What Makes Dutch Art Dutch*

During a trip to Holland I was struck by the indelible imprint this small country makes on its native painters. Environment has always, I suppose, played a strong role, but surely nowhere more effectively than in the Netherlands. Why, I am not quite sure. Possibly because Holland remains a land where continuity results in a recognizably indigenous personality, a fact that does not necessarily imply isolation from the rest of the world but rather the presence of a national individualism rare in our times.

Though one can admire Vermeer, Saenredam, Rembrandt, van Gogh, and Mondrian without knowing the land that produced them, to know it is to understand them better. And by knowing I do not mean merely a nod to the country's more obvious physical characteristics, important as they are. After all, the Lowlands are so named for good reason; they are low, wide, and flat. The cities, if never precipitous in a modern skyscraper sense, have a rectangular verticality resulting from densely organized architecture. In my memories of Holland, steep, narrow staircases are a constant leitmotif.

The lucid angularity that permeates cities like Amsterdam and

The Hague encouraged those so-called seventeenth-century Little Masters to paint affectionate small canvases devoted to the activities of a burgeoning middle class. But Saenredam and Vermeer, despite the modest size of their pictures, were far more than "Little Masters." They transcended purely visual experiences, while using such experiences as points of departure. With pearly light and structured space, they gave daily scenes a noble permanence.

To travel from Amsterdam to The Hague in less than an hour —the train stopping at Leyden, Haarlem, and several other important towns—is to understand why homogeneity pervades this compact nation. No mountains, no plains, no changes in climate, no vast dimensions divide the country. It is all of a piece. As the fields stretch out toward low unobstructed horizons, they allow the skyscape to become more pronounced than the landscape, a phenomenon frequently exploited by such master cloudmakers as Jacob van Ruisdael and Hercules Seghers. The latter also appreciated the boundless space an open sky provides.

During most of the winter Holland is sunless. The mists, which have a strange, remote transparency, seem less gray than a muted ivory gold. And it is exactly this elusive color coupled with an uncompromisingly pure design that turns what otherwise might be a fine architectural composition by Saenredam into a unique masterpiece. The same, of course, is true of Vermeer's paintings. They could end up as little more than exquisite genre scenes, but their indomitable structure and controlled light cause the immediate facts of life to retreat. And yet it is the simple facts of life that are their source material.

What, then, made Saenredam and Vermeer different from most of their contemporaries? It was, I think, their ability to abstract, to take solely what they needed from what they knew, to extract only the kernel from the commonplace. A plump Dutch girl, a map on the wall, a jug on the table—these are the superficial accouterments of Vermeer's paintings. In his hands familiar forms assumed a serenity, a balance, and silence so complete as to create another world. Because tradition played a strong role in Dutch seventeenth-century painting, men like Vermeer and Saenredam could adhere to the past while yet drastically restructuring it. For them, the episodic, so popular with artists of their period, was sacrificed to more timeless investigations.

Saenredam's views of church architecture were less concerned with churches than with what today we might call minimal structures. To humanize his immaculate designs, he rarely used people or events but instead a pervasive tender luminosity. The light plays across his complex spaces like a living force. Other Dutch artists of the period, notably de Witte, also specialized in church scenes, frequently producing limpid white-pillared perspectives, but they never approximated the impersonal majesty of Saenredam's flawless classicism.

As for present-day minimal structurists, very few are more rigorously economical than Saenredam, though I imagine even fewer would accept him as a forebear, or, indeed, know that he ever existed. They would be more apt to admire that famous modern Dutchman Piet Mondrian, who continued Saenredam's search for impeccable order. One questions whether it was coincidence that caused both men to start their careers as meticulous flower painters, an area in nature that suggests at once fragility and resolved definition.

The scrupulous discipline that produced Vermeer, Saenredam, and Mondrian also created a reverse reaction. At times we respond to direct insistent stimuli. At other times we fight against these stimuli because they are too insistent. No country has developed a more deliberately organized or cooler art than Holland, yet no other land has generated more fervently charged canvases than those of van Gogh, Rembrandt (in his later years), and Willem de Kooning today. For it was in Holland that modern Expressionism was initiated, if not by Rembrandt, then certainly some two centuries later by Vincent. Art is often cyclical. Mondrian, Vermeer, and Saenredam pursued a universal harmony. They were not humanists; they were searching for an ideal rationale. Rembrandt, van Gogh, and de Kooning are more properly considered humanists though no less involved with structure. Since their interests centered on the ambiguous passions of man and rarely on utopian values, these three artists

The St. Bavo Church in Haarlem, by Pieter Saenredam

tended to lash out with flail-like brushes. For them anxiety replaced serenity.

En route to Holland I stopped in London, where a large van Gogh exhibition lent by Amsterdam's Vincent van Gogh Foundation was on view in the Hayward Gallery. At the time I wondered, recalling this artist's innumerable American shows, whether there was much left to learn about him, but I was wrong. Because drawings formed the backbone of the exhibit and because they were installed as an introduction to the paintings, one came away realizing that it was less van Gogh's color than his powerfully organized line that gave structure to his work. When he painted, he drew with a stabbing brush, and when he drew, he said it all—all the turbulence, all the autobiographical fire is there. A landscape drawing by van Gogh can be as emotionally revealing as a self-portrait.

Though Rembrandt, too, was a magnificent draftsman, it was his arbitrary manipulation of subjective light that allowed him to probe the human condition. Nor was it Holland's natural light that interested him, but a light of his own invention. Emerging from a hidden source, this light produced form as it kneaded surfaces into deep hollows and swelling protrusions. Of all the great Dutch artists, Rembrandt was the least Dutch. His work ignored the bourgeois security of seventeenth-century Holland. With unfaltering compassion, he pursued one theme—man, man regardless of order or disorder. Rembrandt was totally emancipated because he could not or would not adapt his vision to the demands of a local society at a specific time. To realize how complete was his independence, one need only compare his *Night Watch* with the best of Frans Hals' portrait groups. Rembrandt was Holland's greatest artist precisely because he neither belonged to nor strongly reacted against what existed. He was that rare exception—his own man.

Yet de Kooning, who, like van Gogh, is an expatriate, has remained curiously Dutch despite long years in the United States. The same fury that drove Vincent impels him. One finds it also in the work of Karel Appel. All these passionately intense Dutchmen represent the other side of the coin. They seem to reject the decorous, the temperate, hoping perhaps to escape the uniformity of their background. What they share is an almost frenetic need to tangle with raw color, with raw emotions, and with direct elemental forces. One thinks of the carefully tended, circumscribed fields, the clean, cautious cities of the Netherlands, and one appreciates this rebellion. On the surface Holland may seem as steady and sturdy as Switzerland; yet an impetuous perversity shows itself at unexpected moments—in conversation, in art, in the excessive size of Amsterdam's cavernous airport. The extremes in art that stem from this dualism are the natural concomitants of a land where boundaries both protect and challenge, both reassure and frustrate.

I have often thought that to know Holland well is to understand her artists, but now, on the contrary, I am convinced it is her artists who make us understand Holland.

14. *The Art That History Shaped: Israel, 1966*

On the rim of Makhtesh Ramon, a vast eroded gorge in the Negev, several immense sculptures remain from a recent international competition. Seen there against that ancient myth-soaked topography, these massive modern structures look like trinkets. Though present-day Israeli painting is determinedly abstract (perhaps in unconscious recognition of the stricture against "graven images"), the country itself paraphrases many kinds of art. There is the surrealist never-never land of salt-encrusted crags around the Dead Sea. There is the stark expressionism of Safad, a cabalistic city where medieval scholars minutely reinterpreted every shred of Jewish lore. There is the volatile impressionist light that bounces off the towers of Jerusalem and the humble cubist architecture of nearby Arab villages. Here pure geometric structures, clean and unadorned, take on the coloration of the land because they grow from the land and its needs, a lesson modern Israeli architects have yet to learn.

If ever a country cannot be separated from its art it is Israel, a tiny strip of danger-fringed land where two stark realities are always present—lack of water and fear of invasion. In a single day it is possible to collide with four forbidding borders. To look across at the hills of Jordan, at the mountains of Syria and Lebanon, at the illogical Gaza Strip, at the other half of Jerusalem—a city literally ripped in two—and to realize that these areas are taboo is to understand why European cultures are stronger here than Near Eastern ones. The early influx of Zionist settlers from Eastern Europe had strong impact, too, though at present immigration is heavier from North Africa and Asia. Today Israel is a medley of so many people—Arabs, Druses, Christians, Jews from some seventy-odd countries—that in comparison America's melting pot seems homogeneous. Curiously, it is not Russian, Polish, or German art that has infiltrated Israel; it is almost exclusively art from the school of Paris, and this despite minimal immigration from France. Most contemporary painters elect to study in Paris either before or after they emigrate, though a number are now based in New York.

From a state not yet eighteen years old, it is folly to expect a full-blown national art movement. In a pioneer land where immediate needs are vital, where water is an urgent issue, where housing must keep pace with a constant flow of immigrants from Asia, Europe, North Africa, and the Near East, where guarded borders are daily threats, where every sprinkler, every terraced vineyard, every new tree represents a superhuman effort, it will take time for art to achieve a personal imprint.

Toward this end, however, important help should come from Jerusalem's impressive Israel National Museum, only recently installed in its handsome new home. Facing complexities shared by museums elsewhere, this institution must also cope with the country's incredible diversity. Take only the museum's senior staff and board of directors, a small group comprising people born in no less than thirteen countries—Austria, Poland, England, Israel, the United States, North Africa, Switzerland, Holland, Rumania, Persia, Iraq, Russia, and Germany. Then, too, there are tradition-bound Hassidic Jews in Israel who are closely tied to the orthodox laws of the past and who to this day oppose the use of human images. For them an art museum is a potential threat. The contradictions that divide these devout zealots, still dressed in semimedieval ghetto robes, from their up-to-date sunburnt compatriots create two conflicting worlds.

Clashes are inevitable and frequent. Politics, social life, economics, and inevitably art are all affected. Divergent origins and opposed doctrines fill this small land with simmering tensions. As Teddy Kollek, chairman of the museum's council and mayor of Jerusalem, observed, "We're building a museum in a community with very little background in the fine arts. We have practically no collectors, no museum traditions. Three kinds of people visit the museum—tourists from other countries (about 100,000 in the last half year), people specifically interested in art and archaeology, and people who have never even heard of a museum. This group, of course, includes schoolchildren." It also includes, as Mr. Kollek might have added, thousands of underprivileged immigrants from Tunisia, Morocco, and Iraq. Because Jewish worship has always been a mixture of sonorous chanting and searching self-dialogue, music and literature have taken root more readily than art.

Visitors pour into the museum. Almost a half million have come since the new complex of buildings was opened some six months ago, an astonishing figure considering that Jerusalem's population is less than 200,000. Organized groups from all parts of the country wander through the ample outdoor sculpture garden designed by Isamu Noguchi. In itself a distinguished work of art, this partly walled, partly open area is conceived in terms of tilted space and subtle dipping perspectives. At one with the luminous landscape of Jerusalem, the hillside terraced garden makes history as a new kind of open-air architecture and as a unique setting for sculpture. Familiar bronzes by Rodin, Daumier, Bourdelle, Moore, Lipchitz, and Maillol have never looked better. And a sinewy construction, made by Tinguely on the spot and given to the museum by him, is a harmonious if surprising addition to Jerusalem's skyline.

Nearby is a small pavilion devoted to original plaster portraits by Jacob Epstein. A profusion of famous faces looks out at us with startling spontaneity. These sculptures, ingeniously installed on replicas of open packing cases, precisely as unfinished works should be seen, overflow the gallery and bring to life the personalities of artist and sitters, Winston Churchill and Chaim Weizmann, among others.

Architecturally the new museum is almost as successful as the sculpture garden. Again beautifully geared to the landscape, it encompasses a complex of low-lying connected buildings that include a museum of fine arts and an archaeological museum. Here, too, interrelated space and varied levels have meaning as one moves from section to section. Windows open on matchless views of Jerusalem, sometimes projecting works of art on the very soil that produced them. The building, designed by two Israeli architects, Alfred Mansfeld and Dora Gad, is flexible, capable of growth, and fortunate in its lofty twenty-two-acre site, which it rides with authority. One need only compare the new Knesset (House of Parliament) on a nearby hill to appreciate the difference between organic and decorative architecture. No design could be less suited to the psychological meaning of government than the Knesset's flimsy approximation of a wedding cake.

Also part of the Israel Museum complex is the much-discussed Shrine of the Book, a separate structure designed by the American architects Frederick Kiesler and Armand Bartos to house the Dead Sea Scrolls and other pertinent material. Though this "temple" has been widely acclaimed, for me it is less architecture than romantic symbolism. The fragile scrolls scarcely need such pretentious overstatement to convey their message. Nor should they be worshipped in a "shrine," for they are pre-eminently great archaeological finds, legendary to be sure, but more related to history than to Hollywood.

The museum wisely specializes in Jewish ceremonial art, modern sculpture, archaeology, and a modest but growing collection of graphics and paintings, the latter chiefly from the present century and often given by artists themselves. It is, however, the archaeological section that comes off best and most fully reflects the country, a country gone mad on the subject of digs. Israel is an archaeologist's paradise. Suburban ladies border their flower gardens with pottery shards; school groups swarm over excavated ruins; the foundations of any new house may turn up a masterpiece. Living as closely with these emerging antiquities as with emerging skyscrapers, the people are aware of their many-leveled heritage. For the wind of innumerable civilizations has blown over Israel, a land brushed by every twist of history. Hyksos, Canaanites, Egyptians, Philistines, Israelites, Greeks, Romans, Byzantines, Nabataeans, Crusaders, Turks, Persians, Arabs, and, of course, Jews have all left their mark. Only the British in their brief day made no visible impact, unless an occasional moldering barracks might qualify. Discussing excavations in the Holy Land, archaeologist James Ross once pointed out, "No other civilization offers the tell phenomenon, which makes it possible to trace in one specific spot layer upon layer of civilizations as far back as 7000 B.C. and in as many as twenty-one levels." ("Tell" is an archaeological term for the artificial mounds that cover ancient sites.)

Because the most important objects excavated in the country eventually come to the Israel Museum, this institution has emerged as an outstanding archaeological showcase. Its future is virtually unlimited, since the number of tells in the Holy Land is incalculable. Take Hazor alone, which is only partially excavated and has already yielded rich finds. Located nine miles from the Sea of Galilee, this colossal site is one of the largest in existence, stretching in all directions and abundantly meriting further investigation. So far, work has been carried on for only three seasons, but even this short time has exposed more than twenty layers of intermingled civilizations. Certain specialists feel it could take centuries to uncover Hazor completely. Today it is an awesome experience merely to stand on top of the tell and realize that under one's feet the tangible history of nearly five thousand years is stacked away.

As far as archaeology is concerned, the Israel Museum has a built-in future. But in other fields it faces competition with long-established European and American institutions, a challenge which, if followed, could prove fatal, for the needs and limitations of Israel do not necessarily parallel those of Europe or America. At present, a wealthy donor's name is attached to each building, but as a rule these benefactors are not Israeli citizens. They live in the United States, Canada, or Europe and are rarely involved in the day-by-day struggle to establish a significant national institution. Buildings are not enough; indeed, they can sometimes overpower a museum. One feels that now must come consolidation and a concerted effort to fill these new structures with carefully selected works of art, a feat that cannot be accomplished overnight. Merely to follow in the sometimes frenetic footsteps of American museums seems a pity. Statistics, speed, numbers, publicity—none of this really matters. Far more important are an over-all plan for the future and a wise acquisition policy with quality its keynote. The point is not to fill every wall immediately but to recognize the realistic problems of a late start and assemble an integrated collection.

Ancient art in Israel is sometimes more interesting historically than aesthetically. This land, which constantly adapted itself to invading cultures, simplified imported art by assiduously eliminating strong emotions, human images, and complicated decoration. Since art forms rarely originated here but were transplanted from other countries, the result was often provincial in the best sense of the word. The cultural invasion of Israel today is more financial than physical. One hopes the country will not succumb to foreign benefactors as it once did to foreign aggressors.

Though ruins in Israel rarely approximate the glamour of those in nearby Egypt and Greece, still the land offers sites of surpassing interest. Starting with extensive prehistoric caves near Haifa, where remains of the paleolithic Galilee Man were found, and continuing up to the relatively recent Turkish walls of Acre, this town itself a small masterpiece, the country is interlaced with antiquities. Most visitors go to Caesarea for a brief look at the splendid Roman, Byzantine, and Crusader ruins. Fewer travel a bit out of the way to see the magnificently preserved amphitheater at Beth She'an, surely one of the finest Roman ruins in existence. An equally impressive monument is the Jewish necropolis at Beth Sha-arim on the road between Haifa and Nazareth. Discovered only in 1936, these prodigious catacombs with their skilled marblework and endless tunnels have turned up illuminating Talmudic revelations. Slowly, step by step, each new dig and each newly discovered scroll add unexpected dimensions to our knowledge of religious history. Near Jerusalem, in the all-Arab town of Abu Gosh, a view of Christian chronology unfolds. Surrounded by ancient scent-laden gardens, a well-preserved Crusader church built on Roman foundations dramatizes how much medieval architecture owes to Rome. Everywhere in Israel the indomitable stamp of the Roman Empire persists.

Perhaps the site that most fired my imagination is in the Negev—a biblical city called Arad that has only come to light within the last three years, though it dates back to 3500 B.C. Situated on a remote tell commanding a panoramic view of the wild, dun-colored desert, it is, like most sites, only partially excavated. Yet through the eyes of the archaeologist Ruth Amiran, who was one of the scholars responsible for this dig and who accompanied me there, I was able to envision a large thriving city. The fact that only massive stone skeletons remain to indicate carefully laid out streets and sizable houses did not interfere with the mirage. Here one realized that even thousands of years ago urban planning was practiced, for the entire lower section of Arad is oriented to catch every drop of precious desert rain. The investigation of tells in Israel is a heady occupation, a hypnotic mixture of science and illusion, detection and scholarship, intuition and wishful thinking.

Modern architecture is less interesting, despite or possibly because of the unprecedented amount of construction going on. Housing for new settlers springs up at record speed but sometimes scars the landscape with unnecessary brutality. I cannot forget Nazareth, which for me is an architectural disaster. Above the old city, so closely identified with the land as to have veritably grown out of it, one sees a new, clinically sterile highrise town, awkward, disoriented, and unrelated to the climate of Israel. Modern architects blithely and, may I add, blindly ignore the country's Mediterranean heat and searing sunlight as they build routine European structures with glass predominating. In contrast, I recall a house in the Druse village of Daliyat el Karmil, where I was taken by an artist friendly with a family there. An eighty-year-old Druse patriarch, living in a compound surrounded by nearly a hundred descendants, was the sole member of the family still faithful to a traditional Arab house. On a warm day it was sheer delight to enter this protective structure molded like sculpture and made spacious by a large covered veranda facing the Carmel range. One feels, alas, that this kind

of indigenous architecture is doomed; even the old man was inordinately proud of his sons' new homes, all "époque Grand
Rapids."

If many of the new towns in the Negev are designed with ap-
palling monotony, they are still symbols of incredible courage.
To move whole populations into ready-made cities is no mean
achievement, and to do so in the sandy, arid Negev is little less
than heroic. Schools, clinics, factories, shopping areas, and repe-
titious, boxlike apartment buildings push out of the desert with
demoniac speed. On occasion the water tower is not only the most
crucial structure in the town; it is also the most interesting.
Kiryat Gat, one of the larger new cities, with a population of
thirty thousand, is only ten years old, yet residents from
seventy-two countries are already humanizing their environment by adding to and modifying the stock buildings they have
inherited. The "children of Israel" are no longer "wandering
in the wilderness," but here in the Negev they are still enduring
austere isolation.

Farther south, in the heart of the Negev, Beersheba is a
rapidly growing phenomenon. Skyscrapers rise in the desert
next to the Bedouin camel market, where nomadic tribesmen
congregate at daybreak every Thursday. These travel-poster
contrasts are romantic, yet one feels that the past is on the way
out, that soon the camel market will be little more than a tourist
attraction. Already the government is building permanent settlements for the Bedouins. Whether this last remnant of confident
masculinity will withstand its new security is doubtful. The
symbol of one resolute little girl among 225 boys in a recently
established Bedouin school may be prophetic. There she sat in
a crowded, odoriferous classroom, a proud young feminist half-
shy, half-sly.

Israel is not without modern buildings of interest, but one
rarely finds them in public housing developments or on school
campuses. The universities in Jerusalem and Tel Aviv, the
Technion in Haifa, and Weizmann Institute of Science at
Rehovot, an advanced scientific research center, have elicited
little more than weak echoes of a hybrid international style.
During late November, while leading a seminar at Hebrew University in Jerusalem, I was all but incinerated by ubiquitous

glass. What happens in summer is cruel to contemplate. Only the stimulation of an extraordinary group of students kept me on my feet. However, near Tel Aviv in Bat Yam three Israeli architects, Alfred Neumann, Zvi Hecker, and E. Sharon, have designed a new Town Hall memorable for its structural innovations and its adjustment to climatic needs. Shaped like an inverted ziggurat, the building is composed of three stories, each cantilevered over the one below in order to provide protection from sun and glare. Certain external decorative details may seem superfluous, but the basic design of this structure, inherited from a Middle Eastern tradition, is valid.

In addition to Jerusalem's Israel Museum, the city can be proud of its new Shrine to the Jewish Holocaust in Europe. Built on a bald hill, this solemn, uncompromising monument called Yad Vashem is eminently suited to its tragic theme. Both inside and out one senses the heavy drums of sorrow. Concrete walls and weathered boulders imported from the Galilee keep all light out and suggest a kind of supernatural imprisonment. Abstract, welded iron entrance gates by the Israeli sculptor David Palombo appropriately evoke images of shattered lives.

There are other monuments in Israel, none as noble as Yad Vashem, but each a special tribute to pain or pride. At Beisan, Alfred Mansfeld has designed a towering forty-five-foot concrete structure dedicated to the men and women of that region who lost their lives in the War of Liberation. Inspired by ancient male and female symbols, this stark undecorated memorial speaks for itself, as do even more poignantly the bombed-out bulletproof convoy transports left where they fell on the much fought-over Tel Aviv–Jerusalem road.

The humble Davidka Monument in Jerusalem is another reminder of the War of Liberation. Here an old mortar seen against a heavy, partially carved stone wall becomes a new kind of Pop art. Some of Israel's most impressive monuments take the form of forests planted in memory of outstanding events or people. The sixty million trees that have been added since statehood are practical memorials, designed to control erosion, improve the climate, and beautify the country. One such forest is named after John F. Kennedy.

Tracking down the work of living Israeli artists is a frustrating job. In Tel Aviv, the country's largest city, I visited a number of museums but found no native contemporary painting or sculpture on view. The same was largely true in Haifa. Fortunately, in Tel Aviv at the commercial Galerie Israel I was able to see the work of several promising modern artists, but as yet these men rarely reflect the dynamic toughness of the country. Though Israel is passionately nationalistic, contemporary painting is closer to Europe and especially to France than to the Holy Land. It takes time for art to grow from the roots of a country. For me two artists stand out, neither of them avant-garde, both of them veterans. Anna Ticho's drawings create a composite image of the landscape around Jerusalem. Every crinkled hill, every small twig, every hidden Arab village melds into detailed and yet curiously stenographic panoramas. Web-like calligraphic lines evoke but never describe this ancient land. Mordecai Ardon's work is less obviously related to Israel, yet his authoritative handling of sharp, fluctuating light belongs entirely to the Near East. Though born in Europe, both these artists have withstood the anonymous internationalism so prevalent in Israeli art and architecture today.

At Kibbutz Ein Harod a thriving museum devoted to Jewish art is housed in an excellent building. Here are found specific galleries permanently earmarked for contemporary Israeli art, the only survey of this kind I found in the country. If Kibbutzim no longer act as the moral and social backbone of a fast-developing economy, paradoxically they now offer certain luxuries hard to find elsewhere. Still mostly agricultural, many of these 225 collective settlements have established lucrative, comfortably equipped guest houses comparable to good hotels. And museums are not infrequent, though few compare with the one at Ein Harod. I visited Kibbutz Hazorea and found there a beautiful gallery devoted to Far and Middle Eastern art. Administered with loving care by a member of the kibbutz whose chief work is in the settlement's plastic factory, this sensitive small museum is exemplary. At Kibbutz Kabri, the abstract sculptor Yehiel Shemi lives. Because he enjoys considerable success and numerous commissions, he has been freed of all communal work. Provided with a small home and a good studio, he concentrates on art full-time. The revenue from all sales goes to the kibbutz. Most artists, however, prefer the privacy and freedom of cities, where they need not adapt their work to the strict discipline of communal life.

Whether in kibbutzim or in urban centers, the museums of Israel are expertly installed. Take, for example, the charming separate pavilions that make up the Museum Haaretz in Tel Aviv. Here, among fourteen projected pavilions that together will survey the civilizations of the eastern Mediterranean region, some are already completed, notably the glass museum, which is a small gem. Rare specimens of aged glass are shown so intelligently that even the most inexperienced layman begins to understand the evolution of this craft. In a nearby pavilion the same sympathetic care has been lavished on a historic coin collection. And soon a ceramic museum will open. One is constantly impressed by the dauntless energy that churns behind these multiple projects. In Israel, art and archaeology are everywhere coming to life.

There are certain memories that persist. I remember the new town of Dimona in the Negev just as the sun was setting and the whole community, mostly Moroccan, was gathered in the public square for a funeral. I remember Anna Ticho's wonderful old house and gnarled, dripping garden. I remember her collection of Hanukkah lamps hanging in profusion on white walls. I remember the lacy drawing of a bird by a teen-age Turkish girl who was studying at a Tel Aviv high school for children gifted in the arts. I remember Sodom in its dead moonlike setting, as sinister as its proverbial reputation has us believe. I remember synagogues everywhere that resemble shabby clubhouses more than holy sanctuaries, and that set me to questioning why the Jewish religion, at once rational, ritual-ridden, and mystic, is so averse to sensuous visual experiences. Above all, I remember the fervent love for and pride in their country that most Israelis share, despite widely divergent origins.

Less than five years have passed since this article on Israel was published. The arresting changes that have taken place are proof of how fast history moves these days. The Gaza Strip is no longer "illogical," nor is Jerusalem "a city . . . ripped in two." The half-million visitors who poured into the Israel Museum during its first six months have now multiplied to three million. And the Israeli sculptor, David Palombo, who made the iron gates at Yad Vashem, was killed shortly after I left Jerusalem. Unaware of wire barricades erected by religious Jews to protect their neighborhood on the Sabbath, he was beheaded one dark evening when riding home on his motorcycle.

Added to the "memories that persist" was the day I spent in the Druse village of Daliyat el Karmil, where the "eighty-year-old-patriarch" led me to the homes of his seven sons, one after the other. At each we ate hot bread and drank sweet Turkish coffee, always two cups. It was a wonderful ordeal. I also recall the funeral at Dimona where high-pitched voices wailed for a young man killed by mistake in peacetime army maneuvers. One wonders what has happened during the last five years to that lonely town newly risen out of the Negev. But most vividly I remember those many small synagogues filled on the Sabbath with devout Orthodox Jews importuning their God in passionate, personal confrontations. There, in simple bare rooms art scarcely existed, but eloquent gestures and explosive exhortations compensated for any lack of visual sensuousness.

15. *Alaska's Vanishing Art, 1966*

In Alaska, man is an uneasy intruder. Jagged black mountains geometric with snow, rivers bloated from glacial silt, impenetrable ice wastes, and tangled northern jungles conspire to dwarf human beings. Space in Alaska is on an unprecedented scale. Rivers are wider, mountains are higher (more than sixty-five peaks exceed 10,000 feet), valleys are vaster than eyes can encompass. Here, a burgeoning geology stars nature in the making. At every point one feels the scarring push of glaciers, the beat of gigantic tides (second highest in the world), the harsh erosions of a country still gripped by the Ice Age, still molded by ungovernable winds, snows, and explosions.

The name "Alaska" comes from the Aleut word "Alayeska," meaning "the great land," and that is precisely what it is—not merely another state but a boundless territory of frozen tundra. In comparison, the rest of the country seems tame, middle-aged, even pinched. One thinks of early Chinese paintings where human beings are habitually dominated by nature. But there is a difference. In Chinese art, man, though subservient to the landscape, is yet in harmony with it. Not so in Alaska; except for the old totemic Indian carvings that repeat the vertical majesty of mountains and towering forests, this country's man-made environment is curiously at odds with its natural surroundings.

Urban planning is virtually ignored; recent architecture is vaguely utilitarian or of a semisuburban, semisubdivision variety. Take, for example, Anchorage, Alaska's largest and most modern city. Here, where nature has been particularly lavish with mountains and sea, choice residential sections composed chiefly of hybrid-style ranch houses might just as well be located in the flat Middle West. Singularly, the more prosperous the neighborhood, the less interesting the view. In the business area, too, meaningless high-rise buildings punctuate a sprawl of untidy shacks. Even now after the earthquake, when Anchorage could be rebuilding with an eye to its own identity, the city continues its random growth. And out on the wild Kenai Peninsula a bedraggled little settlement called Seward is challenged by the radiant unfolding of Resurrection Bay. That human beings were able to establish even a foothold in this formidable terrain is a feat not to be underestimated. One can hardly expect them to worry about "good design" when faced with the most elemental difficulties. Nor is it surprising that the architecture best adapted to the environment remains the best-looking. I refer to the log cabin.

After four visits I still find Alaska hypnotic. Its people are warm, responsive, resourceful, and brave; its spirit is free, its mosquitoes monstrous, its wildlife still wild, its possibilities for adventure exhilarating, even though its famous "sourdoughs" are fast disappearing, only to be replaced by new Carol Kennicotts from new Main Streets. "Culture" is on every tongue. There are art societies, art guilds, art classes, but rarely do any of these organizations relate to Alaska; they could as readily be flourishing in Iowa or Minnesota. And why not, since their members are mostly newcomers from the "lower forty-nine"? Contemporary paintings and sculpture are usually competent and up to date, despite numerous artists who still depend on the earlier meticulous Alaskan tradition of Sidney Lawrence, a tradition that tends to reduce incomparable scenery to sentimental clichés. Visually aggressive, especially in summer with its almost twenty-four hours of daylight, the land eludes graphic interpretation. Its limitless reaches stretch beyond the ordinary boundaries of imagination and canvas.

The only art that approximates the magnitude of this country was produced by early Indian aboriginals, whose totemic carvings captured the magic of northern jungle life. Using interlocking symbols to transmute animal images into partly human ones, the Northwest Indian invented a personal, poetic, yet pragmatic mythology geared to placating and honoring his environment. The Indian never attempted to reproduce his surroundings realistically; instead, he distilled and then paraphrased their prime characteristics according to his own needs. What he made was not intended as individualistic art. His superbly decorated, often utilitarian objects resulted from group exigencies. Animistic symbols, both hostile and friendly, became the Indian's dominant themes. Southeastern Alaskan artifacts were produced less for religious than for ceremonial occasions, notably for the potlatch feast, which, as a rule, celebrated some outstanding family or clan event. Hence, the totem pole became a biographical record commemorating specific achievements and identifying specific groups. Sometimes intended as mortuary vessels, the poles also dramatized the prestige that invested every nuance of Indian life.

These lofty wooden monuments were produced only along the southeastern coast, where a relatively mild climate, plentiful fish and wild life, and forests of cedar and spruce encouraged an advanced aboriginal culture to develop. The Tlingit Indians, representing the largest tribe in southeast Alaska, were already well established when the white man first appeared. Later the Haidas and Tsimshians came from British Columbia. Living in permanent settlements, they had evolved a complicated social structure dependent on two separate fratries which, in turn, were divided into numerous clans. Characteristic animals of the terrain became the recognized totems of these groups.

In Ketchikan today, a splendid tottering totem pole called the "Wayward Husband" epitomizes the tragedy of Alaska's vanishing past. Carved by a Tlingit Indian in 1884, this handsome monument, though neglected and disfigured, still bears traces of its original grandeur. Farther north in Wrangell, the famous

"One-Legged Fisherman" pole is suffering the same fate. Names are wantonly hacked on its symbolic eagle, one of whose wings is severely damaged, the other gone—either stolen or eroded. Defaced, debased, dishonored, the noble carving mildews in a deserted section of Wrangell's cemetery, surrounded by tin cans and an encroaching rain forest.

A photograph of this pole made three years later indicated further disintegration. Both wings were now gone and the entire carving had been so abused that any future hope of preservation was almost futile. All of which is the more deplorable since only a quarter century ago the "One-Legged Fisherman" was still a superb intact example of Tlingit sculpture. In February 1970, I received a letter from the Director of the Alaska State Museum saying that finally the State Legislature had appropriated a modest sum and with it the "Wayward Husband" pole had been removed from its present site to undergo possible restoration. She wrote, "It was in amazingly poor condition."

Everywhere in southeast Alaska the same indifference is depleting its heritage. In Old Kasaan, on Village Island, in Wrangell, Saxman, Klukwan, and at many other Haida and Tlingit sites, fine poles and smaller ceremonial objects have either wasted away, have been destroyed, or are so nearly gone as to be hopelessly lost. And yet no tourist blurb about Alaska neglects the lure of its totem poles. Along with Mount McKinley, they seem to have become the official trademarks of the land.

To the average visitor these heroic works are presented as little more than "colorful curios," which, to be sure, they are fast becoming as they are splashed with shiny new house paint totally at variance with the original Indian colors. Ostensibly to protect the wood but more likely to attract tourist eyes, bright pigments now virtually obliterate sensitive surface carvings. Ketchikan, with a false view to economizing, hands all repainting over to ill-equipped prison labor. In our scientific age it is sheer nonsense to believe that only thick house paint can protect monuments of wood. In addition, visitors to Alaska are usually fed a bit of incorrect, if romantic, folklore about totemic symbolism and are introduced to a few recently set up "totem parks," where the carvings are generally anemic copies of old ones.

Often arranged in arbitrary formation, in no way resembling their original Indian sites, these assemblages have little aesthetic or documentary validity.

One questions why objects of undeniably historic importance have not been preserved, especially in the United States, where native carvings of high quality are rare. Comparable at their best to pre-Columbian sculpture of Latin America, these works by Tlingit, Tsimshian, and Haida Indians include not only totem poles but also intricate bentwood boxes, rattles, masks, dance sticks, magnificently woven Chilkat blankets, baskets, potlatch bowls, and richly inlaid ceremonial headdresses. There are, of course, certain extenuating circumstances that explain Alaska's seeming indifference to its past. First come the perils of the land itself. An inordinately wet climate coupled with a wood culture results in the rapid disintegration of carved objects. Dry rot takes over unless care is devoted to conservation. Today, there are relatively few poles still standing that were erected more than a hundred years ago.

Fire is another hazard. Forests, winds, and wooden buildings make flames a daily threat. In 1941, I visited the Indian town of Hoonah, where a large exterior painting on a chief's house gave distinction to an otherwise drab settlement. Five years later I returned only to find that a recent fire had destroyed the painting along with numerous carved ceremonial objects. All that was visible of this town's history was one small totem pole in an overgrown cemetery. The same story repeats itself with sickening monotony. Many of the finest carvings in Wrangell were victims of fire; so also those in Old Kasaan and Sitka. Only a few months ago, Sitka's renowned Russian church was burned to the ground. Now it is to be rebuilt, but copies can never replace originals.

Nowhere is this fact more evident than in Alaska, where certain government agencies operate on the theory that totemic art can readily be reproduced by any qualified carver, a point of view that has led to shocking abuses and that is perhaps the single most recent cause of unnecessary destruction. Some twenty-odd years ago, the U.S. Forest Service, without benefit of archaeological or anthropological direction, instituted a pro-

gram in which the local Civilian Conservation Corps undertook
to rehabilitate—but, alas, more often to dismember and copy—
old poles in Ketchikan, Wrangell, Sitka, Kasaan, Klawock, and
Hydaburg.

There is no doubt that modern copies, even when faithful,
lack the fire, mystery, and obsessive intensity of the originals,
which were made by a people who still believed in and practiced
a totemic culture. The aborigines created records of clan prestige
and designed ornamental potlatch objects because this was their
way of life. Once that way of life was lost, so, too, was the Indian's urge to celebrate it. When the United States Government
benignly banned the potlatch as an impoverishing influence (in
their zeal to outdo each other, clans often gave away their entire wealth at these rites), the social structure of community life
collapsed. What the Indian had created less as art than as symbols
of group supremacy became in fact art, not "relics," "curios,"
"souvenirs," "documents," or "gift shoppe" trophies.

In 1946, I was commissioned by the U.S. Bureau of Indian
Affairs to prepare a comprehensive report on extant totemic art
in Alaska. Wherever the Civilian Conservation Corps had been,
I found remnants of fine old poles, either abandoned in forests
or stacked under open sheds. Since many of these carvings were
still redeemable, I reported on their condition in some detail
and urged that they receive immediate attention. In 1966,
twenty years later, I retraced my footsteps to find my worst fears
justified. Scarcely one of these rare works remained. They had
either been burned to cinders or left to rot in rain forests. Nor
shall I soon forget the public servant who assured me that
"nothing had been thrown away but the originals," many of
which, may I add, could have been preserved rather than poorly
reproduced.

Today, it is a sorry sight to see Alaskan curio stores filled
with horrendous imitations of the past. Gaudy, mass-produced
knickknacks do little to elevate the Indian's self-respect or economic status. Nasty, small totem poles, sometimes only three or
four inches high and frequently imported from Japan, phony
masks, ineptly carved potlatch dishes—the latter two often surprisingly overpriced—are sold in every town or tourist stop.

Neither the glory of Mount McKinley nor the breath-taking ice-blue sweep of Portage Glacier is forbidding enough to frighten away ubiquitous souvenir concessionaires. This unrelieved commercialization degrades the memory of a once vigorous civilization as it also corrupts the taste of uninformed visitors, who themselves are not entirely blameless. Certainly, the time has come for Alaska to encourage a more discriminating tourist trade. To this end, better maintenance of existing monuments plus improved transportation to authentic out-of-the-way Indian sites would be a promising start.

The rigors of pioneering in a wild terrain partly explain why many newcomers to Alaska have tended to disregard the civilization they disrupted and displaced. Ignorance, fear, and a sense of guilt have also caused the white man to underrate his Indian predecessors—their history, customs, and art. Then, too, the natives themselves considered their ritualistic objects expendable. Totem poles and potlatch dishes were designed to honor specific occasions. Since the Indian firmly believed there would always be such occasions, and always skilled artists to commemorate them, he spent more time on future plans than on past accomplishments.

Dr. Erna Gunther, a specialist in native cultures of the Northwest, organized an exhibition for Alaska's centennial celebration in Fairbanks. Called ''The Native Arts of Alaska Come Home,'' the exhibit poignantly underlined the state's dilemma. That most of the finest artifacts are no longer in the land which produced them is an incalculable loss, both aesthetically and financially. One finds these objects in the Soviet Union, in European museums, in Canada, New York, Portland, Seattle, Denver.

Alaska has been denuded and is still being denuded. Only recently, two privately owned Ketchikan poles carved by a Tsimshian Indian named Chief Neesh Loot were sold to a collector in Switzerland. Ketchikan did not raise a finger to keep these carvings, which had long decorated one of the town's main streets. Far more serious was the dispersement some years ago of two important Wrangell collections. The first to go was the Rasmussen collection, assembled by a white schoolteacher who had taught among the Indians. Though Mr. Rasmussen had hoped his collection would remain in Alaska, even going so far as to offer it to the Territory for the nominal sum of $10,000, he found no takers. About the same time, the Alaska Legislature approved a special $3,500 appropriation to acquire several banal pastels of aboriginal types. Painted by a local artist, Nina Crumrine, these picture-postcard potboilers now decorate the State Museum at Juneau, while the Rasmussen collection has become a prize attraction in Portland, Oregon, and has vastly increased in value. Fine North Pacific carvings come high these days.

A few years later the second private collection was lost to Wrangell. Today, in sad contrast to the past wealth of that town, a pathetic little group of innocuous Indian objects is on display at Wrangell's public library. One can only remember with nostalgia the Bear Totem Shop when Walter Waters was its proprietor. The best of his collection, offered for sale in 1946 shortly after his death, came directly from Chief Shakes, one of the last Tlingit patriarchs. Now most of these works are divided between Denver and Seattle.

It is unfortunate that the museums at Juneau and Fairbanks, then under Territorial jurisdiction, did not wheedle or insist on the funds necessary to keep the Rasmussen and Waters collections in Alaska. Though the State Museum at Juneau has a few fine Indian and Eskimo objects, as well as a small group of choice Aleutian baskets, it certainly cannot claim a representative Northwest collection. Nor can the University of Alaska Museum. Here the specialty is prehistory bone and ivory Eskimo carvings, most of them simplified human and animal figures of surpassing dignity. With uncompromising economy, the Eskimos also created powerful masks; some of the finest can be seen at a small private museum connected with the Sheldon Jackson School in Sitka. Because the Eskimos lived in a barren land where unimaginable hardships demanded all their attention, they found neither the materials nor the impetus to produce monumental sculpture comparable to that of the coastal Indians.

Though time is rapidly running out, there are still Indian sites not yet totally lost to Alaska. Village Island and Old Kasaan, originally two of the country's outstanding Indian settlements and now long deserted, are in such deplorable condition that only the most immediate skilled attention can save the little that remains. When, twenty years ago, the Coast Guard took me to Village Island, we found a miraculous strip of land dense with extravagant growth. And there, leaning madly in all directions, were sixteen totem poles, among the oldest Tlingit carvings still standing. I made a crude map of that fantastic island, noting the poles that might be preserved entirely or in part. I did the same for Old Kasaan, Alaska's finest Haida site. Until a few years ago this latter concentration of ancient poles and grave markers was considered a National Monument. Now, apparently, the government has abandoned it. Why, I cannot imagine, and no one at the U.S. Park Service office in Juneau could explain, or, indeed, had ever heard of Old Kasaan.

A recent offer by the University of California at Los Angeles to rescue what still remains of these two sites was discouraged by the U.S. Forest Service, presumably because local groups oppose moving the carvings from Alaska—although the same groups, whether Indian or white, offer no alternative solution. Even the complicated problems related to native ownership that are often cited by Alaskans could be unraveled, given proper legal advice. No one argues against keeping the poles in their original settings whenever possible, but surely it is better to move them than lose them.

During the few years since this article was written, the poles at Old Kasaan and Village Island have suffered severely. Several have toppled over and a number are totally ruined. In the lives of these monuments every month takes its toll at an accelerating rate.

Wrangell, a town with a population well under 2,000, seems more seriously concerned with conservation than any other settlement in Alaska. Yet, due to inadequate funds, most of Wrangell's poles, rated among the best in the state, are in precarious condition. Four ancient, very valuable, unpainted Tlingit house poles, located in a largely unattended wooden Community House on Shakes Island, face daily danger from fire. Impassive and inscrutable, these masterpieces rival great Oriental sculpture. Likewise, in Klukwan a peerless group of smaller ceremonial objects is constantly threatened by possible fire and decay.

No memory of Alaska is more vivid for me than Klukwan, a primitive Indian village located near a glacial river. I spent several days there during the summer of 1946, living in a barren room that stayed light around the clock. I ate my meals (one day we had freshly caught porcupine) with an Indian schoolteacher, his wife, and four small sons. At that time the village was rarely visited by outsiders, so I had some difficulty contacting the chief, who reputedly owned a formidable collection of ceremonial objects. Since the community surreptitiously practiced the potlatch despite the government taboo, these objects

Chief Shakes and his possessions

were still in use. When the schoolteacher learned my father's name was Woolf, he decided this information might prove helpful, since both he and the chief were members of the Wolf Clan. Shortly thereafter the chief received me at his home. ''Welcome, my daughter,'' he said. Then, slowly, marvelous treasures encrusted with filth emerged from superb bentwood boxes. There were potlatch bowls, ceremonial headdresses, Chilkat blankets, dance sticks, rattles, all of a quality to take one's breath away. Now most of these works are gone, destroyed by fire. The chief, quite old and incapacitated by tuberculosis (a familiar native killer in Alaska), agreed that the artifacts could be placed in a one-room fireproof storehouse if the key remained with him and with the townspeople and if the government would pay all costs of construction, which at that time would have been nominal. Today, the value of the lost works represents a sum high in six figures. But more important—the lost art is irreplaceable.

Saxman, a tiny impoverished Tlingit village near Ketchikan, bears most of the responsibility for maintaining a totem park erected there in the early forties by the CCC. Apparently of no vital interest to the community, this transplanted revision languishes in sordid disarray. Several years ago the wife of an old Saxman chief explained the situation to me. She said stolidly, ''Government give, government take.'' Indians in Saxman sometimes even refer to the park as ''the government poles.''

With the exception of the Sitka National Monument, which is under U.S. Park Service jurisdiction, intelligent explanatory data on Indian art are rarely available, not even at Saxman, to which tourists flock by the busload. Well-planned labels and informative folders could do much to educate the layman. And for students, the lack of documentary photographs, particularly of lost and destroyed objects, is little less than catastrophic.

That the U.S. Government allocated sizable sums to save Abu Simbel when it was threatened by the Aswan High Dam is highly commendable; yet why that same government does nothing to save its own landmarks remains an enigma, especially since it did much to destroy them. Perhaps Alaska's developing art guilds and craft societies should appeal for help from the Smithsonian Institution, where specialists in archaeology, anthropology, and conservation are available. To expect small communities

or even the state of Alaska, with its far-flung population of
only 250,000 people—about one-fifth of whom are Indians,
Eskimos, and Aleuts—to generate the funds and technical know-
how necessary for extensive restoration is asking too much. Federal assistance is sorely needed if important works are to be
saved. Scarcely an island in southeast Alaska is not distinguished by isolated carvings that need immediate professional
attention.

If Washington has been lax in matters of preservation, it has
not ignored Indian life on other levels. The Bureau of Indian
Affairs is sometimes accused of overpaternalism; so, too, is the
Indian Arts and Crafts Board, a separate agency of the Department of the Interior that describes itself as ''an informational,
promotional, and advisory clearinghouse for all matters pertain-
ing to the development of authentic Indian and Eskimo arts and
crafts.'' Convinced that a serious arts-and-crafts program depends on pride in native background, I have long wondered why
these agencies are so little concerned with accurate preservation
of the past. Respect for and firsthand knowledge of one's own
traditions are essential if earlier forms are to be creatively
adapted to present-day needs.

Because arts and crafts in Alaska have chiefly become a shoddy
curio business, because at one time missionaries misunderstood
and strongly discouraged native carvings, many younger Indians
today are ashamed of their past. And many present-day Eskimos, though often expert carvers, are repeating *ad nauseam*
the salable little ivory animals that are only slick echoes of
earlier amulets. Eskimos remain the most severely underprivileged economic group in the United States, and it will take more
than kindly arts-and-crafts programs to raise their living standards appreciably.

That Indian and Eskimo history is not incorporated in the curriculum of all Alaskan schools seems an opportunity lost. As it
is, most children are rarely informed about important aboriginal
art, even that in their own communities. There are, of course, exceptions that point the way to a more promising future. In
Wrangell, a high school instructor takes his classes to the beach,
where a number of neglected petroglyphs become a living history lesson. And in Anchorage, a third-grade teacher intro-

duced her students to Northwest Indian art through a potlatch celebration. The children themselves made all the ritual objects with the exception of certain authentic ceremonial robes that a small Tlinget boy brought from home.

ADDENDA, 1967

In a small wooden Community House on Shakes Island at Wrangell, four magnificent Tlingit house poles face the daily danger of fire. Aside from their historic and aesthetic value, these handsome artifacts are worth an astonishing amount in cold cash. For some time experts have advised the U.S. Department of the Interior to fireproof the interior of the Community House, a procedure that would cost little compared to the value of the carvings. Yet year after year nothing is done.

Some months ago in an article entitled ''Alaska's Vanishing Art'' I described how neglect, disinterest, ignorance, vandalism, and bureaucratic bungling were dissipating America's peerless totemic carvings. Among the many letters we received in response were a number also sent to the Department of the Interior offering specialized help. How these offers were answered is a matter worth recording. Citizens eager to provide professional assistance emerged scarred, weary, wary, and convinced that each step forward ended in two steps backward.

Twenty-one years ago a detailed report on extant Indian carvings in Alaska was commissioned, paid for, and subsequently ignored by the Bureau of Indian Affairs. Now rather than hasten to save what little remains, the government recommends that another report be prepared, this time financed by private sources, for, as it admits, many of the important objects described in the first survey ''have in the interim been destroyed by fire, rot, vandalism, or sheer neglect.'' The federal government thus continues to abdicate responsibility as, indeed, it has for the past two decades, during which time little or nothing was done to implement the report already at hand. A new survey, prepared without cost to or effort by the government, might well provide a reprieve long enough to assure the complete destruction of all Indian art in Alaska. And then the matter could be pleasantly shelved.

During the summer of 1965, representatives of the University of California at Los Angeles visited certain remote sections of Alaska and later offered to rescue the few remaining master-pieces they found at Old Kasaan and Village Island. The offer was promptly turned down by the U.S. Forest Service, though neither the state of Alaska nor the federal government had plans for restoring these deserted areas where some of America's noblest carvings are rapidly rotting away. In a letter last No-vember, a professor at UCLA wrote, "A year ago we tried to approach the problem of the totem poles. Unfortunately, we were given the run-around from the Forest Service in Juneau to the Alaska Historical Society to local Indian tribes, etc. Somehow we must cut through this mish-mash." But how?

At the University of California at Davis, the curator of the Laboratory for Research in the Fine Arts and Museology offered his well-equipped facilities to the Department of the Interior, explaining that the laboratory's "prime interest is the preserva-tion of cultural objects." The chancellor at Davis even took time himself to write the Secretary of the Interior suggesting that his department and the university combine forces in "reme-dial action" to preserve Alaska's Indian art. His letter was handed over to someone bearing the impressive title of Director of Management Operations, who in turn assured the chancel-lor that the situation was exaggerated. He then blandly advised the university to prepare a further report. Reports, it would seem, are the government's secret weapon.

Polite letters, aimless requests for reports, vague, oversim-plified statements, and consistent evidence of misinformation characterize the government's approach to art preservation in Alaska. And this is more serious than it seems. For no other area in our country has produced a native art of comparable grandeur, a fact recognized throughout the world by important museums. Canada on our north and Mexico on our south, though not the richest countries in the hemisphere, have protected their Indian inheritance with far greater diligence. The dilemma in Alaska stems less from lack of good will than from ignorance. To be sure, one can scarcely expect Cabinet members to know intimately all the details of their domains, but certainly these vast hierarchies should include a wide range of specialists, and if not specialists, at least informed sensitive public servants who know how and where to turn for the best possible help.

To preserve the Indian art of Alaska is properly the responsibility of the government, which has intermittently had jurisdiction over numerous important sites. Today, there are signs that the Department of the Interior intends to evade this responsibility, to provide no funds for restoration or conservation and no leadership in either organizing or accepting expert help. The over-all funds needed are insignificant compared to those we pour out on routine military hardware. Recently the Commissioner of Indian Affairs said, ''The Indian cherishes the remnants of a culture that once provided bounty; and it is this pride in heritage that must be fostered today. To ignore the cultural ties of the Indian is to destroy his last vestige of pride in self.'' Yet this same official has not lifted a hand to preserve the Indians' past in Alaska, where I understand he represented the Department of Indian Affairs for several years. And, of course, it is not alone for the Indians that these distinguished works of art should be preserved; it is for all of us.

At this point, inventories, surveys, and reports act merely as delaying gestures. Prompt practical action is crucial. Top archaeologists, anthropologists, and conservation specialists are urgently needed for immediate field work. Representatives of the Forest and Park Services have in the past shown little or no professional understanding of the problem. Lacking proper knowledge, they too often have been responsible for abuses and unnecessary destruction. The only hope is to hand over art restoration in Alaska to reliably trained groups of scholars who, working under the aegis of the government, will be free to organize an intelligently planned program without further delay.

Alaska has been my saddest and most forlorn crusade—also my greatest defeat. Since my first trip there some thirty years ago, I've waged a hopeless battle to save that area's great Indian carvings. Why these artifacts mean so much to me is a question, but it is probably because they represent the finest primitive works our country has produced. They are a part of our history that both white man and Indian can view with pride.

To list only a few organizations, government agencies, and responsible people to whom I have appealed for help (always in vain) is a commentary on bureaucracy. At one point I naïvely approached the Secretary of the Interior, who sent his wife to see me after the above censorious articles appeared in *Saturday Review*. She came several times, was charming and voluble, and did nothing. Other people and institutions I contacted were two governors of Alaska, the Alaska Native Brotherhood, the U.S. Forest Service, the U.S. Park Service, the U.S. Department of Agriculture, the Indian Arts and Crafts Board, the Bureau of Indian Affairs (the two latter I found especially parochial), the mayors of various cities in Alaska, the State Museum at Juneau, the University of Alaska, and on and on. I even recall once giving a spirited talk before the Lions Club of Ketchikan. That was long ago when I was still hopeful. The Lions found the whole idea a joke and were inclined to view totem poles (at that time there were splendid ones in Ketchikan) as expendable "souvenirs" and me as an amusing oddity. In those early days, the only other person dedicated to preservation was the mayor of Wrangell, an attractive woman who had inherited her husband's job after he was killed by a brown bear. The town then had a population of about twelve hundred, many of them Indians and half-breeds, so there obviously were no available funds.

The whole wasteful debacle points up our helplessness when dealing with well-meaning ignorance and with a blank wall of officialdom. On the same day in December, 1969, that I clipped an article from the *New York Times* describing "a profit of up to 1403 per cent for a plant doing Air Force work," I received a letter from the new director of the Alaska State Museum, a zealous young woman who is trying to save the few Indian monuments that are at least partly redeemable. With hat in hand she is pleading for a pathetically small handout from either the federal or state government. Now I hear that the State Legislature has appropriated $50,000 for the restoration of what few crumbling poles remain. Too late and far too little, this sum from the richest country in the world is a sad comment on its culture.

PROS & CONS

16. *The Open Eye*

Faces—frontal, inescapable, and repetitive—mesmerize us, especially in art, where the idea of repetition is not new. It has been with us for centuries under auspices as diverse as Byzantine mosaics, Toltec sculpture, Surrealist paintings, and Pop art. And, to be sure, repetition per se is hypnotic. The fact that we see an object repeated irrationally gives it a kind of supernatural importance. Yet all the Campbell Soup cans in the world can scarcely compete with a proliferation of human faces, faces that might seem of little more interest than tin cans were it not for their eyes. Over the years and regardless of period, these eyes gape out at us; sometimes impervious, sometimes incriminating, they assume mythic proportions. As all-seeing archetypes they become at once our alter egos and our super-egos. Even blind eyes conjure up occult powers.

Engraved on stone, etched on metal, painted on canvas, carved from wood, woven in wool, drawn on paper, they gaze at us and we, in turn, at them. It is the unconscionable repetition that rivets us and produces an indefinable sense of guilt. The eyes become a human compendium, meting out final judgments so impartial as to disquiet even the blameless. Take, for example, the fanatic bulging ones in Ethiopian manuscript illuminations that transform otherwise decorative compositions into psychological assaults. I particularly recall an early illumination celebrating the Council of Nicaea that included 318 faces with 636 indomitable eyes. The onslaught was relentless.

When members of a group are highly individualized, they become too specific to function obsessively, but when only mildly varied, they can assume a taut hieratic pitch. Then multiplicity itself takes over, and myriad staring eyes produce a form of incantation. These organs of untold diversity are transparent; we, who look into them and out of them, are also reflected in them. They can be veiled, hidden, or open, but it is the open eye that finally determines the course of art, the eye that is open physically and figuratively. With it we see what exists, what might exist, and what has existed. As a universal iconographic symbol, the eye turns into both the observer and the observed. We not only see it in works of art; we see works of art with it. This duality makes for a provocative interchange, a constant dialogue.

Writers have long treated the eye as a prerogative of romance, and artists, especially primitive ones, have honored it as a separate phenomenon. In compactly designed blankets woven by the Chilkat Indians anatomical details are detached and dispersed at will. Large, half-human, half-animal orbs appear in profusion. Indeed, among many aboriginal tribes the eye often substitutes for the total man. Modern artists, notably Miró and Klee, continued the practice of isolating this organ and allowing it to function symbolically. During the last year of his life, Klee painted a prophetic composition called *Drummer*. Two arms and an open eye, each roughly executed in heavy black pigments, are omens of doom. The beating arms have an implacable rhythm; the eye, a stabbing vision. No need for us to hear the drums; to see them is to understand.

Grinning Maya-Toltec skulls carved on the temple walls at Chichén Itzá are doubly horrifying because of numberless empty sockets. These blank holes have prodigious impact, their very vacuity producing a perverse new way of seeing. Like Klee's *Drummer*, the skulls stare at us with the clarity of death. Far less alive are the six living but sightless creatures in

Breughel's famous *Parable of the Blind*. Lost, stumbling souls, they seem incapable of looking in or out. Their eyes exist— yet are impotent, for the empty sockets of death see more, and see more clearly.

In Barcelona, a Romanesque fresco entitled *Apocalyptic Lamb* depicts a reasonably normal animal except for its seven eyes, each open and alert. Why seven, I do not know, although throughout history this number has been accredited with magic power. It is possible the artist hoped to endow the creature with extra vision and wisdom; usually the lamb symbolizes Christ, the multiple eyes here becoming a transcendental extension of his supremacy. Even today Mexican Indians from Nayarit celebrate a certain festival with objects called ''God's eyes,'' which in reality are woven reed wands decorated geometrically with brightly colored abstract eyes. According to legend, these wands encourage one of their local gods to see more clearly and to understand more fully the mysteries of life.

The most poignant eyes of all were those I encountered in Poland some years ago when visiting Auschwitz. There in end- less concentration camp barracks, interior walls are lined with photographs of the Nazis' victims, taken for identification pur- poses by the Germans themselves, and now installed as a re- minder that actual people and not just nameless digits perished here. The photos are invariably the same size; the faces, always frontal, differ but not enough to break the spell. Young and old, men, women, and children look straight ahead, without hope. Ill, gaunt, and exhausted, these haunted apparitions are curi- ously alike, each touched by the same deprivations and fears. Only their eyes remain alive. Repetition adds up to an unbear- able indictment. The implied accusations are grimmer precisely because thousands of disoriented eyes fasten on us with no sign of emotion.

A group of recent works by the American artist Hedda Sterne recalls Auschwitz. Her studio is plastered from floor to ceiling with disembodied faces that directly confront the viewer. They are never identical, yet they share an unyielding objectivity. Not intended as specific portraits, the heads represent memories distilled from the artist's past. They are executed in somber

Hedda Sterne's studio, 1970

tones on unstretched, unsized, unframed canvases, and are conceived more as free wall hangings than as orthodox easel paintings. Like the concentration camp photos, they have no backgrounds, no additional or softening details; they are compulsive images that nail us with their concentrated intensity. And yet these anonymous personages seem utterly defenseless, almost as if their candor and numbers imperil them with overexposure. A single face or two stand out, but it is the mass that matters.

The whole experience is predicated on exaggeration, on the idea of more and more and more. The individual, who here is deliberately overshadowed by the group, seems appropriately adapted to a sea of proliferation. Though many of these images can be traced to the artist's early years in Rumania, her polyglot ensembles are less related to the repetitions of European surrealism than to American excess. Floating limpidly in crowded quarters, these eyes, always focused on the viewer, are not abstractions. The painter calls them *Everyone*. She could as well have labeled them *J'Accuse*.

Today we are apt to find a parade of human faces more upsetting than our ancestors did, if only because personal involvement always transmutes the familiar. For us, throngs are a commonplace but rarely a reassuring one. I keep wondering, would I see Hedda Sterne's work differently if I had never visited Auschwitz? Her innumerable heads, emerging from bare outlines accented only occasionally by shading, exist less as individuals than as cogs in a mad redundancy. Had they been apples or nuts and bolts instead of faces, would they generate the same tensions, the same anxieties? I think not, for no matter how much we pride ourselves on our objectivity, we still identify more closely with ourselves than with any other image.

In Oriental art, the hand frequently assumes a major role; in the West, it is the eye. Indian and Nepalese ceremonial sculpture stresses multiple arms culminating in ritualistic hands. The hand speaks with the utmost authority. Each slight variation in position and gesture carries a message. The open eye of the West is lost in the circuitous innuendoes that make Eastern art one of the most refined experiences in history. Here lids are

lowered partially or completely, and the eye looks inward, for in
the Orient salvation results from noninvolvement with the outside world. Men meditate; they shroud their eyes in silent secrecy, or lift them toward superhuman heights. The Pantocrator
of the West looks out on us with wide eyes, but Buddha closes
his and directs them toward interior contemplation. Wise men
of the East have long doubted the value of a visible corporeal
world, but for us in the Occident the open eye is central to our
very being. The Oriental looks for universal truths, we for immediate ones.

17. *In Pursuit of Antiquity*

I can imagine no ambition less attractive to contemporary European and American artists than the avowed pursuit of antiquity. For us, today, it is the new that counts—new materials, new methods, new idols, new images, new tremors and shocks. We have deliberately strained to break our ties with the past, convinced that this is the way to the freedom we need, a freedom not shackled by history. For admittedly, looking back can be stifling at times. Somewhat the same mystique may explain our Western devotion to youth and change, two obsessions often confused with growth. In China, however, a homogeneous tradition of painting has endured for well over a thousand years. Artists there accept, even embrace involvement with the past. The very continuity we mistrust sustains them. In the East, the old are respected because presumably they know more; in the West, the young are respected because they dare more.

Nowhere is this attitude more clearly enunciated than in certain Ch'ing paintings. An unprecedented opportunity to study seventeenth-century scrolls and albums from this dynasty is now available in a traveling exhibition organized by Princeton University and first seen there. What makes the show especially interesting is its concentration on the paintings of one man, the versatile Wang Hui, who was a leading member of the Orthodox school, so called because of its preoccupation with the past. As a conscious reaction against the somewhat decorative sterility of late Ming art, the Orthodox group hoped, perhaps futilely, to recapture the strength, purity, and profundity of earlier periods, notably of the Sung and Yuan dynasties (tenth to fourteenth centuries), during which landscape painting turned nature into metaphysical poetry. If the seventeenth century never attained equally rarefied heights, it did at least electrically revitalize Chinese art for a time.

An album Wang Hui made as a gift for his teacher, Wang Shih-min, bears on the title leaf the latter's appropriate inscription "In Pursuit of Antiquity." This tour de force comprising twelve painted leaves, each inspired by a different master, was an undeviating tribute to the past, as indeed were most of Wang Hui's works. He rarely copied slavishly, though, like numerous Chinese artists, he sometimes made forgeries that only a trained eye can detect. And were it not for forgeries and copies we might know considerably less about ancient Chinese paintings, since so many have perished from age and fragility. In fact, certain copies are even copies of copies. Art forgeries in China were not considered disgraceful; they were looked on simply as aesthetic exercises or as a means of extending the pleasure that an unavailable work might provide. Only rarely were they commercialized enterprises. Wang Hui made most of his forgeries during his younger years, no doubt as a learning process.

The present exhibition, including both forgeries by Wang Hui and forgeries of his work, is memorable, too, because it comes entirely from one private American collection acquired during the past fifteen years by Mr. and Mrs. Earl Morse of New York. Wisely advised by several experts, but chiefly by Professor Weng Fong of Princeton University, the Morses are a rare species, for serious private collectors of Chinese painting are seldom encountered these days in the United States, or in Europe. Because of complexities and pitfalls, this is a field little studied by the layman. To present Wang Hui as fully as possible, the Morses have assembled his work in depth, his entire chronological development revealed step by step. In addition, he is shown in historical context, with accompanying examples of earlier masters who influenced him plus those of his contemporaries and successors whom he influenced.

Who, then, was this man Wang Hui? What did he stand for? Why make a comprehensive survey of his work? Because he synthesized many of China's outstanding earlier achievements, his scrolls and albums became a veritable résumé of native landscape painting. Bowing to a variety of archaic traditions, he never entirely sacrificed his individuality. He presented a compendium of the past, but, at best, by revising, editing, combining, exaggerating, and re-creating, he made an art curiously his own even though openly dependent on its antecedents.

That this painter was a formidable virtuoso no one can doubt. Adapting himself to almost any technique, he was the example par excellence of that once popular song, "Anything You Can Do, I Can Do Better." To be derivative in China carries no opprobrium. It implies the decision to honor and to learn from one's ancestors. If we in the West have doubts about the beneficial effects of art history, the Chinese, acknowledging immutable laws of nature, claim we cannot escape what has gone before us.

Wang Hui never concerned himself with originality, yet he became the most popular painter of his era, partly because his sophisticated audience was familiar with the roots that had nourished him, partly because he was highly skilled, and partly because he accepted the past while also reanimating the present. To understand Wang Hui, one should, ideally, know the great periods of Chinese landscape painting, as the enthusiastic following he developed during his life undoubtedly did. He specifically appealed to the educated aesthete who occupied himself with man's delicate and fluid relationships to nature. Art was for the cognoscenti and often about the cognoscenti. Frequently, Chinese landscapes include dwarfed human figures, usually recluses contemplating such natural wonders as contorted pines, omnipotent mountains, bamboo and willow tracery proliferating in haunted wildernesses. And always these forms become mobile forces.

A recent announcement from the Detroit Institute of Arts featured a blurb on the envelope saying, "Art is for All." Whether this euphemism is true I do not know, but I do know it is diametrically opposed to the thinking that made Chinese scholars envision art as a philosophic infatuation, as a unique experience demanding the complete absorption of the viewer. They claimed that to enjoy, one must know, one must do, one must analyze and relate—not merely look. The Chinese artist, too, was at heart a scholar, a man more involved with deductive principles than with his own individualized ego.

As Professor Weng Fong says, "The ancient alliance between calligraphy and painting taught the painter to regard his art as a physical act and a form of self-realization. Great works in the 'scholar-painting' tradition were not illustrations, but impulses of life transfigured into art. . . . A true painting was neither an imitation nor an ornament of life. As a creation equivalent to life, a painting had to become part of the cosmic forces." These words seem vaguely familiar. Not so long ago they might have described certain Abstract Expressionist canvases, especially those of Jackson Pollock and Franz Kline, who also felt that the kinesthetic act became the deed. Possibly they knew about that eighth-century Chinese master who laid silk on the floor, splattered ink on it at will, and, then with the addition of a few lines, turned his accidental composition into a recognizable landscape. The Americans differed from him only because the landscapes they produced were limited to their own immediate emotional reactions. His were open to wider involvement.

Linear vitality is often considered the crux of Chinese painting, and for Wang Hui line as an independent entity was a constant preoccupation. With him line did more than describe; it lived in its own right. All of which may explain why this artist and others before him delighted in winter scenes, where the uncluttered bony structure of nature emerged from crisply conceived contours.

Though Wang Hui is best remembered for his ability to adopt

and adapt the brush and calligraphic techniques of other artists, he is also remembered for his "dragon vein" motif that turned his paintings into pulsating reptile-like enmeshments. According to Professor Weng Fong, "The term 'dragon vein' was borrowed from geomancy and denotes an interconnected arterial system that runs over as well as under the face of the earth." This strange slithering serpentine force operates both visibly and psychologically. The observer's eye is forced through a maze of vibrant curves, but even more compelling is the sense of inner energy that engulfs one. It is as if the earth were created, held together, and yet tormented by some nameless unleashed power.

In Wang Hui's best work the dragon vein kinetically welds all elements of the painting into an integrated throbbing landscape that duplicates nature only in the intensity of its vigor. For this artist, like many of his compatriots, was interested in origins, in growth, in the overwhelming grandeur of the earth as a symbolic force. He was seldom concerned with minute descriptions, though as he grew older his painting lost much of its earlier potency. This, I suppose, was to be expected from a man who lived to be eighty-five. It is not easy to dedicate a life that long to the past. He himself finally became the past and was no longer able to infuse new meanings into old experiences. But it is consoling to remember that the most avant-garde pioneers join the same company when the young supersede them.

There are those who welcome Chinese paintings as poetic evocations of nature while rejecting modern abstractions that are no more abstract than these same Chinese landscapes. Wang Hui, the men who influenced him, and the men he influenced were rarely concerned with realistic definition. It was the spirit of a scene, the interior motivation, the breathing life tensions that engaged them, and it was likewise the brushstroke, the line, the undulating over-all design. For them, the method itself became the symbol (and, let us add, well in advance of McLuhan).

What impressed me repeatedly in Wang Hui's work was how totally his philosophy differed from ours. For him change on its own terms was not significant. Renewal could only come from devoted adherence to the past. Generic conceptions took precedence over individual performance. Art, always a poetic extension of life, became a mystical communion between doer and viewer. It was never intended as a mass medium.

Is there any wonder, then, that our two nations have difficulty deciphering each other? We stem both geographically and psychologically from opposite sides of the earth.

18. *Symbol, Shadow, and Substance*

Twentieth-century art, despite its emphasis on abstraction, has steadily headed toward realism. Today, young painters and sculptors are turning their backs on symbols, metaphors, illusions, allusions, paraphrases, and imagery. They have produced not only an age of reduction, but an age of denial. One asks why. Is it because our world is so threatened that to look inward is too painful, or because our world is so complex that to deal with it requires scrupulous powers of rejection?

Only a few years ago, the Abstract Expressionists, mistrusting the materialism that younger artists presently embrace, looked inward. Fragmenting form, they mercilessly shattered their surroundings in a concerted search for themselves. Paul Klee once observed, ''The more horrible this world, the more abstract our art.'' Hoping to smash through outer boundaries and establish their own personal identities, the Action painters dissolved the object in a crescendo of spontaneous pigment. Their successors, however, are committed to the object per se, the object undisguised, unbroken, impersonal, and uninterpreted. They respect its existence with the same diligence their predecessors lavished on its destruction.

If interest in primitive cultures dominated art in the first half of our century, it is mass production that shapes more recent developments. Yet, our whole period, from its beginnings until today, has focused on a re-evaluation of the real. Even the Cubists engaged in what they called a "new realism." For, by projecting all sides of an object simultaneously, they formally recognized a multiple three-dimensional world. Their methods, it is true, remained curiously illusionistic. As Robert Morris, an articulate spokesman for the present-day structural artists, says of his own sculpture: "The intention is diametrically opposed to Cubism with its concern for simultaneous views in one plane." What the Cubists wanted could not, he felt, be represented on a flat surface, but only in terms of actual form and space. With the development of collage and with the substitution of real materials for simulated ones, another step toward realism was taken. The Futurists, too, tried to approximate actuality when they traced the continuous sequence of speed. But closer to verity was the modern mobile, which in fact moved.

A half century ago, the Dadaists were concerned with *objets trouvés,* with shells, stones, or bits of driftwood. At the same time, Duchamp invented the "Ready-Made," a man-made object that, isolated from its functional meaning, was sometimes further embellished, sometimes not. In either case, the authentic article was basic, and yet it was so dependent on processes of personal selection and irrational juxtaposition as to end up making a voluble comment on life. The visual pun, the metaphor were rarely absent.

In renouncing all symbolism, young artists today go much further. As one of their number, Howard Jones, says, "Let's explore the uncertain world of life itself and forget about art." Are we to interpret his statement as implying that the artist's job is not to make art but to find it? Or are we to believe that every layman becomes an artist merely by the creative act of seeing the world around him? To be sure, the relating of art to life is not a new idea, but when we are told to *forget art* and turn solely to life, then an important part of the equation is lost.

The Action painters were not entirely antagonistic to this way of thinking. They, too, wanted to involve the viewer; they, too, claimed that the work of art is both means and end. The act of painting became the painting, but their works still bore the stamp of temperamental hands. Each brushstroke operated as an emotionally charged autobiographical excursion. What they made, not what they suggested, was the final aim, but what they made were frank extensions of themselves. Take, for example, Franz Kline, whose turbulent paint was at once a swinging experience and an expression of his own turbulence as he worked. For him, paint became an emotional end in itself. Many of today's younger artists repudiate personal handwriting. In fact, with them it is taboo. As a rule, they design but do not make their own structures. The final works, based on the artists' specifications, are often fabricated industrially.

From earliest times, primitive people transformed reality in order to meet their own needs. Carved and painted forms acted as representations of tribal beliefs and as propitiations against hostile forces. The aborigines created half-animal, half-human images, in hopes not of reproducing nature but of celebrating and placating it. They never intended these works as literal portrayals. For them symbolism was a way of life. So, too, in the Middle Ages and the Renaissance, popular concepts, especially religious ones, were clothed in such accepted iconographical terms as to supersede visual veracity. Art throughout history has always dealt with illusion.

But today this is no longer the artists' aim. They tell us frankly how they feel. If you compare their words with those of their immediate forerunners, you will find startling divergences. Says Donald Judd, "A shape, a volume, a surface is something itself . . . things that exist exist . . . they are not images of life—they are themselves—that is enough." It is the physical presence that concerns him—the object itself, but never ideas about the object.

Paul Klee would have dissented. "In the final analysis," he wrote, "a drawing simply is no longer a drawing—it is a symbol." For him meaning went beyond materials and methods. He dealt with allusions: "If I had to paint a perfectly truthful self-portrait, I would show a peculiar shell. And inside I sit like a kernel in a nut.'' Even Klee's words become personal symbols. But today's realists are not concerned with self-scrutiny or with subjective concepts. Avoiding all multiple meanings, they address themselves to specific objects or to series of often identical ones.

Robert Irwin of California feels that ''oil painting has always been a pictorial event, a reference to something else. As long as paintings are about ideas, they're generalizations. But,'' says he, ''I'm involved with specific physical reality. All you can know of my work is what you experience yourself'' (which, by the way, is all we can know of any man's work). At one time, making the same picture with slight variations over and over, he produced monochrome canvases divided by occasional horizontal lines. According to him, ''these paintings give neither a sense of interplay nor composition; they express simply their own physical existence.'' But is physical existence enough? Is all experience to be strictly tangible or purely optical? Are our powers of intuition and inductive thinking to become obsolete?

Lately Irwin has been working with painted disks projected from the gray walls. On these disks he beams crosslights, thus combining in one experience object, wall, light, and shadow. At times, the shadow takes over to dominate the substance, but this is scarcely a new idea. Fernand Léger, in his paintings of positive and negative form, often allowed the echo to become more insistent than its source. Still, there is a difference. Irwin's are not painted shadows; they exist and have a mobility that Léger's lacked; yet both are man-made. Irwin's lighted disks depend on the artist no less than did Léger's painted images. The moment a choice of action is taken, an allusion is set up, be it by literal or invented light. Léger once observed that ''a work of art is a perfect balance between real and imaginary facts.'' He wanted facts and he wanted real ones, but he also demanded the freedom to create his own. Today, realism and abstraction are interchangeable, depending on the aims of the artist and the eyes of the observer. A brushstroke can be ''realer'' than the object it depicts.

Many younger artists deny the validity of invented facts. Says Tadaaki Kukayama, a Japanese painter living in New

York, "Ideas, thoughts, philosophy, reasons, meanings, even the humanity of the artist, do not enter my work at all. There is only the art itself. That is all." This very insistence on material confrontations leads some painters to shape their canvases so that form becomes actual rather than suggested. Donald Judd claims, "Three dimensions are real space. That gets rid of the problem of illusionism. . . . Actual space is intrinsically more powerful and specific than paint on a flat surface," a statement that invites speculation. For, after all, the human mind, freed from facts, can sometimes conjure up a space more potent than any we experience directly. One wonders whether these young realists plan to extinguish all that is chimerical, visionary, illusory, hypothetical, imaginary, and humorous in art.

In his last Manhattan exhibition Robert Morris showed sculpture cut entirely from felt. He chose the material because it had no associative references for him, and because its very pliability determined its form. He avoided conscious composition, hoping to reduce his art to the inherent qualities of felt.

Though Josef Albers may have influenced some of these militant minimalists, still he belongs to the past, concerned as he is with meanings, aesthetics, and ethics. "I've handled color as man should behave," he points out. Preferring to work in series as do so many of the younger artists, presumably because in this way the specialness of individual works is nullified, Albers concentrates on color and its interactions. Yet, when questioned about his habit of making what is seem what it is not, he replied: "A cow sees grass merely as an edible vegetable—I don't believe it sees a lawn as a carpet and it probably doesn't care about all the green possible. But a poet putting his nose into grass can see it as a forest. This for me is reality, the myth behind the fact." Though Albers' insistent reductions may have affected the younger realists, his acceptance of poetic ambiguity sets him apart from them. They recognize no "myth behind the fact." They recognize only the fact.

They would also take issue with Isamu Noguchi's witty series of ceramic forms called *Even the Centipede*. Observing that "when you kill a centipede the two halves just walk off," Noguchi used this idea as a foil for his centipede at the Museum of Modern Art, "a sculpture in sections, each a separate thing, though in actual fact the individual ceramics are tied onto a two-by-four. What happens is that your eye jumps from one image to the other and your subconscious supplies the connection. I also liked the rather quixotic notion of dignifying the centipede by making a sculpture of him—thus indicating the centipede can aspire to humanity, or even to God." In Noguchi's series, there is no uniformity. Each object is a separate symbol reinforcing a larger idea. True, the forms are interesting in themselves, but they are intended as more than purely ceramic forms.

Contrast, if you will, the way Gene Davis, one of the Washington color painters, discusses his works, which are conceived in multicolored vertical stripes of acrylic paint on unsized canvas. "I never plan more than four or five stripes ahead, and sometimes I change my mind before I get to the fourth stripe. To give you an idea of the kind of tightrope-walking involved in my concept, imagine the number of decisions necessary for half-inch stripes on a canvas measuring 10 by 20 feet—some 500 stripes in all." Here, the final result does not depend on the viewer's eyes plus his "subconscious" but only on the viewer's eyes. The artist, in discussing his work, concentrates solely on its physical properties. He describes but never explains, interprets, or questions. It seems consistent that a painter like Gene Davis would avoid all idiosyncratic textures and brushstrokes. He deploys acrylic on unsized canvas so that the liquid paint is evenly absorbed everywhere. Whatever emphasis obtrudes results from scale and color.

For Mark Tobey, however, art paraphrases life; it never competes with life. He once said, "I got the idea of 'writing' cities and city life. At last I had found a technical approach which enabled me to capture what specially interested me in the city: its lights, threading traffic, the river of humanity chartered and flowing through and around its self-imposed limitations, not unlike chlorophyll flowing through the canals of a leaf." Disagreeing with such subjective layers of meaning, Robert Morris explains why "the sensuous object, resplendent with compressed internal relations, has had to be rejected. . . . Control is necessary if the variables of object, light, space, body are to function. The object itself has not become less important. It has merely become less *self*-important.''

And so we finally arrive at an art that is more public than private, an art that demands relatively little of the viewer. True, he must look with great care, yet he must neither interpret what he sees nor relate it to the past. For him, knowledge of history is unnecessary, since much of contemporary art grows only from immediate stimuli. Art is frankly intended today as an alternative of life—a stern, optimistic, impersonal alternative.

Ironically, we seem to have come full circle—back to making art real, not representationally real as did the nineteenth-century academicians in their hope of recapturing classical and Renaissance humanism, but real in a physical sense. Unlike the earlier Constructivists, the present structural painters and sculptors are not trying to improve society by imposing a new visual order on it; instead they are facing their surroundings in terms of total material actuality. Whether what they offer us is as interesting as the environment that spawned it is a moot question.

And one I would like to pursue further. I have yet to see a single kinetic light experiment that can compete with the exploding neon signs on Times Square. Why reproduce in art what daily life does better? Why must everything be real? I cannot agree that art is unequivocably married to its medium and hence has no other function beyond the demands of its own material. If this is true, mass-produced objects often make more sense than those specially designed by artists and fabricated industrially. For, since the latter usually end up as unique pieces or are produced in small series, the whole idea of modern technology is subverted. Likewise, though many minimal sculptures have impressive architectural dimensions, they rarely compare with the structures that influenced them.

Recently I rode on the Metroliner from New York to Baltimore. The landscape, filled with oil tanks, smokestacks, colossal chimneys, sprawling factories, and strange industrial shapes and colors, was quite marvelous—indeed much too marvelous to be reduced or reproduced. For without its cumulative impact, much of this landscape's power is lost. Fragments of industrialization like pipes, tubes, and sheets of gleaming metal have a grace of their own, but in the end, when isolated, they become sterile. And no imitation machinery can ever approximate the intricate beauty of the real thing. Like nature, technology is only a point of departure for the artist, not a model to reproduce.

19. *Place, Time, and Painter*

There was no reason to compare the two paintings. They represented totally different worlds, and perhaps that was precisely why I found myself doing so. True, they both were hanging in the same building and both were variations on "the Virgin and Child" theme, but kinship ended there. I encountered them separated by several rooms in one of America's star institutions, the Worcester Art Museum, rightfully celebrated for its superior collections hand-picked over the years by a succession of knowledgeable experts. And should one question whether knowledge makes a difference, a visit to this sophisticated art gallery will dispel such doubts. Also, should one question the advantages of a well-pruned smaller museum adapted to normal human intake, Worcester is proof that size and geographic location are not what make an institution parochial.

Among this museum's holdings is a group of rare seventeenth-century American paintings climaxed by an anonymous double portrait called *Mrs. Freake and Baby Mary,* often considered this country's outstanding canvas of the period. Much less famous but far more urbane and technically accomplished is Bartolommeo Montagna's late fifteenth-century *Virgin and Child,*

Virgin and Child, by Bartolommeo Montagna

probably painted in Vicenza, where this Italian artist spent most of his life. Viewed on one level, both Worcester pictures are interesting works of art; viewed on another, they are reflections of wholly different periods in time, thought, and place, each offering a brief résumé of the land and mores from which it came. Worth investigating, too, is why one painting is so highly prized, the other merely accepted with polite respect.

Mrs. Freake and Baby Mary, artist unknown

Though nothing could be more egregious than confusing
aesthetic reactions with historical documentation, art has always
served as a valuable clue to the past. What better way to understand the elegant frivolity of eighteenth-century France than
through Boucher, Watteau, and Fragonard? What better way to
understand our own abrasive scene than through its ebullient Pop
imitators? Yet, *Mrs. Freake and Baby Mary* is not typically na-

tive. It is all the more provocative because method and message are somewhat divergent. The subject is clearly American, the technique not necessarily so. As Louisa Dresser, the Worcester museum's curator, points out, this carefully delineated composition might well pass for a French provincial painting—one of those crisp, slightly awkward works found frequently in France's excellent smaller museums. If technical methods have been refined by mixed memories of Europe, the sitter, her child, her costume, her stalwart character are strictly early American. Indeed, most of the details in the picture probably provide accurate data on the period in which it was painted—about 1674.

Where its anonymous artist came from we do not know, but most likely from England. One thing is certain: he was never a member of the Dutch Patroon school that settled chiefly in New York State, producing a legacy of brutally frank, brilliantly strong portraits that lack the sensitivity of Mrs. Freake. We also do not know too much about Elizabeth Freake herself, except that she was born in Dorchester, Massachusetts, in 1642, thus making her thirty-two at the time of the portrait. Her husband, John Freake, whose likeness hangs next to hers in the Worcester Museum and came no doubt from the same hand though at a less inspired moment, emigrated from England around 1660 to settle in Boston as an attorney and merchant. A year after the portraits were finished, he died in a Boston Harbor explosion.

The question immediately confronting us is why the woman's portrait is hailed as a major—possibly *the* major—example of primitive American art. Surely not because of the puppet-like child, the bourgeois sitter, the affectionately recorded garments, the wealth of subtle whites. Rather, I think, it is the quiet, the purity, the trusting record of an authentic person that come through to us with touching impact. Whether this same painting would be regarded so enthusiastically in any country other than its own is doubtful, though Daniel Rich, director of the Worcester Art Museum, reports that "interested Europeans respond to the portrait, because they sense in it the primitive quality we admire today. Since Le Douanier Rousseau," he adds, "Europeans as well as Americans have been interested in self-taught artists who are involved with direct, fresh discoveries."

But it is more than quaint primitivism that attracts us to *Mrs. Freake and Baby Mary* (a title, by the way, I find wonderfully American). This strong, measured, plain woman is part of a heritage we like to remember, especially today under less serene circumstances. She seems eminently respectable, secure, and non-Freudian. As we emerge from historical adoléscence and begin to value our past, American art daily assumes greater importance. Yet, admiration for this particular work goes beyond pride in home production; it is rightfully based on the appeal of a painting that probes deeper than the usual early American portrait. The picture has its own individuality, its own uniqueness. The unfaltering linear design—rigid, proud, and simple— echoes similar characteristics in the young mother, providing us with an eloquent glimpse of an early American personality.

All of which brings me back to Montagna's *Virgin and Child,* painted two centuries earlier than Mrs. Freake. If one were to ask a casual viewer, who knows nothing specific about the antecedents of either picture, which he prefers, he would, I think, choose the Montagna. To appreciate this tender religious work presupposes little previous knowledge. One need not be told that Montagna lived in Venice at one time, that the present painting may have derived from a print by Mantegna and may have also been influenced by Giovanni Bellini. The close relationship of Mother and Child, the beautiful candid Virgin, the undulating gracious design are all part of a southern European Renaissance tradition we have long understood and accepted. But Mrs. Freake's portrait, even more Protestant than American, is related to an austere New World where denial of sensuality was basic to survival. In order to relish the picture fully, one must recognize the stern realities of the land and the time it came from. Montagna's deeply Catholic panel combines idealized symbolism with warm human emotions. This dichotomy, implicit in much Italian Renaissance art, was characteristic of an indulgent faith. Here, though religious iconography was omnipotent, there was none of the Puritan restraint that inhibited early American expression.

In the long run, however, the American portrait remains inimitable, a special and unusual encounter. I recall no other seventeenth-century painting produced in the United States that in any way duplicates or, for that matter, approximates it. The Montagna Virgin is not an individualized personality but a type dependent on familiar traditions. She is part of a safely established period, not a brave preview of a new one. More articulate and more polished than Mrs. Freake, she is the heroine of a universal story. So, too, is the American mother, but her story is related to the mundane facts of life, while the Virgin, despite her human fervency, is nonetheless a supernatural being.

The Montagna, of course, is not a primitive work, though it is dated some two hundred years earlier than the American canvas, demonstrating how geography can become as important as chronology. It is the place *and* the time, to say nothing of the artist, that make a picture tick. But it is more than place, time, and painter; it is the audience, too. What in the second half of the twentieth century is considered a masterpiece might have seemed merely an adequate historical document to viewers a hundred years ago. And what Americans consider a chef d'oeuvre today might appeal to contemporary Europeans as little more than a typical regional work of minor importance. It is rare that a country's primitive beginnings turn into a world-wide inheritance. During relatively recent centuries this has happened in Italy, the Netherlands, and, to a degree, in Germany, Spain, and France.

With great works rapidly dwindling from the market, Americans are turning back on themselves with almost hysterical zeal. Prices for older and sometimes third-rate indigenous canvases are skyrocketing unrealistically. These paintings often have value only here and now, only to us in these United States. They are scarcely negotiable elsewhere. Yet, we must not forget that on occasion a blunt early American work can hold its own with more worldly examples from abroad. *Mrs. Freake and Baby Mary* is a formidable case in point. Here honesty and innate dignity compensate for technical naïveté. And, curiously, it is this very naïveté that intensifies the picture's uncompromising integrity.

20. *Letter to a Nature Lover*

Dear Aunt Mary,

Knowing how interested you are in nature study, I thought I should tell you about some strange goings-on that are quite the rage here in New York. It's really like having your cake and eating it too, for now, of all things, avant-garde artists are bringing the great outdoors to our asphalt canyons. Yes, that is exactly what's happening. I thought you might like to come for a weekend and see for yourself. The exhibitions I have in mind will probably be down by the time you get here, but no doubt there will be others to take their place. You see, nature-study-art (here they call it "earthworks," "environmental art," or "ecological art") is the *dernier cri*.

I'll try to give you an idea of what it's all about. Take, for instance, the case of Robert Morris. It seems he was commissioned by the Museum of Modern Art to make a "space." So what did he do? He planted a whole bunch of dear little pine trees (you would have loved them) right in the museum. I don't believe he planted them himself; a gardener was there looking after them—you know, spraying them and adjusting the temperature in the room just like specially trained art conservators do for old masterpieces, so I suppose the gardener must have planted them, too.

Anyway, a press release the museum got out described the venture as "an interior room where 144 trees have been planted on large eye-level pedestals faced with Cor-ten steel and separated by narrow paths of Cor-ten." It was fascinating to learn that the tiny Norway spruce trees were donated by Kimberly-Clark Corporation. The museum even told us all about the Kleenex, cellulose wadding, and barber towels this great firm manufactures. It did seem quite a lot of palaver for just 144 dwarflike trees. The Cor-ten steel, I was happy to learn, was donated by Joseph T. Ryerson & Son, Inc., whose products, according to MOMA, "are burned, cut, and shaped to customer's specifications." The wall labels were downright scholarly, as they always are at the Museum of Modern Art. There were also data about "horticultural services" (the gardener, I guess) provided by The Manhattan Gardner Ltd., and about a refrigeration company, to say nothing of a light corporation, each cooperating with the museum and with Mr. Morris and, of course, with visitors like me who might not otherwise have known about the products and services these companies offer.

It was all most educational, but I was confused. Maybe that was because I had just suffered a rather nasty fall in a nearby "space" (there were six in all) designed by Larry Bell. In there it was very dark and I lost my footing. A kind guard with a flashlight helped me up and soothed me as he led me out. I considered suing the museum but since my arm was not broken—only severely bruised—I went on.

And I am not sorry, for it was then I found the pine trees. Jennifer Licht, associate curator of painting and sculpture, who directed the exhibition, says Mr. Morris "contrasted human proportions with miniature groves of fir trees, planted in diminishing size to create impressions of distant vistas." Maybe I was stupid but there were no distant vistas for me— just a lot of little trees looking uncomfortably crowded in there. I think it would have been better to transport us bodily to the woods and mountains. Some of those giant airplanes

might have provided study trips in return for the same kind
of credits the other firms got. Miss Licht also revealed that
"originally the air (in Mr. Morris's space) was to be imbued
with an additional fillup, negative ions, which induce feelings
of euphoria, but," she confessed, "this aspect could not be
realized."

I'm wondering, Aunt Mary, if it's "the real" they want,
why don't they go the whole hog? As long as they use real
earth and real trees, why not real scale and real distance?
Why not just go outside and look at nature the way you do? I
suppose they'd say I'm missing the point, that it's precisely
because part of what they do is real and part is not that they
finally come up with something new. The fact is, it doesn't
seem very new. It's not so different from the old-fashioned
painted way; both imitate nature, only one is flat and pretends
to be 3-D and the other is 3-D. So what! I wouldn't mind if it
weren't boring. However, I'm happy to tell you that some of
these "ecological" artists are beginning to move outdoors,
but we don't go with them; we stay inside and read what they
have to say, or look at their photographs.

I found out about this particular kind of nature-study-art
syndrome the other day when I visited a New York gallery
called John Gibson Commissions, Inc. The gallery sent me a
seven-page single-spaced mimeographed brochure by Peter
Hutchinson describing how he had transported 450 lbs. of
Super Wonder Bread to the top of Paricutín, a remote Mexican volcano, and then how he had covered all those loaves with
300 feet of thick plastic sheeting. You may wonder why. He
wanted to produce bread mold on the rim of that wild crater—
not for any scientific reason but just for the sake of art, just
so he could fly over it several days later and take photos. I
thought you might like this romantic idea—so wayward and
whimsical with no pretense at a final solution, and that's rare
in a materialistic age.

The idea was not to take highly professional photographs.
In fact, Mr. Gibson explained to me that the exhibition wasn't
supposed to be just another photography show. Yet when I
went to his gallery there wasn't anything to see except color

photographs (rather indistinct ones) of moldy bread on a vast yawning volcano. I suppose the contrast was what interested Peter Hutchinson, but then contrasts in nature are an old story. We're always marveling at them. A field of wild poppies near patches of snow on Mount McKinley or sand blowing against crazy boulders in the Negev—oh well, you know.

In the brochure Mr. Hutchinson described the hardships he and his companions endured, also the expenses he incurred while making bread mold on Paricutín. In addition to chartering planes, he had to employ an entourage of Indians, and, of course, the expedition needed horses, pack donkeys, and camping equipment. One problem was keeping the Indians from littering the wilderness with all those plastic wrappings from the Super Wonder Bread, the way our astronauts leave that discarded junk on the moon. Once Mr. Hutchinson was almost overcome by poisonous gases and he also suffered from extremes of heat, cold, and altitude, but he persevered because this mountain met his requirements. Had it not, he planned to head farther south and consider a volcano in Costa Rica that he'd heard about. He says all he was after was ''to juxtapose a micro-organism against a macrocosmic landscape, yet in such amount the results would be plainly visible through color changes.'' Well, they weren't plainly visible to me. Of course, I wasn't there, so I have to believe the artist even though his photos didn't work for me. They're not supposed to, I guess. I got more out of the mimeographed brochure because Mr. Hutchinson writes very well. Perhaps it's a book he ought to be doing. And I imagine the Super Wonder Bread, instead of just any old Mexican bread, was an ''added fillup,'' as Miss Licht might say. It suggested the idea of conspicuous American waste and gave the whole project a philosophic slant.

I keep remembering my own experience at Paricutín more than a quarter century ago. I wrote you about it. A group of us traveled over nonexistent roads—really nothing but cactus and ruts—to see that fiery new, fiercely exploding volcano. We stayed all night, awed by its violence, noise, smell, and magnificence. That was a real earthwork or should I say a work of earth?

By the way, Aunt Mary, I'm sending you a book for your birthday. It's called *Art Povera* and it's all about nature study, about how different artists use what Donald Judd calls "the specificity and power of actual materials, actual colors, actual space." It seems a shame to use such long words about actual things we can see without too much help, but maybe the artists want to make us see them more clearly and in a new way. I don't object to guidance. What really bugs me is that these earthwork men claim they are producing a "noninstitutional art," not for museums, not for collectors, not for critics, and yet they end up showing it in the very museums and galleries they pooh-pooh.

In *Art Povera* there's a project by Lawrence Weiner, who advocates "3 minutes of forty pound pressure spray of white highway paint upon a well-tended lawn. The lawn," he continues, "is allowed to grow and [is] not tended until the grass is free of all vestiges of white highway paint." Do you think he's trying to prove how hardy grass is? Well, I think nature proves it better.

Anyway, I hope you'll come soon and see for yourself. Let me know in advance so I can prepare a list. Sometimes the shows don't last very long. This winter I was invited to a champagne back-to-nature exhibition based on melting ice but it was all over before I got there, nothing left but the champagne—so I just went home and looked out of the window.

Love from Katharine

21. *The Story of a Picture—or What's a Museum For?*

In 1950, Willem de Kooning painted a large and now famous abstract composition called *Excavation*. A year later the canvas was invited to the Annual American Exhibition of Painting and Sculpture at the Art Institute of Chicago. There a jury composed of Hans Hofmann, Peter Blume, and Aline Saarinen awarded it the top purchase prize. Unfortunately, the funds for this prize were less than the price of the painting, which, as I recall, was around $5,000, a modest sum even then for a canvas 80 by 100 inches. I would guess that during the intervening nineteen years, the value has increased at least thirtyfold, but it is not extravagant monetary figures that interest me; it is the picture itself and its story. Now on view in the de Kooning exhibition at Manhattan's Museum of Modern Art, the canvas stands out as one of the artist's definitive works and also as one of America's most important mid-twentieth-century paintings.

Filled with a nameless malaise, the tumultuous pigment whips in and out, over and under, to suggest natural and unnatural forces at work. De Kooning once told me the idea for the painting came to him while looking at the movie *Bitter Rice*. He still remembered, he said, the wet fields with peasants spading up and

Excavation, by Willem de Kooning

into the rich loam. On many levels the composition becomes
a synthesis of excavating. The earthlike color with its occasional
iridescent glints reveals hidden treasure beneath the surface.
And sinuous brushstrokes suggest the process of gouging out
and scooping up. One feels a kinetic excitement at work here, yet
the whole restless maze interlocks to produce a kind of personal
iconography.

A year after de Kooning painted *Excavation,* he wrote an article for *transformation* in which he said: "The attitude that
nature is chaotic and that the artist puts order into it is a very
absurd point of view, I think. All that we can hope for is to put

some order into ourselves. When a man plows his field at the right time, it means just that.'' Several years after the Art Institute acquired *Excavation,* de Kooning saw it in Chicago for the first time since it had left New York. He examined it carefully and then, questioning its scale, wondered if it wasn't too large. I think not. The composition seems to fill the canvas, and even push beyond its boundaries in a continuous burgeoning assault.

The painting department at the Art Institute shared the jury's enthusiasm for the picture. I remember we voted secretly before the jury assembled and unanimously selected *Excavation* as the top work in the show. I also remember that Hofmann, after his initial day in Chicago, was attacked by a virus infection, but even from his hotel bed made clear that his first choice was the de Kooning. None of us was clairvoyant. It was only that we were more accustomed to looking at art than the various committee members who a few days later were to reject the picture with record speed. Perhaps there should be a rule that anyone responsible for the public acquisition of a work of art must be locked up with it for at least one full hour before coming to a decision. With part of the cost already available because of the purchase award, the staff urged the acquisition committee, composed chiefly of trustees, to authorize the necessary additional funds. But the committee members, as is often true in American museums, were chiefly businessmen or pillars of civic life who, little informed about contemporary art—indeed, often about any art—regarded the painting with jaundiced eyes. However, certain members of the staff, after considerable outside canvassing, discovered two friends of the museum willing to supply most of the needed money. The rest was contributed by the artist and his dealer, who agreed to accept a lower price for the canvas, though, let me add, at that time de Kooning was far from prosperous.

But even a gift must await trustee benediction. In this case, the committee, not wanting to offend generous donors, accepted the work with strong reservations, cynically recommending that it be kept in storage for as long as possible. Thus came *Excavation* to the Art Institute of Chicago. Shortly thereafter the painting was invited to an exhibition where it was seen by James Thrall Soby, then the able art editor of *Saturday Review*. In his column he found *Excavation* the most distinguished modern American work of art to be acquired that year by any museum in the country. Each committee member promptly received a reprint of these reassuring words. The softening process had begun.

While the de Kooning retrospective was on view in London at the Tate, art critic David Thompson covered it for the *New York Times*. He wrote, "Almost every reviewer has singled out for mention the great *Excavation* of 1950 from the Art Institute of Chicago, which stands as an indestructible masterpiece." After world-wide approval, the painting triumphantly returned to Chicago, when the exhibition moved to the Art Institute. Many trustees who excoriated the picture are now dead, but some are still around. As they proudly led guests through the show and stopped before their museum's renowned canvas, did they, I wonder, recall the truculent reception it had received nineteen years before? Star billing in New York and Europe plus accelerated monetary appraisals are not necessarily the only reasons these men were apt to accept what once they and the local press vehemently denounced. Time, familiarity, and a bit of knowledge are helpful, too.

Because *Excavation*'s history is not an isolated episode and because similar experiences are frequently repeated in American museums, we have reason to question whether businessmen as trustees are in fact good businessmen. Turning down an Alexis Rudier cast of a great Rodin priced at a pittance because they considered it lascivious, or the gift of an excellent black-and-white work by Bradley Walker Tomlin (later promptly accepted by New York's Museum of Modern Art) because they considered it not at all, was scarcely astute. I doubt whether the most skillful handling of stocks and bonds can approximate similar increases in value, not to mention the added dividend of emotional enrichment.

It is not, however, the Art Institute of Chicago that is at fault; it is the entire system. I have merely used this specific museum because I am acquainted with its history. And, also, I am told that in recent years trustees are better informed about the present, though at times they become so fastened on the contemporary scene as to ignore the past. Now, ironically, the new is safer than the old. When we think of the innumerable splendid works lost to our civic institutions because of unnecessary roadblocks, we can only grieve. The best curators are always slightly fanatical collectors. Otherwise, they might give up too easily. When finally they track down their quarry only to lose it for purely arbitrary reasons, they lose more than the work of art. Somehow, their future usefulness is eroded.

The moral of this story is obvious. It is concerned with the function of trustees and staff. The former's responsibility is to provide their institutions with top professionals in the field of art, and then to respect these experts, at least in their special capacity. When trustees lose confidence in their staff, there is only one solution: get a staff they do trust. A rational and clear division of responsibility is mandatory. Supervision of community relations, financial investments, over-all policy, and fund raising are rightly the domain of trustees. Where the acquisition, preservation, and presentation of art are concerned, specialists are needed. And in these days museums are hard-pressed to find them. Tired of interference and money-raising gambits, art experts are looking elsewhere for satisfaction. The search for experienced personnel is literally turning into a scramble. Meanwhile museum directors and curators are heading toward teaching, research, writing, and publishing. They are seeking avenues where they need not cajole, compromise, or laboriously lobby in order to do what they have been trained to do.

After all, what is an art museum for? In my lexicon its chief functions are to preserve, acquire, educate, and give pleasure. Art museums are not normally social gathering places or sociological workshops; they are not music halls or film theaters; they are not political forums or scientific laboratories; they are not restaurants, bars, or travel agencies—though from time to time these extracurricular activities can be combined with art in useful if minor context. Art museums are for the preservation and presentation of art. They offer islands of relief where we can study, enjoy, contemplate, and experience emotional rapport with history's finest man-made products.

No matter how much we rant against the idea, art museums *are* repositories. How else are the greatest relics of our past to be preserved and conserved for future generations? Why else would dedicated curators (like those at the Hermitage during the siege of Leningrad) take chances with their own lives in order to protect historic works? It is scarcely news that great European museums when sponsoring special exhibitions, notably controversial modern ones, often install these shows in buildings far removed from the central galleries that house irreplaceable masterpieces. To be a repository does not presuppose the breath of death, for works of art can be juxtaposed in meaningful, even dramatic, relationships if projected with sensitivity.

Established museum routines, inherited over the years, are not always as square as reputed. There are legitimate reasons why art museums are ill-starred rivals of far-out, "much-in" events and happenings. Picket lines and unruly throngs held back by restraints make for newspaper headlines but not for the security that rare objects require. Too many important masterworks have already been lost through wars, fires, neglect, ignorance, and the erosions of time. What remains must be preserved. Today we have the scientific know-how, but do we have the simple good sense?

Our *bête noire* is publicity, a valuable activity when deftly controlled, yet one that ceases to serve as it becomes less a tool than an end in itself. Expanding American museums, not surprisingly, are borrowing Madison Avenue techniques. Funds, funds, and more funds are needed for exhibitions, purchases, operating expenses, and new buildings. Competition for donors turns into a full-time occupation. Attendance digits in annual reports carry more weight than enlightening information about art. Acquisitions too often command public attention purely because of spectacular prices. When museums no longer analyze but merely advertise, they abrogate their birthright.

22. *Art's Voyage of Discovery*

To predict the future of American art demands a soothsayer and fool. A review of the first fifty years of our century provides certain clues, but it is history in the making that sets the course. For no matter how subtle its communicative powers, how evasive, elusive, and oblique its message, art worth its name is always geared to life. From cave symbols to non-art protests, graphic expression has dealt with man himself. During an interview several years ago, the American artist Mark Tobey observed, "The content of a painting is tied up with time, place, and history. It is always related to man's beliefs and disbeliefs, to his affirmations and negations. How we believe and disbelieve is mirrored in the art of our times." This is not to say that each school of art identifies with parallel contemporary events, for art grows from more than life. It also grows from art and is often closely enmeshed with the work of earlier men. How explain, otherwise, the earth-shaking impact of such figures as Leonardo and Michelangelo, or more recently Mondrian and Picasso?

The best way to consider the future is to examine the immediate past. We may, of course, be too near our own century to evaluate its meaning or pinpoint the main currents art has followed and the sources that have forged these currents. But it is worth a try. The fine arts have been shaped by many of the same forces that affected modern literature, music, theater, and dance. Each has responded to the accelerated tempo of our time, to the implacable power of speed, to a new bewildering awareness of space, and, not least, to the advances of science. The danger, however, is to overemphasize the authority of science, for where art is concerned external sources are sometimes less cogent than hidden ones. The painter and sculptor do not report on world affairs; they may reflect these events but, at best, always distilled through their own personal bias, their own atavistic memories.

In trying to condense present multiplicity into tangible form, artists turn to certain short cuts, to transparent, fragmented, reconstructed images where two compelling illusions—speed and space—act as basic source material. A persistent and insistent manifestation of twentieth-century art is its preoccupation with breakup, breakup of color (inherited from Impressionism), of form, surface, time, line, pigment, content, light, space, and design. In many cases, the immediate if not final explanation for this consuming interest in dissolution stems from modern technology. Take the Impressionists, who in the nineteenth century were bent on capturing realistic atmospheric effects through broken color. Had it not been for the optical experiments of various contemporary scientists, it is doubtful whether artists like Monet and Seurat would have been so involved with color. Yet, surely, it was not science alone that caused an entire generation of painters to focus on realistic light; more likely it was the same urge that motivated both artists and scientists. As usual, the painters were searching for wider horizons and freedom from past conventions. In fleeting nuances of light and color they found a poetic escape from the more prosaic facts of life. For them, sunlight was so evanescent as to deny its own reality and, in fact, propose the ephemeral aspects of all reality. Objects as such assumed minor importance; it was how light shone on these objects that counted. And thus the first tentative steps toward modern abstraction were taken.

The Surrealists, too, borrowed from science. Were it not for certain Freudian discoveries, they might have hesitated to shatter content and time sequences with such total abandon. However, they went beyond orthodox psychoanalytic methods to invent a new kind of awareness. Their brand of superreality deliberately made what is seem what it is not. By forcing us to recognize the duality of daily experiences, they proved that facts are never infallible. A rock on second glance becomes a man; a tree metamorphoses into human form, and so, too, does a test tube. Witness the paintings of Dali, Max Ernst, Tchelitchew, and Duchamp. With these men nothing is precisely as it seems. The same object assumes perverse and multiple aspects, not too surprising in an age anxiously aware of the unconscious.

As for the Abstract Expressionists—such men as Jackson Pollock and Willem de Kooning—the invention of atomic destruction may have accelerated their emphasis on splintered surfaces, for in a world where upheavals and explosions are commonplace, the artist scarcely remains immune. Indeed, there is no place for him to hide, except perhaps in his own work. The painter Morris Graves was right when he said, ''You simply can't keep the world out any longer.'' Fallout reaches even the most remote studios. Still, I doubt whether the knowledge of atomic devastation acted as an important influence on contemporary art, except indirectly as it infiltrates all our thinking. The whole concept behind it is on such an inhuman scale as to elude graphic interpretation. A wildly tangled painting by Pollock tells us more about his personal conflicts than about any scientific inventions. Slashing away ruthlessly at his canvas, he was not merely seeking a catharsis; he was also annihilating the world of material security. And this is again what Giacometti did, only with greater refinement. By reducing his figures to an absolute minimum, he dematerialized them. They became the apotheosis of isolation. Robbed of all substance, they live only as gestures of frustration.

Though modern methods of destruction have undoubtedly affected all the arts, I am convinced that our century's emphasis on dissolution—on scarred surfaces, segmented compositions, and smashed forms—results less from direct technological developments than from the artist's consuming desire to escape the overmaterialistic world that technology has produced. Some claim that painters and sculptors with their supersensitized vision intuitively predicted an atomized landscape long before "the bomb" became a *fait accompli*. But a more telling motive, I think, was the artist's need to dematerialize his environment in order to block out the banality of mass-produced abundance. He purposely disintegrates his surroundings, sometimes out of sheer fury, more often to reconstruct them according to his own needs. This is precisely what the Cubists did. For them, dissolution was a disciplined process, the artists breaking up form only to reassemble it in fresh and unexpected relationships. They literally remade the physical world around them.

We cannot discount the overwhelming impact of modern speed on present-day art. It, too, fragments our vision. The act of racing past stationary objects makes them seem to coalesce and overlap; yet while our eyes applaud these phenomena, our spirits reject the efficiently lethal machines that make possible this very velocity. For that matter, artists have been grappling with the machine for well over fifty years, at times with undisguised admiration, at times with scorn, more often with defiance and fear. According to their lights, they see it as a knight in shining armor (Léger), as a whimsical man-made gadget (Klee), as an obstinate rival (Duchamp). They see it as witty, willful, wicked, and wanton. It is for them a never-ending source of stimulation.

And so, too, is motion. That the art of our period deals so dynamically with speed is not surprising, but I question whether the influence of high-geared modern communication is the sole explanation. For motion is often employed less as a representation of present-day life than as a suggestion of growth. The unfolding sculpture of Pevsner and Gabo, the boundaryless paintings of Pollock, Klee, and early Kandinsky all imply that containment is an illusion, that final beginnings and endings are nonexistent. Vision is a continuous experience the artist cannot duplicate but can approximate with shorthand symbols. Broken, overlapping, transparent forms and over-all compositions without specific centers of interest result in a new kind of realism, a realism that seems abstract only because it deals with volatile growing processes. Inevitably, this preoccupation induced a sharp break with classical traditions, with all symmetrical humanism. An observer exposed to a Greek sculpture or a Renaissance portrait sees a finished object, complete and intentionally permanent. However, when he examines a modern painting he often joins in an unfinished experience that only his own powers of projection can complete. Classical art, despite its idealism, replaced illusion with fact. Contemporary art deals with less finite matters. Classical sculptors made idealized form their panacea; modern artists make nonform theirs, and in the process of dissolving form they in turn find a boundless release in space. For them, voids take precedence over substance; negative becomes positive as space turns into a tangible force energizing their work. They recognize that all vision is interpenetrated by space, that even solids are not impervious to its pressure.

As the world becomes larger our sights tend to shrink, in repudiation, perhaps, of an expanding universe. Today the artist condenses his symbols, allowing a single detail to assume multiple meanings. Fernand Léger claimed that under certain circumstances an enlarged close-up of a fingernail could be mistaken for a mountain. Brancusi sometimes merged attributes of both sexes in the same sculpture, hoping thus to celebrate the origins of life. For Miró, only an isolated eye and ear were needed to recapture the nostalgic sights and sounds of his youth. Whole macrocosms were thus abbreviated into small familiar symbols.

The present century often tries to escape its own materialism by exploring shadows and exposing hidden meanings. Modern artists repeatedly depict not the object but its ambiance. They show us the process of growth rather than specific growing organisms. This concentration on abstract metaphor turns the spectator into an active participant. He must identify personally with these diverse symbols, with these subtle visual puns, if he is to understand the artist's intention. A tenacious characteristic of modern art is the heavy reponsibility it places on the viewer. His involvement becomes an integral part of the finished work.

We hear a great deal these days about non-art. There is no

doubt that a strong nihilism has marked our period. It shows itself in many guises—in an emphasis on breakup, in the repugnance certain artists feel for aesthetic traditions, in a frank desire to shock. This obsession with anti-art started during and immediately after the First World War when the Dadaists, disgusted with the world they inherited, tried to demolish it with every possible desecration. As artists, they denied all accepted conventions; as human beings, they denied life, at times allowing their total nihilism to drive them to suicide. These were men who firmly believed in their causeless cause. It is a mistake to imagine they were insensible simply because they were negative; the truth is they judged society with plausible rage. Their dilemma was only one of many signs indicating how sorely the church had failed modern man. In the past, as art's chief *raison d'être,* religion dominated painting and sculpture. Now it is less a whipping boy than an afterthought.

I have never understood why certain moralists attack works of art they consider destructive. When they claim that the word ''art'' presupposes exalted emotions, they restrict us to a Pollyanna world of good deeds and pure thoughts. But since life is not always sublime, inventive men will continue to find fresh ways to illuminate the truth. And it is the truth, not morality, we are after. Ardent, brutal statements can on occasion become art's lifeblood. One need only recall the tortured Christs of Grünewald, the sadistic imagery of Bosch, the furious lampoons of Goya. The Dadaists, who were accused of lacking discipline, made a new kind of discipline out of chaos, not only visual but psychological chaos. Their very negations became a language that is still nourishing the art of our century.

What artists choose as source material is indicative of their own needs. Though exposed to innumerable images from the past, painters and sculptors of late have concentrated to an astonishing degree on primitive art—and possibly for the same motives that led them to non-art. The aboriginal carver did not think of himself as an artist; he was merely performing a ritualistic duty. Modern man, surfeited by a mechanistic environment of his own making, turns thirstily to more earthy experiences. Escaping from his complicated surroundings, he attempts

to renew himself through the direct, sometimes savage statements of primitive societies. Jacques Lipchitz, in discussing
Gauguin, once said that this nineteenth-century pioneer was less
important as a painter than as a missionary promoting the cause
of native art. Like Klee, Lipchitz claims it is only through redis-
covering our own roots that we free ourselves from sterility.

Were we to predict the future of American art we might
readily oversimplify the situation. For example, we might logi-
cally decide that art will become increasingly international, but
it is just possible that the more available the outside world,
the more avidly painters and sculptors will withdraw into themselves. Though the idea of internationalism is widely accepted
today, often the best of modern art stems from national sources.
Artists, notably during their early years, turn for support to
memories of their homelands. Nostalgic images associated with
youthful experiences can persist throughout the entire span of a
man's work, reappearing in different forms as his art matures.
Indeed, it sometimes seems that the more insistent the outside
world, the more reassuring are the symbols of home.

In the past, art influences usually followed an orderly sequence. Painters and sculptors were apt to revert step by step
to earlier traditions, starting with their immediate antecedents
and only gradually discovering more remote periods. Moreover,
with travel and communication limited, artists were often restricted to their immediate surroundings. But today they can
pick and choose at will, referring to all periods in history without obligation to chronology or geography. If this wealth has
widened the artist's vision, the overwhelming freedom has sometimes driven him back more deeply into his own protective roots.
And the kaleidoscopic variety of new material has only helped at
times to intensify his need for familiar images.

Present-day art is closely related to present-day life, both as
a positive outgrowth of contemporary culture and as a strong
reaction against it. Twentieth-century painting and sculpture
reflect and reject the world around us, though the drive to
escape at times seems more urgent than the desire to identify.
Occasionally painters, like Gauguin, abandon their own culture
in order to find relief from it. Sailing off to the South Seas or

to other exotic retreats is one way of avoiding the pressures of modern life. Most artists, however, remain at home. Some are inventive enough to break with antipathetic surroundings by recreating their world in new terms. It would be folly to under-estimate how much the legitimate need to escape has encouraged the spread of abstract art, but one must remember that this movement is not merely the result of escapism. At best, it has opened up radically new ways of seeing and thinking; it has freed us from oppressive surroundings; it has forced us to par-ticipate more actively in the process of looking; it has created poetic equivalents for modern life, and, above all, it has attacked basic problems with shattering intensity. Brilliant as the nine-teenth century was, except for Cézanne and perhaps Seurat, its artists never approximated the revolutionary vision of our own turbulent century. It is not only our vision that has changed; it is our attitude toward this vision.

This brief survey of twentieth-century art was written some years ago, before Pop, Op, and Minimal art had taken over—yet already even these movements are being displaced. To keep up with present-day art requires a peripatetic zealot.

23. *The Art Education Myth*

The education of art teachers in American universities is, as a rule, unwieldy, unrealistic, and stultifying. From undergraduate ranks come young hopefuls armed with a smattering of art techniques plus an overdose of bland educational theory and methodology. No sooner out of college than they gravitate to grade schools, which are generally the chief source of jobs for neophyte teachers. Graduate art education students, on the other hand, strive with almost incestuous enthusiasm to perpetuate their recently acquired knowledge in institutions of higher learning, often in teachers' colleges, where salaries and working hours are more salubrious but where new ideas are rare commodities.

Thus, the younger the child, the less experienced his art teacher. The age levels and blighted neighborhoods that most need creative guidance are apt to inherit precisely the reverse. Add to this the absurd forty minutes of so-called art per week that are allotted the average pupil in many underprivileged public schools and one doubts whether the game is worth the name. Crayons, paint, or clay are produced and attacked so briefly that most of the time is spent getting ready and cleaning up. Only a genius could reach the children in more than routine measure under such circumstances. Too often, bewildered young art teachers or harassed older ones preside over classes that become virtual cathartic interludes in a dizzy schedule where any hint of experimentation is lost in a welter of discipline. That such instructors might connect the process of making art with the process of looking at it is asking too much. And too much, also, to expect these teachers to relate art to the child's daily surroundings or, for that matter, to have any idea themselves of what place art should occupy in present-day life. Somehow we proceed on the basis that art is good for people, that it is ennobling, uplifting. But I suspect that a Chinese boy in a Bowery school was right when he told me he wanted to study art in order to find out about himself.

Moreover, the art education departments that indoctrinate teachers-to-be have had relatively little contact with the nitty-gritty slum schools where many of their students will eventually work. Though art equipment is often good in teacher-training classrooms and studios, it is the curriculum that is the *bête noire*. Based on the false assumption that methods are more important than involvement, teacher education too often tells *how* rather than *why*. It presupposes "right ways" and "wrong ways"; it encourages qualitative judgments from young acolytes who have neither the knowledge nor the accomplishments to make such judgments.

Not infrequently, three separate art departments compete with one another in the same university, thus splintering a field of study where close interrelationships are basic. Why should the history of art, the making of art, and the training of art teachers be fragmented into autonomous hierarchies? Why, indeed, shouldn't the teacher of art be trained as an artist rather than as a semitherapeutic dabbler? After all, any teacher worth his salt will invent his own methodology depending on his skills, experience, intelligence, and dedication. The expense of duplicate studios for divided art departments is minor, though wasteful, but faculty rivalries are major. Professors actually begin to stake out certain areas as their own special domains. Petty politics proliferate as art becomes a battleground. Funds, space, prestige, equipment are all excuses for intramural squabbles. And even more serious are the blackouts that often stifle communication between student artists, art-history students, and design and teacher trainees.

For several years I was a consultant to a large Midwestern university where my job was to acquire original works of art, not for a specific museum but for such public areas on the campus as libraries, theaters, meeting halls, dormitories, and classroom lobbies. Our hope was to humanize the environment while introducing the students to art on an intimate level. The collection, which comprises a sizable group of first-rate drawings, sculpture, tapestries, original prints, and photographs, was both ill-cared-for and inadequately used. Some of the finest pieces remained in storage for years. A curiously competitive art department, instead of welcoming the original works as valuable study material, actually set up petty road blocks. Far from cooperating with the acquisition program, it discouraged the activity. To my chagrin, I discovered after five years with the university that most of the graduate art students did not even know the whereabouts of numerous important works. For me, it was like dropping pebbles into a bottomless pit. Distinguished painters- and sculptors-in-residence complained of similar alienation. Students rarely met them. Their names were proudly listed in a promotional folder, but their ideas remained top secret.

It is depressing to look back on the many time-consuming and relatively costly round tables, panel discussions, seminars, and similar powwows recently devoted to art education in America, only to realize how limpingly change comes to obdurate bureaucracies. If we remember nothing else from the Bauhaus, we should at least accept the fact that all learning operations related to creative processes are indivisible. Making art, looking at it, teaching it, investigating its labyrinthine past are varied facets of one integrated experience. For that matter, the fine arts cannot properly be separated from the other arts. Painting, poetry, music, the dance all stem from common roots.

Today, the young art teacher-to-be learns a bit about the techniques of painting, drawing, ceramics, prints, collage, sculpture, weaving, and whatever else seem obligatory. There are also timid stints with art history, methods of teaching (ad nauseam), and art appreciation. The latter, by the way, should be promptly scuttled. Children don't "appreciate" art; hopefully they are involved with and in it. And, to be sure, no smorgasbord of techniques ever compensates for in-depth experience. Every child does not need exposure to multiple materials and methods. Far better that he come in direct contact with one enthusiastic artist who follows no rules but his own. At least then the youngster will acquire some understanding of that excitation we call "the creative process."

Recently, I visited a junior high school where the hesitant young art teacher asked the class to make an abstract design out of primary colors. There didn't seem much rhyme or reason for the assignment, but the children dutifully complied. One boy traced the outline of his hand, then added a sixth finger and painted each finger in a primary color; the result was handsome, but the teacher was dismayed because for her the design was not abstract. Had she, however, been a practicing artist herself, she could not have helped but applaud, nor would she have arbitrarily suggested an abstract design. For though abstractions are very much "in" today, they become empty exercises without some organic *raison d'être*.

What can a child be taught about art? He can be freed to enjoy making it. He can be freed to enjoy seeing it. In art there are no final answers; there are only questions that lead to new ways of understanding. For this reason, when I was teaching summer school a number of years ago at the University of Wisconsin, I stipulated that my course appear in the catalogue as a "Workshop in Looking," realizing that the majority of my students would be teachers and would need such refreshment. But, characteristically, the university willed otherwise. The class was listed as a more acceptable "Survey of Modern Art," though modern art was not its theme.

And while we are on the subject of specific university art classes, it seems inconceivable that such institutions are still dealing with marks and semester hours. How can we grade a young painter's work? Judging from history, often the man most denigrated in his youth becomes the outstanding artist of his period. And the number of hours spent in the studio are also no gauge of ability. Cézanne took months to paint a canvas; van Gogh took minutes. Both, nonetheless, passed most of their waking hours grappling with the problem.

Of course, the knotty question is whether one can be taught to teach art. Surely the greatest teachers in this field have always forged their own methods from their own convictions, and these methods, doubtless, had nothing to do with prescribed ones. Techniques, it is true, can be learned, but where art is concerned it is never techniques that make a teacher. Indeed, they often act as blinders.

I recall a young woman who said she was attending a workshop I was leading in order to learn how to evaluate art qualitatively. This would, I explained, necessitate years of study, travel, and comparative looking. In one short course all we could hope to do was show her how *not* to evaluate, how to withhold judgment. Before any evaluations can take place, one must learn to see, to *see* in terms of immediate surroundings. After discovering a wayward shadow on the wall, a dirty sidewalk, a broken pine cone, a puddle of water, a bird, and after accepting these visual experiences both in and out of context, then perhaps the time has come to face the *Mona Lisa*, to approach this overfamiliar masterpiece with the same sense of discovery. Nor are the woods and sea more absorbing than a ride in the subway, a look through a window, a walk on a crowded street. Here, then, is the crux of the matter. Before any understanding of art can exist, both teacher and student must learn to use their eyes, to look, to take nothing for granted visually.

All we can hope to do, I suppose, is play it by eye. A middle-class suburban school may need different stimuli than a slum school because of local variations, but teachers and children in both can be equally blind. They hear the same dreary art jargon, the same meaningless moral adjectives about nature and beauty. They rarely look; they are inured to listening and being told. In an active New York grade school, the art instructor was demonstrating how to make artificial flowers. The boys, not unexpectedly, were drooping with boredom. Interchange of ideas was strictly *verboten*. Inane soft music acted as a further narcotic. Conversely, a splendid art teacher in the Bowery, who helped the children relate images of trees to their own nervous systems, was in danger of being dropped because she was unable to pass all the proper methodology tests.

One can be taught mathematics; one cannot be taught to see, but one can be encouraged to look. Seeing comes later. It takes ingenuity, compassion, wonder, and self-confidence to open the eyes of a child. It takes more perseverance to open the eyes of an adult, for here so much first must be unlearned. What it does not take, however, is a plethora of words. Seeing in depth is a composite operation that results from all manner of visual comparisons and from nonverbal as well as verbal communications. To draw an acorn after feeling it, and then again after looking at it, is to know an acorn in double dimensions. To observe a familiar tree from a distance, to approach it slowly so that the tree gives way to branches, leaves, and finally to a bit of bark—this is one way of seeing a tree, a way that may appear oversimple but in fact is not. Like a Cubist who represents all aspects of an object, so a photographer might capture the wholeness of a tree through its arbitrarily superimposed parts. It wouldn't be the familiar tree we first saw, or would it?

Why not, then, do away with orthodox art education and substitute in its place practical workshops in looking for all teachers? Why not do away with art teachers as such and substitute in their place artists-in-residence who would act as resource reservoirs for both teachers and students in our grade and secondary schools? Of paramount importance is the inclusion on a part-time basis of creative artists. The present method of full-time art teaching drains even the most gifted enthusiast. Arriving early each morning and rushing from one forty-minute session to another, the instructor rapidly becomes a robot. And as for those forty or fifty minutes a week, it might be better to write them off in the debit column. "Reading, writing, and 'rithmetic" could benefit from a tie-in with the real visual world. After this world is explored, the transition to art is painless, since the two are inseparable.

Recently the federal penitentiary at Leavenworth, Kansas,

presented its Annual Inmate Art Show. Some sixteen hundred paintings were on view. If the forty-four works reproduced in the catalogue were typical, then one cannot but wonder what makes these men tick. There were stiff ballet dancers, banal still-lifes, copies of everything from maudlin religious scenes to Toulouse-Lautrec posters; there were slick landscapes and a curious pervading aura of fake buoyancy, but not one iota of personal expression was evident. We would scarcely expect passionate autobiographical outpourings, yet the prisoners might have been encouraged to *see* their own world, painful as it is, and deal with it, at least on some level that betrayed human involvement. For isn't that what art is all about, about what we know, not about what we are supposed to know?

A single episode haunts me. One of the black teachers in a New York workshop I was leading invited me to spend the day in her Harlem schoolroom. She taught only retarded children. Toward the end of the morning a small boy, nose running and stockings drooping, decided to pummel a little girl. Much wailing ensued. The teacher finally separated the children and sent the boy back to his seat. After a few minutes he escaped into the hall and, despite her gentle urging to return, he remained there where we could hear him repeating endlessly, "I'se in trouble. I'se in trouble." And those were the only words he spoke all day.

24. Mending Damaged Treasures: Florence, 1967

Today the words "preservation" and "restoration" trigger conflicting emotions among art experts. Controversy boils nationally and internationally. Differences of opinion are so intense that the once little-noticed vocation of art conservation is rapidly become a *cause célèbre*.

During the last two decades art curators, conservators, and historians have tended to renounce the nineteenth-century philosophy that often allowed restorations to turn into virtual reconstructions. Now, modern scientific discoveries, analytical equipment, and advanced technology are revolutionizing art conservation. In 1967 the National Gallery of Canada announced a conference in Ottawa focused, as the press release said, on "recent research and scientific solutions to present-day problems of conservation." High on the agenda was a discussion of Florence and its recent catastrophe. After the flood, this city had become a mecca for art experts from Italy, Europe, America, and even from Africa. So it was to Florence I traveled in order to interview foreign and local authorities, to find out what progress had been made since the flood, and, if possible, to clarify the many shades of opinion surrounding modern art conservation.

St. John the Evangelist Resuscitating Drusiana, by Giotto, detail. Left, before removal of nineteenth-century repainting; right, with repainting almost entirely removed.

The terms themselves can be misleading and are too often used indiscriminately. Conservation describes a specialized field including both preservation and restoration, the latter referring to repair after damage, deterioration, or loss has occurred in works of art. It is precisely in this last area that dissension proliferates.

Preservation, as a rule, is concerned with preventive care. Different environments, climates, and materials demand different preservative methods.

Before flying to Florence, I took a brief refresher course in late nineteenth- and early twentieth-century restoration techniques by visiting Crete, where the Englishman Sir Arthur Evans, with single-minded devotion, excavated the labyrinthine (indeed, that's where the word comes from) Palace of Knossos, restoring it with such aplomb as to suggest Hollywood in its heyday. It was not, however, this architectural reconstruction that baffled me; it was the restored frescoes unearthed at Knossos and now on view in Herakleion's nearby Archeological Museum. Because these Minoan paintings were produced almost four thousand years ago, it is small wonder that only the barest fragments remain. Under Sir Arthur's supervision, the frescoes were less restored than reconstructed. What we see is rarely the work of Minoan artists; we see projections of what Sir Arthur and his colleagues, after extensive study, thought the Minoans might have painted. All of which is provocative but perilously fanciful in light of present attitudes. To create complete compositions from nothing more than a few minor details seems extreme even for Sir Arthur's day.

Now the pendulum swings in the opposite direction, at times with such uncompromising integrity as to offend romantic eyes. The over-all tendency is toward less imaginative flights of invention, toward more realistic acceptance of the ravages time exacts. After all, what no longer exists no longer exists. Yet, even today differences of opinion are frequent.

In Florence, I went first to Santa Croce because I had heard conflicting reports about the recently cleaned Giotto frescoes there. Though this church was cruelly damaged by the flood, the Giottos, located in the famous Bardi and Peruzzi Chapels, were well above water level and thus escaped injury. On first encounter, the frescoes, appreciably changed from when last I had seen them, were startling apparitions. For now, with all earlier repaint removed, only the work of Giotto and his associates hold the stage. The slightly sweet nineteenth-century restorations are gone, and in their place one sees large empty gaps resulting from prior losses, but one also sees the strong, unedited hand of a great master. I felt for the first time Giotto's work was presented as it was intended to be and not as later generations have seen fit to interpret it. No one can deny that the original unmarred frescoes would be more satisfying than damaged ones, but neither can the scars of six hundred years be ignored. The Giottos point up methods diametrically opposed to those practiced by Evans in Crete; yet little more than a half century separates these two approaches.

Today the frescoes in Santa Croce arouse as much censure as admiration. Bates Lowry, at that time national executive chairman of CRIA (American Committee to Rescue Italian Art), felt that "there must be a middle ground between the two extremes now practiced in restoration. No one wishes deception by total repainting as was sometimes done in the past, but the practice of no repainting can also be deceptive because the viewer is not able to comprehend the total effect intended by the artist. This is particularly evident with the Giottos in the Bardi and Peruzzi Chapels. Here, even areas of flat blue sky above the spectator's head are left scarred by the scruples of an overly conscientious reaction to past abuses."

Ulrich Middeldorf, director of the Kunsthistorisches Institut in Florence, agreed with Dr. Lowry. He thinks that "ruthless removal of all past restorations is unwise. It may be scientifically interesting," he notes, "but aesthetically intolerable." He prefers retaining a good restoration from the eighteenth or nineteenth century rather than revealing a hole or repainting that hole again. But who, one asks, is to say what constitutes a good restoration? How can we know? What frame of reference permits us to intuit an artist's original intention if he and his associates are no longer around to verify facts? True, other works by him can supply valuable clues, but the best of painters have always been unpredictable. Creativity follows no set rules. Even after the most exhaustive study of an artist and his *oeuvre,* to replace lost areas in his work seems presumptuous to me.

(In this connection I remember once seeing three early drawings by Picasso. The owner wanted my opinion on their authenticity. I found them doubtful and suggested he show them to two experts whose knowledge was considered impeccable. Both men examined the drawings separately and both felt they were spurious. Later we sent photographs of all three to Picasso, who promptly acknowledged them as his own, which merely proves how "presumptuous" it is to chart an artist's course on the sole basis of stylistic evidence.)

In any case, Dr. Middeldorf doubts that the Santa Croce frescoes—"from which," he admits, "everything has been removed that Giotto did not put there"—have meaning for the average person, filled as they are with yawning gaps. "But for the art historian and experienced connoisseur," he adds, "the Giottos are a revelation." Disturbed that paintings might turn into little more than archaeological relics if purists are permitted total latitude, Dr. Middeldorf asks, "Have we become too rigid— too antiquarian during the last two decades?"

And, to be sure, these are pressing questions. In Florence and in many other European cities one frequently finds three separate art audiences—specialists; the general public, including tourists; and religious worshippers, whom we sometimes tend to overlook. Each of these audiences has different needs. I strongly doubt that any single approach to art restoration could satisfy them all. Yet it still seems advisable to rely on the hand of the artist himself and hope that eventually the public with intelligent guidance will come to understand and enjoy works that have suffered unavoidable losses. The fact that many museums in America and Europe lull their visitors with overrestored paintings is no reason why this habit need continue. Not infrequently, the art market offers canvases which, when examined by X ray and ultraviolet lamp, turn out to be distressingly repainted. That museums, aware of these discrepancies, are occasionally willing to acquire such pictures seems more than shortsighted. And one shudders to think of how many private collections are similarly blighted.

The man responsible for Giotto's "new look" in Santa Croce is Leonetto Tintori, a well-known Italian conservator who was heading a team of restorers working on frescoes damaged by the flood. In the Boboli Gardens on one side of the Pitti Palace he had set up a workshop where under his supervision a group of former students were busy cleaning mud and diesel oil from detached frescoes and subsequently transferring these priceless compositions to new supports. Having lunch in that workshop was an unforgettable experience. It is not every day one eats pasta in casual communion with famous masterpieces. There, leaning against the wall, was Andrea del Castagno's haunting mid-fifteenth-century fresco of *St. Jerome with Two Female Saints,* from the Church of the Santissima Annunziata. And nearby was the sinopia, the artist's sketch on the original plaster wall, that had been used by him as a preliminary guide. Now for the first time, thanks to modern scientific methods of preservation, we were figuratively able to go behind the scenes and see how Castagno worked, how and even why he departed from his preliminary design. Striking is the loose, free drawing of the sinopia in contrast to the final fresco with its tightly mannered intensity.

Though Florence's flood was an incalculable disaster, certain unexpected advantages accrued. One was the uncovering of preliminary sketches (the sinopias) and the new insights they provided. Another was the removal of old, dirty restorations. Some works were emerging with fidelity for the first time in many generations. Other gains resulted from new scientific laboratories, improved equipment, and specialized technological assistance, all provided after the flood.

Professor Tintori, who wherever possible is unequivocably opposed to inpainting (retouching the lost areas) or any form of reconstruction, does not try to conceal the weaknesses that time has inflicted. "I feel it's more important to let the original work speak for itself," he said, "despite all the abrasions and scratches that may exist. My major effort is concentrated on preserving what is left of the original. Today, Leonardo's *Last Supper* is the sum of multiple reconstructions carried on over a long period of time. Finally we lose the original and have nothing but a myth."

In Florence's Limonaia, row upon row of wounded panel paintings were still drying, receiving first aid, and awaiting more extensive treatment. This huge greenhouse, which was once devoted entirely to lemon culture (hence its name), was filled with tragedies, for both the wood and pigment of numerous panels had been severely damaged. Some conservators feel that the two materials most vulnerable to water are bone-dry wood and ancient leather. At the Limonaia, the first painting I encountered was Cimabue's *Crucifix*, surely the greatest single art loss Florence suffered in the flood. Little was left, for here Nature had been relentless. In the future, these mutilated remains can hope to act as little more than an archaeological document. Umberto Baldini, who heads conservation at the Uffizi, assured me the Cimabue will be left exactly as it is, for it would be wiser, he felt, to make a copy than to try to reconstruct the original. So this painting will not become a myth. The Limonaia, I hear, is no longer a repository for damaged paintings. And the surviving sections of the Cimabue have miraculously been removed from the wooden cross which still three years later has not completely dried out.

The Limonaia evoked memories of a hospital where seriously ill patients passively await treatment. For conservators, the mere task of setting up priorities was no easy matter. The importance of the painting and the nature of its ailment were, of course, deciding factors. These hundreds of panels, especially the large ones, for some reason seemed curiously defenseless. One felt like an interloper gazing down at works that always before were seen proudly displayed in lofty churches. Now they lay in tiers (no pun intended) undergoing humiliating cures. Some were totally covered with Japanese paper to prevent flaking during the drying-out period. Immediately after the flood, so many reams of this paper were used that the supply gave out and, in desperation, restorers turned to Kleenex. Some works were still undergoing cautious removal of diesel oil and caked mud. On some, conservators were laboriously trying to consolidate tiny pigment fragments that had fallen off but fortunately had been preserved.

When works in the Limonaia were ready for more detailed treatment, trained experts from Germany, England, the Scandinavian countries, the Soviet Union, Poland, Hungary, Switzerland, Holland, Belgium, and the United States joined their Italian colleagues and often remained for long periods of time. Short-term visits were not always advisable, for it can take months to restore a single work. And to change restorers in midstream is dangerous, particularly in a field where differences of opinion are valid and frequent. Take, for instance, the attitude of Louis Pomerantz, a Chicago restorer. For him, conservation boils down to his "own interpretation of what the artist intended." When asked how he compensates for losses in a painting, he replied, "Depending on the area in which loss exists and its size, I either reconstruct the void to the best of my ability so that it matches surrounding areas or I leave the void void. In reconstructing where no interpretation is required I try to follow the painting's continuity. Where major interpretation is required I do not try to reconstruct.''

On the other hand, Lawrence Majewski, chairman of the Conservation Center at New York University, feels differently. He, too, is primarily interested in preserving as nearly as possible the original state of the object and in closely respecting the artist's intention. But where losses have occurred, ''one cannot,'' he says, ''make hard and fast rules because one must consider the purpose of the object, the information we have about it, and the extent of the damage. One should never attempt to reconstruct missing parts.''

Divergence of opinion is more often related to methods of procedure than to over-all aims. How to protect the artist's original conception is the pivotal problem. Since art restoration like psychoanalysis is not an exact science, variations in procedure are inescapable. Most conservators today, however, agree that each object must be considered individually.

Sir Kenneth Clark, English art authority, once said, ''The more nearly a picture can be made to resemble its original condition the better. . . .'' Yet René Huyghe, a French specialist, claims, ''It is . . . idle to expect to restore a picture to its truly original condition.'' Because he finds that time chemically alters color relationships, he disapproves of total cleaning. Instead he advocates retaining a light covering or film from past restorations in order to tie the composition together harmoniously. Like Dr. Middeldorf, René Huyghe deplores the sometimes overcleaned wrecks that hang on our walls, but other experts deplore the overrestored inventions that hang on our walls. So the argument persists.

One thing is certain: Almost all factions today defend the use of advanced scientific aids whenever possible. The Florentines, who, from generation to generation, have acquired remarkable facility in the restoration of frescoes and panel paintings, are not always familiar with the latest technological developments. Realizing this, the Italians, under the auspices of CRIA, welcomed to Florence several American scientist-restorers who were widely experienced in physics, chemistry, or both.

The most far-reaching scientific assistance resulting from the flood saw the establishment of a Conservation Research Center in, of all places, the Palazzo Davanzati—a splendid fourteenth-century Renaissance residence but scarcely an ideal home for a thoroughly modern laboratory. At the time, however, this was the only available space. Later the Italians hoped to integrate the Research Center into new, enlarged and centralized conservation quarters under the supervision of the Uffizi. The Conservation Research Center, alas, is no longer in the Palazzo Davanzati. Most of its functions, now concentrated in a building near the Uffizi, were to be financed by CRIA until the spring of 1970, when the Italian government was to take over, but it now appears no funds are available. Newspaper comments are biting, but the Italian government seems blithely unconcerned.

The morning I visited the Davanzati, American and Italian colleagues were checking a new X-ray diffraction machine lent by CRIA. No greater anachronism can be imagined than this ascetic, efficient mechanism in its ornamental setting. The machine, which any up-to-date laboratory would covet, is concerned with the atomic breakdown of materials. It analyzes every fragment fed into it and then informs the restorer precisely what he is dealing with, thus eliminating considerable guesswork.

A serious problem that developed shortly after the flood concerned critical damage caused by crude oil that swept in on the waters of the Arno. When finally scientists hit on a solution, various marble carvings emerged rejuvenated and often nearer their original state than they had been for generations. Special talc applied to the stone soaked up oil and dirt, yet did not erode the material. For paintings, alas, the oil proved more lethal.

At the Davanzati in a small hermetically sealed room lay Donatello's wood carving of Saint Mary Magdalene, rescued from the battered baptistry. Small experimental areas had been cleaned to reveal successive layers of earlier dark brown repaint. Underneath was evidence of clear flesh tones and gilded hair, both of which may well have been hidden for more than a hundred years. This semi-expressionist, semi-Gothic work dating from the mid-fifteenth century shows the Magdalene, as Vasari noted, "consumed by fasting and abstinence." Coming unexpectedly on the celebrated figure lying on its back was a unique encounter. Rarely does one confront an old master in such unorthodox intimacy, and rarely can one predict its new image so dramatically. For the Magdalene will surely shine with unfamiliar radiance when years of grime and dreary repaint are removed. (Recently a friend who lives in Florence wrote that the Donatello is now "totally cleaned of grime and repaint and looks better than ever! Less like a witch and more like a poor devil. . . .")

The fact that considerable progress was being made in Florence did not hide the staggering hurdles that still remained. New ailments result from new cures. Like people, paintings develop compensatory illnesses. The much-needed heaters going full blast in many churches had drawn out various salts from aged walls, salts which in turn were plaguing numerous frescoes with crippling bubbles and flaking. Wherever possible, conservators tried to tunnel behind the walls so that dryers could operate from the rear and thus not endanger painted surfaces.

Most of the heaters, fed by bottled gas, were gifts from West Germany. The outpouring of help from all parts of the world was heartwarming. Not only were individual countries supporting the expenses of their own specialists, but they were also underwriting specific projects. In the March, 1967, issue of *Harper's* John Fischer wrote, "When floods ravaged Florence and Venice last winter, very few wealthy Italians gave a single lira to rescue their damaged art treasures. They were confident that contributions would flow in from America—as they did." It is true that the United States collected more money than any other country, but both the Germans and the British were proportionately generous.

CRIA and the English sponsored the Conservation Research Center, where volunteers from England, Austria, and Germany worked. CRIA allocated its funds wisely and widely. Firmly opposed to reconstructions, it concentrated on restorations whenever possible. It earmarked help for such varied projects as books, archives, sculpture, paintings, architectural monuments, and frescoes. When one realizes that at least twelve hundred pictures alone were damaged—and untold numbers of valuable books—the job that confronted Florence seemed herculean. Speed was likewise of importance, for the city could not hope to maintain its role as an intellectual center without the full participation of its museums and libraries. Some of Florence's outstanding antiquities were involved. One thinks immediately of the Museo Archeologico, where irreplaceable Etruscan artifacts were hard hit. As Dr. Middledorf aptly put it, "Once these objects were dug out of the ground; now they're being dug out of the mud."

Though the Italian government is now involved with art restorations in Florence and Venice, and though donors from Italy and elsewhere contributed to the Palazzo Vecchio Fund for this purpose, still Mr. Fischer was correct when he said that very few well-to-do Italians offered substantial help. I heard of only one case, that of a rich widow from Milan who re-equipped Professor Tintori's destroyed laboratory and in addition underwrote the restoration of the Ghirlandaios in the Sassetti Chapel. The cities of Milan and Verona supplied funds for special projects. And various important Italian newspapers raised money. But the lack of public help from wealthy individuals is baffling and perhaps is only explained by the country's unfortunate tax system. Italian citizens are, in a sense, punished for being generous. Instead of receiving tax deductions, as is customary in the United States, they are more heavily assessed once their contributions to communal projects are announced.

It was not always easy for the Italians to accept such open-handed aid from other parts of the world. Recalling Egypt's warm gesture of gratitude when that nation offered the Temple of Dendur to the United States in return for American help in saving threatened Nubian monuments, I wondered why the Italians did not consider similar if less lavish symbols of reciprocal good will, particularly for those countries that proved most cooperative. Numerous sinopias are being uncovered. Where will Florence find room for them? The city is already so packed with art that to see even its greatest works, let alone study them, requires a lifetime. In 1968 the Italian government lent a magnificent group of restored frescoes, often with their sinopias, to New York's Metropolitan Museum. The exhibition, made possible by the generosity of Olivetti, was subsequently seen in Amsterdam and London, and presumably was organized as a grateful gesture.

During the days I spent in Florence, the two most unsettling sights were the scarred Cimabue and the lacerated National Library (Biblioteca Nazionale Centrale). Though here archives and catalogues were ruined beyond words, it is good to report that the photographic archives at the Uffizi, contrary to earlier reports, were largely saved.

In the Library, a sense of the overwhelming work still to be done swamped the imagination. Every page of every soaked book, manuscript, and periodical demanded separate processing. A million and a quarter wet volumes in the Biblioteca Nazionale alone needed attention. And nearly fifty smaller, often specialized libraries were also affected, bringing the total number of damaged books close to two million.

At the National Library I was shepherded around by a young Ghanaian, Joe Nkrumah, who, originally trained in Rome, Brussels, and London, planned to return to Accra and work there at the National Museum. He in turn introduced me to an English team of book restorers, a group that was providing inestimable technical assistance. In fact, the British considered the Biblioteca Nazionale their major project in Florence.

At the time of my visit, the British team included four experts; earlier there had been as many as fifteen. Peter Walters, leader of the group, reported that some sixty thousand to eighty thousand rare volumes, dated between 1500 and 1820, represented source material of such extreme importance that they were receiving first attention. Most of them, he felt, could be saved, but the process would be long, arduous, and costly. Rumor has it that the restoration of this library (the largest in Italy) demands approximately the same amount of money required to build twelve kilometers of a superhighway, a comparison that should melt even the most obdurate bureaucrat. I heard of only one library that was totally destroyed, a collection devoted exclusively to books on Etruscan art.

The endless steps connected with the restoration of a single volume are stupefying. Shortly after the disaster, in order to absorb as much moisture as possible, good old-fashioned sawdust was lavishly sprinkled on, under, and even in wet books, which later were interleaved several times with absorbent paper to facilitate drying and to prevent pages from sticking together. Innumerable other treatments included hand vacuuming, sterilizing, applying fungicides to protect the surface of paper, washing each book section by section, mending, sewing, binding—to say nothing of combating constant ominous molds. The variety of these growths was as numerous as their hues were iridescent. In Florence, new circumstances produced new molds. All the old familiar ones were there, but so also were a plethora of unknown ones. Paradoxically the same mud that punished the paintings protected the books. At times, caked mud prevented diesel oil from infiltrating. If one doubts the practical advantages of modern technology, a visit to the Biblioteca Nazionale will dispel such uncertainties. Nowhere have I encountered a more cogent argument for the value of microfilm than in this gravely menaced library.

The flood has now joined other historic events in the life of Florence. Small metal tabs commemorate date and water levels. To the resilience of the Italian people much credit is due, for the city once again blooms with confidence. And its art, damaged but indomitable, still remains the Renaissance's finest hour.

In 1970 the English are still working at the National Library, which they hope eventually to turn into an International Center for Book Conservation.

Italy is now faced with additional menaces. Venice is sinking, and unless that city is rescued soon, there won't be much left to rescue. An American committee is zealously soliciting funds and organizing restoration procedures, but until the Italians themselves take charge, the future looks bleak. Obviously they need help. No one country, and least of all a relatively small one, can afford to preserve such an array of endangered treasures. The

Leaning Tower of Pisa alone will take two years and $5 million to repair. The tower, about fourteen feet off center, each year sags more perilously.

Most depressing is the news that nothing serious is being done to protect Florence from possible future floods. Almost every month an outcry in the press falls on deaf ears.

25. *New Breeds in Art*

Art is spawning curious new breeds that often adopt familiar labels no longer related to their original meanings. Take the word "research," for instance. Not so many years ago art historians dedicated to research spent long hours in museums and libraries ferreting out secrets about specific artists, periods, or objects. Such students traveled widely, read source material in original languages, sat at the feet of renowned scholars, and followed each lead with breathless attention. Indeed, they became so immersed that at times, lost in dates, dogma, and details, they all but forgot about art.

The scene is changing rapidly. Scarcely a week goes by that some pleasant young man or woman fresh out of college and armed with nothing more than an undergraduate degree and a major in art history complacently offers his or her services as a research assistant. The expression now substitutes for an inefficient secretary who has a yen for "Art," no knowledge of dictation, and a term paper or two as credentials. The dictionary describes research as a "careful, systematic, patient study and investigation in some field of knowledge. . . ." Today the words "careful," "systematic," "patient," "study," "investigation," and "knowledge" are gone. What remains is merely "in some field," and this field is fast becoming a happy hunting ground for any well-intentioned neophyte who identifies art with romance and research with condensed references in an encyclopedia.

The awesome title "curator" is also in danger. Museums still try to retain a degree of professionalism where this once prestigious word is concerned, but many newly arrived private collectors are installing dulcet-voiced young ladies as their art babysitters. They call these glorified secretaries curators. For those who once struggled through graduate school, through years of humble museum apprenticeships, such effortless recognition is unnerving. Formerly, a curator was supposed "to take care of" art, a responsibility demanding special training, since not even prima donnas are more temperamental than paintings and sculpture. Pigments crack, bronze casts multiply, canvases disintegrate, prices change, authentications vary, provenances are elusive, watercolors fade, and fakes are always with us. In medicine and other sciences, misleading professional titles are suspect; in art anything goes today, even instant curators.

Another new gimmick is providing short cuts to college degrees even at the doctoral level. University students specializing in the fine arts have come up with a painless method for producing ready-made theses. They simply blitz art critics with questionnaires so designed as to avoid any future work for themselves. First comes the bootlicking letter, obviously mimeographed for wide distribution, urging the critic (always the student's favorite writer) to document his opinions fully so that his words may act as a major contribution in an important research project. Herewith a few typical questions: "What is your opinion of modern art? What has it contributed to the life of our times? How would you characterize Surrealism? What do you recommend as a good bibliography on Expressionism? What is the basic influence of Japanese prints on modern art?" Because these requests are multiplying and, let me add, growing more banal daily, I have been forced to mimeograph a standard reply. It reads, "How about doing your own work?"

Perhaps the most astonishing new art breed is the bidder at

auction sales. For years this once anonymous personality hid behind his monocle, his handkerchief, or his agent. His face was unknown to the public. He felt, and rightly, that he could make the best possible financial deal by bidding secretly, by not letting on that he, a concerned collector, was vitally interested in a particular work. There is little doubt that the best bargains acquired at public auction were usually engineered discreetly. Today, it would seem the aim is less to buy advantageously than to make news, to be seen, to be televised, and to be generously described in the press. Now private bidders resemble actors. They arrive at the sale dramatically; they wave, bow, and even pose for photographers. In fact, the auction house has become a top public relations stage, and, as a result, an arena for ever-accelerating prices.

If we have instant curators these days, we also have mini-patinas. The latter reach us mostly from France, where foundries are turning out a stream of posthumous bronzes by distinguished sculptors who are, alas, no longer around to object. And they most certainly would. For to see familiar masterpieces by Rodin, Daumier, and Bourdelle, their surfaces sprayed with paint and further vulgarized by varnish, is distressing. When the demand for art was still rational, casters in bronze considered themselves skilled artisans. Because they were not rushed, they took time to polish and work over each piece until the surface of the metal acquired a life of its own. And often they were fortunate enough to have the full cooperation of the sculptor himself. For craftsman and artist alike, the integrity of the patina was paramount. To obscure the metal's surface with paint and varnish was little less than sinful. But now avid and inexperienced collectors accept shoddy mini-patinas, produced hastily to satisfy a frenetic market. Our message to the buyer is be wary, be informed, and be adamant.

From Europe comes another novelty, this time from London. Last year I spent a few weeks in that city and visited some fifty galleries, many of them dealing in old masters. Heretofore, the prospective customer was regaled with impressive facts about the past owners of a given work and, of course, about the illustrious artist who created it. As impeccable pedigrees and names of fame become less and less available, new ploys are invented. We no longer hear that "this canvas by the immortal Titian belonged for two centuries to the family of Lord So-and-so," but rather that "this fascinating composition by a little-known, seventeenth-century artist's artist is in mint condition and is enhanced by a peerless period frame." Dealers begin to scrape the bottom of the barrel when frames become a lure. And as for that "mint condition," it sometimes seemed too minty, almost as if an agile modern chef had freshened up the sauce.

The living artist himself is often a new breed, a man harassed by income taxes and by his own ubiquitous image. He suffers from an updated kind of exposure—not from cold and hunger but from sudden adulation and equally sudden neglect. In less than a decade he can skid from affluence to poverty, from stardom to abrupt oblivion. Gnawing fear is a concomitant of his life. For him success is a new kind of torture, an ephemeral insecure illusion that may vanish overnight. Today, accountants and lawyers are the prosperous artist's advisers, the former for tips on taxes, the latter for counsel on complicated lawsuits, usually directed against dealers. Time was when galleries exploited artists by purchasing their works at sub-bargain prices. Now artists are busy suing dealers and often paying their lawyers with valuable paintings. Dealers tended to gamble on unknowns, but attorneys are more cautious. They rarely represent a man who has not arrived. Galleries and artists no longer maintain stable relationships; they shop around for one another at a dizzying pace. No one counts on even a modicum of permanence—a dilemma which finally takes its toll in nerve-wrenching anxieties.

Last but not least baneful in the new hierarchy is a modern coalition between critic, artist, and dealer. What does this mean? It means that John Doe, influential writer on present-day art, publishes a number of laudatory articles on an artist he admires, touting him as the master of all masters, whereupon certain dealers in America and abroad rush to show this man's work. But what perhaps is not so clear is the business relationship between John Doe, the dealers, and the artist in question. What are we to believe if critics, who are theoretically impartial, join organized combines that demand not their business acumen alone but the virtuosity of their pens? The critic thus assumes a dubious role behind the scenes; he turns into a manipulator of public taste who himself materially benefits from his own words more as entrepreneur than as writer. That such an unannounced Janus figure wields power is indisputable.

If the boundaries dividing painting and sculpture are no longer visible, neither are the boundaries defining other peripheries of art. Critics become businessmen who, as advisers to artists and dealers, emerge as leading personalities in an already overpersonalized field. The scene is absorbing, cynical, and open to any taker. Euphemistically we might call it exciting; realistically we must call it depressing. Again the final watchword is—beware.

26. *Denials and Affirmations*

Can it be that the brutalities, ambiguities, and bitter frustrations of contemporary life are triggering a cool and bloodless art? We find prolific evidence in such current trends as the Constructionist, Post-Painterly, Hard-Edge, Abstract-Concrete, Synthesist, Systemic, Reductionist, Primary, and Minimal schools. Never mind the labels; they multiply with each new exhibition. But the fact remains that art today is often pared down to rigorously elementary forms and to an all but anonymous impersonality. This phenomenon was brought home to me forcibly last month when I happened to visit a Barnett Newman show immediately after a long de Kooning confrontation.

Though these two men are contemporaries, they reflect a troubled world with drastically opposed means. De Kooning mirrors the frenzy of life today; Newman reacts against this frenzy with rational restraints and serene authority. One man produces heavy, dense, measured canvases where strict economy adds up to an aggressive unyielding presence; the other creates frayed, knotted, nervous, and evasively anxious images which interact in a multiple shifting kaleidoscope. Some art historians feel the great European classical tradition ended with de Kooning while the true American avant-garde began with Newman. This is perhaps an overeasy assumption. In any given period there have always been dichotomies based on the art that submits to overwhelming forces and the one that escapes from these forces.

When Mondrian was creating pure space with pure color, the Surrealists were excavating their own involuntary urges. While Cézanne was deploying formal elements to achieve the finality of permanence, van Gogh was shredding these elements in a blast of self-revelation. Go back earlier if you wish. Ingres and Delacroix lived at the same time in the same country but worked at diametrically different eye levels, as, for that matter, did such contemporaries as Michelangelo and Raphael. The art historian Max Friedländer once wrote, "Among the great masters some are like fighters, others like victors." He listed Michelangelo as fighter, Raphael as victor. When Cézanne said, "I am the primitive of my way," he implied, no doubt, that he was battering down past traditions in his fight for what we now call "the new vision." And, to be sure, every period has its own new vision. Otherwise there would be no history. Painters like Derain and Vlaminck, who came after Cézanne and inherited his findings, sweetened and diluted the master's hard-hoed truths until their works became little more than popular pastiches, if highly accomplished ones.

This is not to say that either de Kooning or Newman is a victor, despite their late but bountiful public recognition. Yet, during the last decade it is Newman whose influence pervades "the scene." In the fifties, it was de Kooning, Pollock, Kline—men who relied on their own uninhibited drives. Today the younger artists see in Newman's vast simplified color areas a degree of reality they can respect. These paintings, they feel, are not involved with any form of symbolism or personal identification; they are based on color and they *are* color—nothing more, nothing less. With certain Newman followers, this idea is carried so far as to limit an entire canvas to only blue or red or yellow. For them, the amount of color and the color itself are all that count. Even in the nineteenth century, Gauguin, reacting against impressionistic breakup, claimed that a meter of green was greener than a centimeter.

Yet bigness can dilute as well as intensify. Gigantic paintings from nineteenth-century Russia and Poland are often little more than pretentious history lessons. In present-day America, enormity can be equally sterile. Unless these vast areas of color crowding our museum walls are more than vast areas of color, they fast become superfluous. I find large second-rate paintings more reprehensible than small ones, for the latter are easier to store. Is it possible these yards of monolithic color are a direct result of our common yearning for clean, pure, uncluttered surroundings? Is our chaste new art a reaction against urban blight? If so, minimal structures, for all their pride in self-identification, end up as the same old escapism we have always known. Yet, to burden Newman with all his followers is hardly fair. He deals with more than color.

His paintings at best are evocations of burgeoning space gashed by deep vertical cleavages. But his canvases are also tributes to the power of sheer color. In America, where urban elbow room is dwindling daily, where ten thousand people work in one building, where the clutter of visual and physical life is almost unbearable, where noise, confusion, and pollution are omnipresent, an art of denial is both welcome and salutary. The aim is no longer to distill our surroundings but to vaporize them. This is not a new idea. When Malevich painted *White on White* during 1918 in Russia, that country had been caught up in war, destruction, and revolution for several years. His uncompromising composition of one white square tilted on a white canvas represented for him "the supremacy of pure feeling." Thus did he geometrically and philosophically obliterate surrounding complexities.

Newman's paintings, unlike those of numerous disciples, are not denials alone; they are affirmative reorganizations. He combines real color with the illusion of space, relying always on scale and degree. Size and intensity are his tools, and not infrequently the latter is the result of the former. Though Newman's work differs totally from Mondrian's in intention and appearance, when their paintings are seen together in reduced black-

and-white reproduction, it is similarities that obtrude. Yet there is no basic connection between these men unless it is their joint insistence on the elimination of all naturalistic allusions and their emphasis on starkly controlled organizations. Mondrian depended only on severe line and pure color. In Newman's work, line as such ceases to exist. Instead, a long palpitating brush-stroke splits color into vibrant activity.

Mondrian was after "a new esthetic based on relationships of lines and pure colors, because," said he, "only the pure rela-tionships of constructive elements can lead to pure beauty." But for Newman, beauty is irrelevant. As early as 1948 he wrote in *Tiger's Eye:* "The invention of beauty by the Greeks . . . has been the bugbear of European art and European esthetic phi-losophies." Eliminating "memory, association, nostalgia, legend, myth," he hopes through art to evoke "a new way of experienc-ing life." In his stringent denial of all irrelevancies, it is not purity he seeks, but intensity. Both Mondrian and Newman, and for that matter Malevich, too, deal with a kind of metaphysical morality, with the underlying ethics of art. And this morality is involved with what they consider reality—not realism but reality.

Who is to say which artist is the more potent social commen-tator, the one who squarely confronts the tangle of life or the one who rejects it? Both stem from the same roots. But surely the only painters who survive must irrevocably pursue their in-dividual convictions rather than hand-me-down stereotypes. De Kooning's early fury when his own influence was not yet haunt-ing him and Newman's awkward experiments in minimal op-timism reach us with authentic impact. Too often the works of their followers do not. Validity is sometimes impaired because, though art can grow from art, it grows best from personal dis-covery.

Again to quote Friedländer, who found van Gogh "a genius without talent," I would suppose most artists have talent with-out genius. They are apt to follow the lead blindly if correctly, not only because following can be easy and profitable but also because it can represent the limit of their ability. These men, then, are the minor victors, the losing ones in the end. Still we need them as norms to judge by, as aids in our long journey from peak to peak. Lesser artists have their place both for the valid periphery experiences they provide and for the helpful padding they give to history. True, these men do not make history; they embroider it. Through them we come to understand more fully the artists they emulate.

I would imagine that soon the pendulum will swing again. It vibrates rapidly these days. Shortly all those stripes of bright color seemingly painted by the same hand and all those endless minimal structures seemingly turned out by the same machine will give way to the reign of another ''new vision.'' Who knows —minimal may now swerve to maximal. It is rarely the school but more likely the man who finally launches a transformation, yet the school cannot be written off. It ends up as a revealing résumé.

27. *Maturity and a Touch of Madness*

I can remember when the German Expressionists fired my blood. I looked on their acid color and warped forms as exciting emotional catharses. Their violence attracted me, but recently, after seeing a large group of their paintings, I find my enthusiasm ebbing. The years have not always dealt kindly with this school. What I originally mistook for passion now sometimes seems closer to overwrought posturing. Many of the distortions I once regarded as brave social comments impress me today as "modernistic" clichés.

Though it is dangerous to generalize about an entire movement, one cannot help wondering why so much of German Expressionism begins to look tarnished. Possibly our present cool attitude toward art makes us renounce all stark emotionalism. German Expressionism, so-called because it blossomed in that country during the teens and twenties, differed from similar movements elsewhere in degree and in its emphasis on romantic conventions, especially those abrasive deformations that were often superfluous structurally and psychologically. Expressionist artists deliberately took liberties with nature in order to "express" deep-seated feelings about a chaotic world instead of directly portraying that world, but at times their feelings seem scarcely deep-seated enough to justify the liberties. Several outstanding members of the group, however, were not misled by stereotypes. Such men as Corinth, Beckmann, Kirchner, Kokoschka, and Munch invented corollary forms that parallel their passions.

Exhibitions can clue us in on new ideas or encourage reappraisals of old ones. Seventy-three twentieth-century northern European paintings from the Morton May collection shown in New York offered an excellent opportunity to evaluate this school in present-day terms. All the right German names were there: Pechstein, Heckel, Hofer, Schmidt-Rottluff, Kirchner, Marc, Mueller, Nolde, Macke, and, of course, Beckmann—the last with by far the largest representation, too many paintings I felt for such an aggressive assault in comparatively crowded quarters. Mr. May, who lives in St. Louis, came to know Beckmann when the artist left Nazi Germany to settle in St. Louis and teach at Washington University. The Beckmann group overshadowed the rest of the show, partly because of sheer numbers, partly because of undoubted power, and partly because of an ambivalent brutality that characterizes much of the work.

Vacillating between semireligious adumbrations and censorious indictments, Beckmann's message sometimes is weakened by overstatement. With him everything is emphatic and final, yet at the same time ambiguous. His paintings, solidly constructed and vertically oriented, are so carefully composed as to seem inevitable. One feels they had to be the way they are. Deliberately compressing his figures and objects into overcrowded spaces, he created an aura of anxiety, almost as if his enlarged forms were trying to break out of invisible chains.

Devotees of Beckmann, and they are legion, discuss his work in terms of esoteric meanings. That his symbolism related closely to the disillusionments sparked by both world wars is clear. For that matter, most German Expressionism was directly related to catastrophic political and social events of our century. Beckmann's contorted figures, especially those in his triptychs, resemble actors performing ritualistically in agonizing morality plays, but plays that somehow elude us today. Grünewald, who

was born five hundred years ago, seems closer to us than Beck-
man, possibly because the earlier artist was ushering in the
Renaissance, while the twentieth-century one was looking back
to the Middle Ages and specifically to those awkward medieval
German prints that are among history's most portentous works
of art. Whereas Rouault, the celebrated French Expressionist,
was indebted to the sonorous stained-glass windows and stone
carvings of medieval France, the Germans reverted to their own
heritage and especially to the unmitigated vigor of Northern
Romanesque and Gothic images. Early German art, preoccupied
as it was with cruelty, dripping blood, and sadism, graphically
foretold Northern Expressionism and also the horrors of modern
concentration camps.

For me, Beckmann excels as a portrait painter, surely one of
the greatest our century has produced. His self-images are stark
comments on a troubled world. Here he had no need of obscure
symbolism or medievalism, for in personifying his own stiff
body, bullet-like head, and eloquent hands he required only himself to expose the suppressed tensions of an entire age. Beckmann's invectives were not muted during his years in America,
though his German colleague George Grosz lowered his voice
under similar circumstances and in so doing impoverished his
art. With Beckmann there was no diminution of power. He was
at his peak when he died in 1950, the year he painted *Self-Portrait in Blue Jacket,* a canvas in the May collection that ranks
with his best.

German Expressionism was fertilized by two non-Germans,
the Norwegian Edvard Munch and the Austrian Oskar Kokoschka. If the May collection is long on Beckmann, it is short on
these two precursors, for Munch is not represented at all and
Kokoschka with only three canvases. Of the seventy-three paintings on view, I found Kokoschka's 1924 *The Painter (Artist
and Model II)* the star. In this hallucinated double self-portrait
the artist sees himself as a cross between a cadaver and a sculpture hacked from some nameless material. He even initialed his
bare body with the familiar OK signature. Near him lurks a
woman, possibly the ubiquitous Alma Mahler, whose overwhelming personality haunted Kokoschka for years, even after their

love affair ended. He was an artist genuinely obsessed, whereas most German Expressionists were merely trying to be. Unlike Beckmann, Kokoschka did not concern himself with the age-old opposition of good and evil; he was too involved with himself and with the anomalous compulsions that dominate all human activity. He was less missionary than visionary.

The Painter (Artist and Model II), by Oskar Kokoschka

In comparison, Nolde seems naïve today. His oil paintings, with none of the fluid spontaneity of his watercolors, are luridly romantic. One senses that he was after savage emotions, but what he produced was often little more than sentimentality. Despite strident color, his pigment has a sticky, almost gooey quality like the primitive finger paintings of children. And yet this artist was not without force, which is more than can be said of such associates as Pechstein, Mueller, Heckel, Hofer, and

Schmidt-Rottluff. Occasionally, it is true, these men successfully manipulated dissonant color surprises to communicate the intensity of their feelings, but taken by and large, they adhered to most of the orthodox rules, and this despite their deceptively jazzed-up surfaces and misshapen figures. At heart, they remained academic; they only *seemed* to break the rules.

If their work appears dated, that of the French Fauves, who antedated and strongly influenced them, remains relatively timeless. Even lesser artists like Vlaminck and Derain produced vibrant, biting paintings in their Fauve days, paintings that never allowed emotions to overwhelm structure. Fauve color was as discordant, Fauve line as tough as that of the Expressionists, but the Fauves, for all their "wildness," insisted on discipline. With them, exaggerations of color and line created a new kind of flattened space and a new kind of magnified presence. In their work everything seems nearer, fresher, more immediately at hand. We are there participating, not at second hand through the artist's emotions but through our own. The Fauves shared the German Expressionists' desire to shock the viewer, to give him new eyes, to free him from the monotony of naturalistic appearances, yet they were never possessed by the methods they used. The Expressionists often were. And the Fauves, too, were less introspective. The outside world concerned them more than involvement with their attitudes toward it.

A few Expressionists, to be sure, were not intoxicated by their own rhetoric. Kirchner in his early years and Corinth later made paintings that still come through to us with magnetic energy. Corinth's feeble (and too early) representation in the May collection gives little evidence of his eventual brilliance. His mordant introspective portraits and Kirchner's fierce early scenes epitomize the best of Expressionism. These paintings do not "express" simple emotional reactions; they dig deeper to penetrate recalcitrant layers of experience where sensations are too conflicting to be easily categorized. For, after all, what is Expressionism (German or otherwise) if not an attempt to divulge the inner workings of a man's personal relationship to his particular world? Artists of this group addressed themselves more to the feel than to the look of things, if indeed the two can be divided.

The undeniable master of the school was the Norwegian painter Edvard Munch, who relentlessly identified his own fevered nightmares with the cold, threatening landscape of the north. No one was better able to make outward appearances correspond to personal excesses and yet retain a rational stance. His portraits, often rigid, are filled with nervous turmoil, his frigid landscapes with untold terror. For him, outside and inside became one. The line was tenuous, but it held.

Almost always the most successful Northern Expressionists were admirable draftsmen, although we tend to associate them more with color than with line. Munch, Beckmann, Corinth, Kokoschka, and Kirchner are distinguished as much for their drawings and prints as for their paintings. Each of them made line a personal form of calligraphy and frequently a virulent one. Beckmann and Kirchner slashed wide and deep, Corinth and Kokoschka concentrated on trembling evasive illusions, and Munch's line was as cold and decisive as his color. At their best, these men never capitulated to the amorphous emotions that often vitiate orthodox Expressionism.

Expressionism is hardly a new idea. Though unlabeled until this century, the movement has been with us for a long time. Hellenistic sculpture, paintings by Grünewald, Rembrandt, El Greco, and van Gogh all qualify for the title. If an artist lives long enough, he frequently turns to Expressionism, possibly as an antidote for old age but more likely because he has at last found security. With technical problems solved, he can afford to turn inward. Titian, Turner, Cézanne, Monet, and Degas all allowed themselves greater freedom as they grew older. Brushstrokes were looser, color moodier, light inscrutable, and focus more interior. To be an authentic Expressionist, regardless of period, demands maturity plus a touch of madness.

28. Buying and a Sense of History

The art market is steeply inflated these days, but there are still excellent works that can be bought for considerably less than a king's ransom. This does not mean merely tracking down out-of-fashion oddities; it presupposes the ability to evaluate history so that the entire spectrum of art becomes a continuing experience rather than an episodic one. Only then can individual works from all times and places be judged comparatively. To be frozen into any one period, whether past or present, is as stifling in the fine arts as it is in music or literature. The whole world of man's creativity from prehistoric times until today is open for the taking. I do not deny that art of the present is closest to us and demands our serious attention, but surely not our exclusive attention.

Why certain sculpture and paintings are currently out of favor is a question worth investigating, for what we neglect is as revealing as what we pursue. Any number of causes can elevate art prices. It is not just supply and demand that determine what we pay. Jazzed-up promotions, earlier influences that either parallel or predict current moods, novelties that titillate, art as an investment, the collector's personal prestige, tax considerations—all can influence prices. In addition, there are people who simply buy what they like or what looks best in their homes. Finally, however, it is quality that counts. Just what quality means is anyone's guess; perhaps it is the magic imponderable that makes for staying power.

This article is not intended as a practical manual for the young collector, or for the older, better-heeled one either. The acquisition of art by the unwary and, indeed, by the wary is full of pitfalls. Even blue-chip names can discolor. Two don'ts, however, might alleviate a few perils. First: Don't buy art as an investment. It's not that viable. Precisely when you want to convert a work into cash, the market for it may have temporarily or permanently evaporated. At the risk of seeming a pseudomystic, I am convinced that paintings languish, fade, disintegrate, when relegated too long to safety-deposit vaults. Like people, art needs attention and affection. Then, too, there's something repugnant about viewing art as a purely monetary commodity; it was never intended to double for stocks and bonds, even though there are moments when it outshines them economically.

In the end and despite recently organized art-investment combines, I feel the whole idea will boomerang, if only because well-trained experts refuse (let us hope) to cooperate. Without benefit of specialized knowledge and wide experience, the most ambitious investment houses are apt to lose their cool when confronted by questions of authenticity and quality. And the second don't: Never buy art as decorations to fill empty walls or to add that "dash of color." Any painting worth its salt has too strong an identity to accommodate such simple-minded demands.

One acquires art differently for different institutions. In museums, it is sometimes those very areas already best represented that determine acquisition policies, for well-selected concentrations can make more sense than thin historical surveys. Museum curators buy in relation both to strengths *and* to weaknesses; they fill gaps and they broaden specialized collections. Universities have other needs, chiefly those of their students. Ideally, a university gallery provides art for study purposes and for the enlightenment of the entire academic community. In corporate institutions, in banks, hotels, stores, and other business establishments, art plays a humanizing role. It can civilize forbidding surroundings and give pleasure to employees, visitors, and clients. I see no reason why these institutions need limit themselves to contemporary works, as so many do. A broader visual base makes for broader participation. Specially privileged, however, is the private collector who buys solely for himself and who is restricted only by funds, space, taste, and knowledge.

Today, the objects most pursued, not unexpectedly, are the most inflated. I think, for example, of the French Impressionists. Shortly before these men crystallized their own style, several lesser-known artists, such as Gustave Doré, Georges Michel, and Eugène Isabey, antedated them in France. Too romantic for modern tastes, the earlier painters were nonetheless highly accomplished. Yet, a fine picture by one of them often brings considerably less than one-hundredth the sum lately paid for a Renoir. Recently a prophetic exhibition in New York featured neglected French painters of the nineteenth century. In addition to the three men mentioned above, the show included such names as Théodule Ribot, James Tissot, Antoine Vollon, Gaston Latouche, and Jean François Raffaelli. There is no doubt that several of these artists already occupy assured slots in history, though they are still not "in" as far as public popularity is concerned. One need only refer to the luminous landscapes of Doré and Isabey to realize how much both men foretold Impressionism. It is absurd to think that distinguished oils by Doré sell for less than feeble pencil scratches by some of our here-today gone-tomorrow idols.

And for that matter much of contemporary art is overpriced. Lest we appear "old-hat" for boycotting the "new" (shades of the late nineteenth century), we are apt to embrace the present with permissive indulgence. At times astronomical figures are justified when artists emerge as indisputable giants, but this is hardly a daily occurrence. Too often plush prices result from artificial publicity and overcredulous purchasers, though many unknown painters and sculptors languish in undeserved anonymity.

If one cannot glibly generalize about the current scene, one can about earlier American art, which is escalating out of all reason. I question whether the exalted six figures attached to certain nineteenth-century native paintings can endure. If supply is the answer, then they can, but if comparative quality is, then they cannot, for, although these works have a fenced-in American audience, someday they must be judged in relation to their European contemporaries. At present, they have little meaning and no market abroad. After all, it was not painting in the United States that changed the course of nineteenth-century art; it was painting in France and, to a lesser degree, in England.

Other works with sharply and sometimes irrationally rising prices are original prints, whether lithographs, linoleum cuts, etchings, engravings, or woodcuts. The thousands of dollars paid for certain modern graphics, as well as the soaring price level for the entire medium, seem unreasonable to me. Prints were originally intended for a large audience, which is why they were produced in multiple issues, but recently the emphasis on small editions and on the preciousness of individual examples is subverting the *raison d'être* of printmaking. Graphics in many cases are becoming more costly than original drawings. The latter, by the way, are among the best buys available today, and this includes a variety of drawings from a wide chronological range. Those with world-famous names attached are the expensive exceptions, though even here an occasional windfall is possible. I know of a fine Giandomenico Tiepolo that was acquired a few months ago for half the cost of an Oldenburg drawing or for the same price as one by Ellsworth Kelly. And last winter several large pencil studies by John Singer Sargent went for less than various signed reproductions pawned off as original prints.

Just as certain precursors of Impressionism were too romantic for present consumption, so drawings are perhaps too intimate and often too small. Art is going public these days: It is big, brassy, and basically architectural. Drawings are the opposite: introspective, tentative at times, and always best when frankly personal. In addition, they are frequently limited to black and white, which may explain why contemporary prints are more popular. With their strong emphasis on color and size, graphics decorate a wall; they come out to meet you, whereas drawings recede, almost demanding to be tracked down.

Yet, drawings rarely present the tricky problems that plague the print market. One need not worry about restrikes, about reproductions being pawned off as originals, about falsely numbered editions, about lack of supervision by the artist. And while we are on the subject, the whole gamut of silk-screen prints bears careful reclassification. Drawings, on the contrary, are unique statements that provide valuable clues to the artist's working processes. Over the years some of the most knowledgeable collectors in history, notably the English, have concentrated in this field.

London currently offers the best hunting for good out-of-fashion paintings. Here one can encounter excellent seventeenth-century still-lifes by reputable if not always famous artists from France (rare), Holland, Belgium, Spain, England, and Italy, the last particularly well represented by Naples. Still-lifes of fruit and flowers are in great demand, but compositions of animal, fish, and "vanitas" themes are available at relatively modest sums and frequently surpass in intensity the blander, more popular subjects. One can acquire sober, beautifully painted seventeenth-century English still-lifes of inanimate objects (books, pipes, and table ornaments) by respected artists for a fraction of what similar subjects by certain late-nineteenth-century American trompe l'oeil painters bring—an illogical situation if the works are dispassionately compared.

Another field still underpriced is Far Eastern Indian sculpture, much of which is perhaps too intricately symbolic for contemporary Western audiences, who prefer a more immediate attack. We like to be shocked into seeing. The Indian artist with his complex hierarchy of sophisticated gestures persuades us to see. And yet he is franker about life and love than we are, although he adheres to ceremonial procedures that must be decoded to be understood.

Different ages respond to different stimuli. Where art is concerned, the wise buyer will go beyond the obvious favorites of his own time and country to consider less thoroughly exploited periods. As for museums, wealthy ones that acquire million-dollar treasures are fortunate but not always as astute as smaller galleries that at times lead the way by recognizing the importance of neglected works. Some years ago, the art museum at Oberlin College purchased most expeditiously a major painting by Hendrick Ter Brugghen. The artist was then little accepted in America, but now this northern follower of Caravaggio is highly prized, and museums throughout the country openly compete for his work. It is ludicrous that institutions and collectors receive more acclaim for paying exorbitant prices than for acquiring "good buys." To obtain a top work of art advantageously requires expertise, temerity, and a sense of history. Sometimes a modest budget is a benefit. It forces us to operate underground where uncovering hidden treasures is one of the few adventures left in the cynical world of art.

Over the years I have bought art for many institutions—for an important museum, for a Midwestern university, for a large bank and its international branches, for an occasional private collector, and, in a very modest way, for myself. Each experience has been different and has demanded a different approach. But always there remains the delight of buying, the almost fanatical game that ends up not necessarily in personal possession but in tracking down elusive works, in studying and acquiring them, and finally in seeing them installed (one hopes not in vain) for other people's pleasure. I am convinced that given some knowledge, one learns more about art from intelligent buying than from any other activity. For those addicted to this pursuit, it can be endlessly engrossing, entailing as it does research, sleuthing, travel, and all kinds of unexpected encounters.

Years ago, for example, when I was a curator at the Art Institute of Chicago, I saw a huge unstretched early canvas by Picabia in a Paris gallery. I wanted that picture with all my heart. Already visualizing where we would hang it, I cabled the museum but got no go-ahead. A year or two later, the artist Fritz Glarner wrote me to say the painting was installed in his New York studio, still for sale but now double the earlier price (and well worth it). I continued to yearn for the canvas, so I went to see it again and found it more exciting than on my first encounter, but still no O.K. from the Art Institute. Years passed. By this time I'd given up all thought of the Picabia

when miraculously out of the blue the picture once more crossed
my path. While I was assembling a retrospective Léger exhibition I visited various private collections in Europe and America.
Among them was a New York architect whose name was unfamiliar to me but who was reputed to have an interesting
group of Légers, several of which he agreed to lend. And then
as I was leaving his apartment he asked if I still remembered
the Picabia. He had heard I'd been after it. It seems he had
bought the painting but found it too large to hang. Now came
more negotiations. After well over ten years the prize came to
the Chicago museum in the form of a loan. And there it remains,
for the lender eventually turned into a donor. The picture was
worth the wait. It is one of Picabia's three greatest works and
a landmark in the art of our century.

I recall another episode. The museum was considering a fine
seventeenth-century Spanish canvas, but after a comprehensive
report from our conservation laboratory we decided against the
purchase. X rays and an ultraviolet examination indicated the
picture was better than fifty per cent repainted. Years later I
unexpectedly came on the canvas in the collection of a venerable
Eastern institution. It looked better than ever. I am still wondering whether modern technology deprived us of a masterpiece,
even though a partly spurious one.

29. *The Selective Window*

A window is to look through, both into and out of. Though often considered the symbol of an eye, it is not an eye, but a vehicle for light and for that volatile mirage we call atmosphere. A window is selective; it can frame nature in sweeping panoramas or in magnified close-ups. It provides access to inner visions more vivid than real ones. It can be nothing more than a blank, a vacant opening, or it can reproduce the unedited reflection of one's own image. Because windows imply secret revelations, because they are outlets to both the inside and outside world, but, unlike doors, are rarely tangible passageways, they take on a variety of guises. Frequently exploited in art as compositional devices, they have come into their own only recently since Freudian discoveries infused them with new meaning.

In the past, windows were largely decorative afterthoughts, providing additional dimensions to otherwise circumscribed scenes. Sometimes, especially in portraits, these dimensions went beyond the purely physical to mirror psychological idiosyncrasies. Take Dürer's painting of Oswolt Krel. Here one side of the picture opens up to filter light through a grove of trees almost as obsessive as the sitter himself. Landscape and portrait

Portrait of Colonel William Taylor, by Ralph Earl

share a slightly contained madness. More conventional is Ralph Earl's eighteenth-century American painting of Colonel William Taylor featuring a window through which a nondescript, if romantic, view unfolds, a view that frankly borrows from traditional English scenes of the period. At first glance the aperture appears little more than an excuse to relieve a monotonous wall, but a second look adds an amusing postscript. For now the same landscape emerges as a sketch by the stiff-backed colonel, an unlikely "gentleman artist."

It is the picture within a picture that saves the day. And oddly enough, the scene through the window could well be a painting itself were it not for the realistic trappings of frame and sill. Ralph Earl's window opens up the wall no more than do Vermeer's familiar maps, which were never intended as atmospheric outlets but as rectangular divisions in consummately organized compositions. With Vermeer, one rarely looks directly into or out of a room; yet a casement's oblique presence is always there, sifting mellow gold over modest objects. This artist, Dutch though he was, focused less on substance than on the light he felt gave life to substance. In his paintings air circulates; a limpid glow transmutes and makes permanent the most banal interiors. No Impressionist was more accomplished at capturing trembling nuances of light than Vermeer, who lived two hundred years before the term was coined.

Until the present century, windows in art were chiefly adjuncts to portraits or to occasional architectural and genre scenes. One thinks of paintings by the Dutch Little Masters where buxom young women lolling in flower-decked windows were always more important than the windows. At other times, such apertures turned into tasseled vestibules looking out on faintly absurd Arcadian landscapes. But today the window is no longer a supplement; it exists in its own right. As a central motif, as a symbol of light, sex, frustration, escape, or indescribable loneliness, it can direct the entire course of a canvas.

In 1963, the Belgian artist René Magritte painted *La Lunette d'Approche*, a large surrealist composition in which a partly open window looks out on a total void. Two glass panels, seen arbitrarily from inside a room, reveal wispy clouds drifting

above a doubtful sea. On closer examination the scene becomes a capricious invention. Deceptive, ambiguous, and disturbing, Magritte's window is not an outlet to the world but an excursion into the unconscious or, should we say, the artist's unconscious. Characteristically, the two glass panels open inward. Architectural details, though meticulously defined, are strictly irrational, thus making the ephemeral skyscape all the more improbable. What is, is not; what is not, is. How are we to evaluate actuality? Is it what we see, what we know to be true, or what we dream? The painting, which initially strikes one as serenely empty, culminates in an experience of unrelieved anxiety.

Different in aim but not always in end are certain contemporary American canvases that celebrate the city at night. These are less mythical probings than forthright representations of how artificial light revises visual facts. New York is a favorite target. The confusion, vulgarity, and ambivalence of the metropolis by day is obliterated, leaving only a dark vertical cityscape. What goes on behind these numberless lighted openings does not concern us. There are no psychological overtones. What we do find, however, is a new kind of space unrelated to its daytime equivalent, and likewise unrelated to night scenes of the past. Modern man-made light has produced apparitions almost as deceptive as Magritte's Freudian ones, but the intention is not deception. These iridescent compositions punctured by irregular areas of luminosity are often close approximations of what we actually see. Unfortunately, most of us are so occupied with immediate demands, with tangled traffic, store windows, signs, noise, words, words, and more printed words that we miss the poetry of electrically lighted cities. From necessity we look down, not up. Much of the beauty eludes us.

Involved with a highly personal kind of luminosity, Mark Tobey turned his *Window* into an abstract idea. For after all, what is more abstract than light? You might say motion. With Tobey these two gossamer goals become one, yet for him light always takes priority. Quite naturally he turns to reflecting and translucent surfaces as source material. Through his openings, rays of light dance in myriad white and silver cadences. His light describes nothing; it is merely light for its own sake, an

La Lunette d'Approche, by René Magritte

intangible fleeting element that speeds across his paintings in interlocking choreography. Like the Oriental artists he admires, Tobey comes to grips with the mobile aspects of nature, with the interaction of forces too fragile to document. He can only suggest. And what he suggests is demanding. He asks us to realize that the world of light, of flux, has meaning only as it remakes itself. He offers no easy status quo. His delicate, evasive vision explores the balance that nature extracts from chaos. For Tobey, perhaps more than any other modern artist, is aware of the imperceptibly subtle conflicts that shape our surroundings.

One could, of course, go on indefinitely examining how our century has relied on the window as a specific theme, and how individual artists have adapted the subject to their own special interests. In 1911, when Henri Matisse was living near Paris at Issy-les-Moulineaux, he painted a view from his bedroom window and, because of the picture's pervasive color, called it *The Blue Window*. Outside one finds trees, sky, a cloud, and the top of Matisse's studio. In front of the window are isolated objects on a table—vases, flowers, a lamp, toilet articles. There is no distance; hieratic still-life, bushes, and trees merge on a single flat plane, and it is finally color that takes over. The window is virtually a backdrop, allowing voluptuous curves to play against a rectangular frame, and shimmering color spots to intensify the experience of blue.

However, when Josef Albers painted his windows, he was mainly interested in them as geometric objects, as architectural elements that permitted him to experiment with changing relationships in size and tone. By manipulating these rectangular areas, by varying their linear divisions and color, he forced himself to concentrate on a narrowly restricted problem, and in so doing turned the window into a speculative microcosm. Edward Hopper's windows are as stark as Albers', but his are designed to be looked into. And through them, in impersonal offices, hotel rooms, and diners, a silent frozen loneliness takes over. Never have our harsh surroundings been more ruthlessly exposed. Hopper occasionally includes an impassive human figure flooded by hard cold light, a light that hides nothing, though the artist himself has already stripped away every unnecessary detail.

His windows open into an existential world that offers no escape, no outlet from sterility.

Then there is van Gogh's window in the hospital at Saint-Rémy. It is barred, yet it deals gently with the pain of incarceration. Hopper lets us look in; van Gogh makes us look out, but out to a view that is blocked. In either case we learn something about the man who painted the window, for these transparent surfaces provide valuable autobiographical notations. Ivan Albright reveals himself, too. Long concerned with the processes of dissolution, he makes his window—a painting he worked on for some twenty years—testify to the vitality of death. (See illustration on page 6.) Every dusty object in it reminds us that what lives must die, that material possessions no more than human beings can vanquish time. So his window, which we view *at once* from the outside *and* the inside, exposes a crowded array of eroding objects from the past while also offering a philosophic comment on the present.

And this, of course, is the entire point. In different periods the same theme has different meanings. Today, the idea of a window assumes new proportions, not alone because of psychoanalytic investigations but also because of modern architectural break-throughs. Buildings now are frequently transparent, conceived entirely of steel and glass. At times, one can look in and out too readily. All protective cocoons are vanishing, leaving us with no place to hide. The window is a symbol of exposure as well as a token of withdrawal. Loren MacIver once made a painting of nothing but a battered window shade. What went on behind it, what we could not see but only surmise, was what counted.

Twenty years ago, Ben Shahn in a picture called *May 5* juxtaposed windows in an occupied building with those in a wrecked one, the latter a potent comment on American obsolescence. More unnerving, however, was the uniform anonymity of the openings in both houses. Whether they were dreary holes in a ruined shell or the dead eyes of an inhabited dwelling, they managed to give off the same barren miasma. Lyonel Feininger also worked with multiple windows, yet for him they were less human documents than structural punctuations. The architecture itself concerned him—its clarity, power, and rhythm. If both men were social commentators to some degree, it was Shahn who attacked immediate human problems. His windows, like everything he painted, bore witness to man's endless struggle for a modicum of the "good life." Feininger was more optimistic, more confident in present-day technology. His vitrines are generalizations. Shahn's are individual indictments.

All of which is simply another way of saying that each artist reconstructs familiar images in terms of his own convictions. Still, the fact remains that certain considerations at certain times take precedence over others. The window is now a reappearing phenomenon in art as, let's say, the still-life was earlier. Because windows are less final than doors, because their functions are more varied, because recent architecture has liberated them, because the openings themselves embrace conflicting images, they have become a virtual symptom of our period, a new kind of portrait—the face of today.

30. *A Panorama of Nineteenth-Century America*

Nineteenth-century American art when seen en masse can be a bore or a delight depending on the audience and the works involved. Ideally, the viewer should have some previous knowledge of the period, for where our native art is concerned, tolerance results less from final standards than from an understanding of the sources, interrelationships, and difficulties that produced this art. The show currently at the Metropolitan Museum in New York is a triumphant compendium of wit, history, genuine quality, naïveté, and local color. Carefully chosen, beautifully installed, and accompanied by two first-rate catalogues, the exhibition called "Nineteenth-Century America" juxtaposes lesser-known, sometimes superior works with long-familiar favorites that range from excellence to mediocrity. One senses, decade by decade, how life was lived in nineteenth-century America, for this survey is both a gratifying aesthetic experience and a social commentary of broad dimensions. Painting, sculpture, glass, and other decorative arts cover a culture that included Louis C. Tiffany and Frank Lloyd Wright, Raphaelle Peale and John Singer Sargent, Hiram Powers, and Frederic Remington, plus all the other contrasting and supplementary personalities who gave the 1800's their special character in the United States.

Somehow the exhibition saddened me. I felt a sense of loss, a nostalgia for the innocent America we have irrevocably abandoned or, should I say, that has irrevocably abandoned us. Often benignly literal and uncompromisingly honest, the best of the paintings are a graphic record of the sturdiness, self-reliance, and trust that characterized life in the earlier years of the century. Later, in the final decades, the influence of French Impressionism was strong, but never strong enough to wean the Americans away from a certain primness. Theirs was not a sensuous art. Particularly moving are the numerous romantic landscapes that describe a still unspoiled terrain waiting to be explored, also the portraits invested with stability and permanence. Even trivial genre scenes recall a rational world.

In the Metropolitan's comprehensive panorama of the century, certain idiosyncrasies repeat themselves. Portraits of men, as a rule, were more searching than those of women, possibly because male sitters were less concerned with flattering images, possibly because women had scarcely emerged as public figures. What could be greater proof than the show itself? Among the ninety-odd painters included, Mary Cassatt is the sole representative of her sex. An emphasis on unvarnished honesty was scarcely an idiosyncrasy, but it was the backbone of nineteenth-century American painting. Take Rembrandt Peale's portrait of his seventeen-year-old brother Rubens, a remarkably realistic likeness of a young man with weak eyes who not only wears spectacles but holds an extra pair in his hands. The picture, painted with crisp authority, softens no single fact of life. Or take *Samuel Coates* by Thomas Sully. Although at times this artist turned out artificial likenesses of ladies, his portrait of the Quaker merchant from Philadelphia is memorable for its direct integrity. Only an American would have handled the subject so simply, so without flourish or foible, and this despite Sully's years in London and his respect for English portraiture.

Humor also was important, although rarely subtle. Sometimes unintentional, sometimes ironic, often heavy-handed, it permeates the work of such artists as Quidor, Mount, Browere, Edmonds,

Woodville, Blythe, and Vedder—the last an unwitting wit as evidenced by his endearing, if ridiculous, *Questioner of the Sphinx.* Except for Quidor, who occasionally was an inspired satirist, most of these artists approached humor via the obvious anecdote. Were I to level one criticism against the show, it would be this overabundance of genre paintings, some of which, to be sure, are amusing but most of which are merely simple-minded. It comes as something of a shock to realize that Daumier was producing his biting lampoons in France at the same time Americans like Woodville were painting their provincial little jokes. In retrospect, the chasm dividing the two cultures seems wider than the ocean between them.

Although nineteenth-century American paintings could rarely compete with French ones, they were not overshadowed everywhere in Europe. There are unexpected parallels between the United States and Russia. Differing only in the local customs depicted, quaint genre scenes much like ours were immensely popular during the nineteenth century in Russia (and, alas, on a more vulgar level still are, as reflected by Socialist Realist aggrandized imitations). Perhaps the funniest American picture in the show was painted in Germany by Emanuel Leutze, who is considered an American despite his long stay in Düsseldorf. *Washington Crossing the Delaware* has all the bombast and ludicrous overstatement one finds in equally theatrical Russian and Polish historical canvases of the same period.

But the best American paintings from the first half of the last century were less tied to European influence. The more American, the more unpretentious their format, the greater their validity. The elegance of English portraiture lost its inbred urbanity when exposed to the rigors of a raw young country, and languid memories of Greece and Italy were scarcely relevant. John Vanderlyn can pall with his superficial derivations from Renaissance and classical sources, but more robust contemporaries, like Samuel Morse and the Peales, although rarely immune from European influence (what nineteenth-century American artist was?), were free enough to develop their own authentic styles. They saw America not in terms of foreign stereotypes, not as a pseudosophisticated upstart, but as a new adventure that demanded new thinking. The sober dignity of such canvases as Morse's *Old House of Representatives* and Charles Willson Peale's *Exhuming the Mastodon* set the pace for an indigenous frankness that was to persist for many years.

As I went through the show, I asked myself if anyone other than an American would find it as absorbing as I did. The answer is probably no, for much of the exhibition is closely tied in with our own history. Full enjoyment of many works, especially those by minor artists, requires an understanding of local mores. Yet, there is no question that a number of paintings at the Metropolitan could hold their own in distinguished company anywhere. And these deserve special mention.

Two canvases tower above all the others. *After the Bath* by Raphaelle Peale is an undeniable masterpiece. Its ingenuous handling of an unconventional theme, its bold design and consummate technique put it in a class with fine seventeenth-century Northern European still-lifes and even with Magritte's modern Surrealism. No less impressive is Thomas Eakins' *Gross Clinic,* a painting of such profundity as to rank it with the greatest, regardless of time or place. One thinks immediately of Rembrandt's *Anatomy Lesson,* which undoubtedly influenced Eakins, but the American was able to avoid enslavement. His intensely recorded portraits, his unorthodox composition, his undeviating involvement with the decisive moment are all very much his own. The color is dark, somber. Not a single concession to sentiment mars the picture's objectivity. Painted in 1875 for Philadelphia's centennial, the canvas was denied proper installation because of its relentless probity.

Another picture that could hang in international company without apology is Thomas Cole's *The Oxbow*—a wide, spacious view of the Connecticut River with a moody sky, a stormy foreground, and a sunlit valley. There on a hill sits the painter himself, a tiny figure near a large, unopened umbrella, the latter a bit of practical Americana. Except for *The Oxbow,* Cole does not emerge, however, as the giant I have always considered him. Something counterfeit in his extravagant symbolism becomes slightly suspect.

Surprisingly, Cole's pupil, Frederick Church, stands up better, although he was no less extravagant. Two of his large canvases, *Niagara* and *Cotopaxi,* do more than portray specific scenes; they are philosophic comments on the phenomena of nature, on the grandeur and power of rioting water and boiling clouds. George Caleb Bingham's *Fur Traders Descending the Missouri* also transcends its subject to become a silent lyrical celebration of a half-wild, still-expanding country. Here it is the utter purity and joy in the land itself that touch us. There are other paintings that could happily survive European exposure. Whistler's famous *Portrait of Thomas Carlyle* habitually does. It belongs to the Glasgow Art Gallery and is one of two pictures among the more than 170 on exhibit that come from abroad.

Why nineteenth-century American painting completely outclassed sculpture of the same period is an interesting question. Almost without exception artists who worked in stone, usually marble, based their carvings on classical themes totally unrelated to the New World. These posturing figures, although skillfully executed, indicated a growing bourgeois society intent on symbols of prestige. And what could have been more prestigious than these simpering white nudes and mythological figures gracefully (and absurdly) removed from any semblance of life's nitty-gritty realities? Bronze sculpture, as a rule, attitudinized less, but was so unrelievedly detailed that it often seemed closer to literary chronicle than to metal.

Certain decorative arts of nineteenth-century America were more vigorous than the sculpture. For my money, the most exciting three-dimensional objects are found in the Tiffany rooms. There a madly exuberant punch bowl ornamented with lapping waves recalls the lavishness of Irish design, if not in form at least in feeling. Another opulent object—an enameled silver vase—was created by Tiffany and Company during the last decade of the century. Flowers, plants, leaves, and scrolls turn this art nouveau container into an exotic emblem of America's accelerating wealth. If these prodigious fantasies sometimes exceeded credibility, at least they were never boring, never sterile like their marble counterparts.

Any American curious about his roots should not bypass this show. Nor should he bypass another nineteenth-century American show currently on view in New York at the Whitney Museum. This one, called ''The Reality of Appearance: The Trompe L'Oeil Tradition in American Painting,'' is engrossing on several levels. Yet why so many American artists devoted themselves to trompe l'oeil (fool the eye) painting toward the end of the nineteenth century has always puzzled me. There are, I suppose, plausible reasons, but none is persuasive enough to explain the persistence of this movement well into the early years of our own century. What triggered the yearning for optical deception and what kept it alive so long?

Each artist in the group seems to have hit on a special theme which he exploited in depth. Richard LaBarre Goodwin painted innumerable hunting-cabin doors; John Frederick Peto alternated between such neglected objects as dusty books and frayed letters, the latter usually attached to the wall under taped racks; John Haberle went in for compositions that fooled the eye with paintings of paintings and with paper money any forger would respect. The only woman in the show and the only habitual watercolorist, Claude Raguet Hirst, devoted herself to meticulous representations of messy table tops covered with old books, pipes, ashes, and matches, a repertory she borrowed from William Harnett, whose studio was next to hers.

For that matter, all these artists owed something to Harnett. Even though he frequently repeated himself, he was the most vigorous, the most varied, and the most authoritative member of the group and no doubt one of the prime stimuli that perpetuated the trompe l'oeil tradition in nineteenth-century America. During its heyday the movement was enormously popular and so also was Harnett, who masterminded much of it. He could turn out impressive large canvases or fastidious miniatures. He was sober, organized, and technically more than proficient; yet when he tried his hand at the human figure or face, his élan dried up. Almost every subject the other still-life painters tackled, he had introduced earlier—Goodwin's dead game and hunter's paraphernalia, Haberle's American currency, Hirst's table tops, Peto's secondhand books and racks of old letters.

Most of these themes had originated earlier in Europe. The table tops recall seventeenth-century Dutch Little Masters, and, of course, the hunting still-life with dead animals was long a favorite decorative device abroad, but the idea of conscientiously simulated currency and taped letter racks was more indigenous. And even more indigenous were the methods used by the Americans. Dry, cool, unsensuous, their tight textures, except for those of Peto and occasionally of Pope, were a far cry from the painterly pigment of their European forerunners. Peto, more than any artist in the group, went in for warm, soft, almost velvety surfaces suffused with chiaroscuro. He was a lyricist able to compromise with detail in order to achieve structural designs that seemed spontaneous but in fact were carefully organized. His paintings were nostalgic comments on the mystique of simple beat-up objects. As for Pope, one of the outstanding canvases in the show is his *Trumpeter Swan,* a magnificent dead bird spread out and hanging head down against a geometric door. White feathers painted with tender attention highlight a brilliant design. This lesser artist produced a veritable masterpiece, a work that went beyond the quaint, the Victorian, and the specific. So also did Harnett's *Golden Horseshoe.* A few nails and nail holes in weathered wood, a slip of paper, and a curved metal form add up to more than merely a charming bit of Americana. The small painting has both monumentality and silence. Somehow it manages to convey a sense of serene secrecy, the horseshoe taking on the quality of a totemic symbol.

Perhaps I am reading too much into these domesticated works. It could be that familiarity with Surrealism, where trompe l'oeil played such a crucial role, has influenced me. And, indeed, is it because of Surrealism that we have rediscovered and elevated to prominence and high prices a school relatively neglected during much of the present century? For the same reason we are perhaps reassessing baroque sculpture and delighting in its nonfunctional marble carvings of rich velvet and filmy lace along with its mad trompe l'oeil figures sprawling over balustrades and swarming across ceilings. We see with new eyes because new artists have reintroduced us to old ideas.

This thought was uppermost when I went through the show at the Whitney. I was amazed how much Raphaelle Peale's painting *A Deception,* done around 1802 (and surely the father of all later rack compositions), reminded me of Kurt Schwitters' collages. Obviously there is no direct connection, but well over one hundred years earlier than the European, the American had realized the evocative power of stray papers, tickets, newsprint, stamps, and bills. Technically the work of these two artists is at opposite ends of the spectrum. Schwitters relied on the real, the tangible, and made it look fabricated; Peale made the painted object look real. In the end, they pursued the same goal. They fooled the eye and mystified the viewer with the magic of discarded trash. Their experiments raise the age-old question: What *is* realism in art? Is it a simulation so faithful as to appear real, or is it a tangible manifestation so agilely juxtaposed as to appear a simulation? The truth is: Realism in art does not exist.

Alfred Frankenstein, who organized the show, points out in his fine catalogue that many trompe l'oeil American painters were legitimate ancestors of those modern Pop artists who intermixed actual objects with painted and sculpted prototypes so that method and meaning overlapped. Both schools were attracted by folk art and by the phenomenon of cumulative repetition. Haberle's *Fresh Roasted,* an amusing small painting of 1877 featuring a bin of peanuts seen through a broken glass lid, somehow reminded me of a courtyard strewn with real rubber tires which I saw several years ago at the Martha Jackson Gallery. Conceived by Allan Kaprow, a leading innovator in the field of Happenings, the carelessly abandoned tires carried the same message as Peto's dusty books and Haberle's torn currency. Even in the nineteenth century, America's casual attitude toward obsolescence was an important theme. Pop and trompe l'oeil artists were concerned with mundane objects as aesthetic experiences. Each used the vernacular with gusto. Jim Dines' bathrobes and S. E. Harlow's (a little known trompe l'oeil painter) socks have much in common.

Artists of both schools often worked tongue in cheek. The humor that made nineteenth-century American still-life especially beguiling came from native roots. Such canvases as Rubens Peale's *Magpie Eating Cake* is soberly painted but waggish nonetheless. Humor pops out everywhere, in Pope's *Do*

Not Feed, a picture of dogs, a rooster, rabbits, and monkeys locked up behind chicken wire in a crate marked ''Boston, Mass.'' The deception is all the more engaging because these living creatures (rare in trompe l'oeil art) hang on to the wire, poke their heads through it, and gaze out at us as if we were the picture, not they. In 1894 another little-known artist, F. Danton, Jr., produced a canvas called *Time is Money,* which represented an old door from which hung a clock and paper bills. A projecting wooden frame (a real frame) was painted with boards and nail holes to continue the idea of the door, but an added hoax of several actual nail holes gave the ensemble an illusory character. One asks, What is real, what is fabricated? Where is the dividing line? The painted holes are as convincing as the physically correct ones. The viewer is left wondering and worrying, but titillated, too, by these ambiguities.

So I return to my original question: Why did this school of minutely recorded still-life painting capture the imagination of nineteenth-century America? Possibly Victorian mores, growing out of a familiar, secure, somewhat stuffy environment, encouraged a wry, materialistic art. All the little household trinkets, all the oddities that cluttered American homes a hundred years ago contributed to the movement. But the paintings themselves were rarely stuffy. True, they were concerned with the object per se (not surprising in a period of practicality and economic growth), yet their treatment was often refreshingly backhanded. Though the trompe l'oeil artists projected a world of modest dimensions, they nonetheless turned their canvases into such equivocal experiences that even today our eyes and psyches are piqued.

31. *From Nature to Art*

In the summer I live on a small Cape Cod marsh. From my sundeck I look out on a glistening carpet of wild cranberries and a hillside of pines, among them a dead one leaning perilously. It is the dead tree that seems most alive to me, its naked, knotted branches insistent against the sky. The more I observe it, the more I find myself thinking of the romantic early nineteenth-century German painter Caspar David Friedrich. His trees, often denuded of leaves and silhouetted against a winter landscape, were infused with the same linear energy. I have no doubt I see the dead pine more intensely because I see it through the eyes of Caspar David Friedrich.

It has long been a truism that art grows from nature, but it is equally true that art transforms nature, at least for the viewer. To be sure, our vision of natural objects is heightened only by those painters who uncover hidden secrets or reassess familiar traits. Take van Gogh. When this artist humanized and yet demonized his cypress trees, he guaranteed that never again would they act merely as static punctuations in a landscape. Or take Turner. Since he, Whistler, Monet, and a host of other painters experimented with atmospheric effects, fogs have become shrouded in poetic mystery. For the real fogs that inconvenience us, we now substitute eloquent paraphrases—or could it be that the painted versions have become our real ones?

Not that man improves on nature; it is rather that he helps edit our visual and psychological reactions so that we accept more fully what he chooses to emphasize. And that may explain why nature's confirmed imitators rarely add to our understanding. We have already experienced first hand everything they have to say before they say it.

Going a step further, if art deepens our delight in nature, it can also diminish it. Who doubts the impact of a dazzling sunset; yet since this phenomenon became a favorite theme for hack painters, it has been so oversentimentalized as to seem little more than a trite stereotype. Even in travelogues the symbol is identified with banal finales. Today it requires considerable effort to observe a luminous setting sun purely in terms of itself. We tend to complain, "It looks too much like a picture postcard," or should we add, "It looks too much like a painting."

From my little sundeck I also begin to wonder why the simple act of gazing down diagonally on a straggly marsh can become a pleasant experience. I question whether it is the surrounding enclosure of pines that makes the open marsh more welcome, and whether the vagaries of light playing on birds, sand, cranberries, and water increase my interest. We are told that paintings filled with light and space are particularly rewarding. Are we to believe, then, that the sheer existence of these intangible elements lends added excitement to works of art?

I think not; I think there is more. At times space can suggest a special kind of freedom. But, curiously, it can also be frightening if it is too vast for human control. In daily life we unconsciously search for varied spatial experiences, for the freedom of unhampered dimensions, for the protection of circumscribed limits, and for all the intervals in between. The same variety we seek in life we pursue in art, but in art it is never real space, it is painted space that confronts us.

When the Germans demanded more *Lebensraum* they were asking for extended physical boundaries and for extended power. Space can at once represent the most subtle aspects of personal freedom and the most vulgar symbols of group authority. A glance at Hollywood films of the thirties reveals how closely space was related to affluence. The proverbial American millionaire was always pictured in a grotesquely outsized mansion where pretentious scale became more a liability than a liberation. In art, too, space reassures us only when related to human understanding.

Artists manipulate space to emphasize movement, which, after all, is just another manifestation of freedom. Unshackled motion is as kinesthetically agreeable as it is psychologically sustaining. To circulate freely from one area to another encourages improvisation both in life and in art, but in art one does not move, one merely senses motion.

Even more than space, light evokes motion and actually is motion. Sometimes staccato, sometimes languid, sometimes speeding faster than eye can grasp, light itself moves and makes everything it touches seem to move. The artist who grapples with luminosity is up against an idea as evasive as space. Distance is something we can cope with (it has limits), but space and light are abstract conceptions that we feel more than we see. They are life-giving elements, especially light, which man repeatedly connects with physical well-being. And yet too much light can be devastating. I remember June nights near the Arctic Circle when the sun became a burden, when darkness would have come as a welcome release. For it is never bright light alone that invigorates, it is changing cycles of light. In art, not surprisingly, we crave parallel atmospheric variety, responding as acutely to somber retreating light as to its blazing counterpart. Though painted light gives off no heat, it can arouse sensations of warmth.

Paintings that try to simulate real space and atmosphere are doomed to failure, for how can such indefinable experiences be materialized? Clearly it is not the artist's job to untangle nature's structure; it is the scientist's. Using methods adapted to his specific medium, the artist constructs his own view of nature, though only after intimate association with his motif. This personal process of reconstruction accounts for multiple interpretations of the same theme and also explains the painter's willingness to take liberties with nature. The artists who seem to conquer space and light tend to combine poetry and science, relying on the former to escape reality, on the latter to analyze it.

Unraveling the paradoxes that separate nature from art requires more than passive observation. It requires concentrated involvement, prophetic intuition, and above all, an open eye.

INDEX

Numbers in *italic* refer to illustrations.